Real
Sports
Reporting

Real Sports Reporting

Edited by
Abraham Aamidor

INDIANA
University Press
Bloomington & Indianapolis

This book is a publication of

Indiana University Press
601 North Morton Street
Bloomington, IN 47404-3797 USA

http://iupress.indiana.edu

Telephone orders   800-842-6796
Fax orders   812-855-7931
Orders by e-mail   iuporder@indiana.edu

© 2003 by Indiana University Press

Library of Congress Cataloging-in-Publication Data
Real sports reporting / edited by Abraham Aamidor.
p. cm.
ISBN 978-0-253-34273-7 (alk. paper) — ISBN 978-0-253-21616-8 (pbk. : alk. paper)
1. Sports journalism. 2. Sports journalism—Authorship.
I. Aamidor, Abraham.
PN4784.S46R43 2003
070.4'49796—dc21
2003002448
2   3   4   5   6   13   12   11   10   09   08

To
Shirley, Joe,
David, Sidney, Jonah,
Isaac, and
Judith

CONTENTS

Preface

This book is intended for young sportswriters at smaller media who want to move up, advanced journalism students, anyone in sports management or media relations for a team, and even general readers who have always dreamed about what it would be like to be a sports reporter.

It's a collection of essays, retrospectives, and even jeremiads written by sportswriters from some of the very best print media in the country—the *Chicago Tribune,* the *St. Louis Post-Dispatch, Soccer America Magazine, The Miami Herald, The Denver Post, The* (Louisville) *Courier-Journal, The Indianapolis Star,* the *Fort Worth Star-Telegram,* and more.

You'll recognize some of the heavy-duty sluggers included—Danny Robbins, Michelle Kaufman, Elliott Almond, Adam Schefter, and more than 15 other top writers.

The book is divided into two parts. Part I deals with specific beat coverage—football, basketball, soccer, and so on. Chapters give an inside-out look at the job of reporting major-league sports. Even if you don't want to become a full-time sportswriter, you'll learn what it's really like to cover a football game in blizzard conditions, an auto race when the asphalt is 120 degrees and climbing, or an Olympic venue half way round the globe. You'll find that it takes equal parts madness, passion, and skill to do what these sportswriters do for a living. Each chapter is full of personal anecdotes, mythic personalities, and sage advice. Most chapters include a full-text sample of the writer's work, together with a candid self-appraisal. You'll find that good writers become great writers by being brutally honest with themselves.

Part II deals with important issues that play a big role in sports coverage but that don't always spill over into the public's consciousness. Should sportswriters accept free meals, tickets, and even rides from the teams they cover? Should they even become friends with coaches and players? John Cherwa of the Tribune Company tackles these and other ethical questions in his chapter in Part II.

What if you want to write about sports part-time? It can be done. Read about Steve Salerno's surprisingly humble origins as one of the nation's top sports freelance writers, also in Part II.

But mostly, enjoy!

Acknowledgments

The ancient Greek philosopher Aristotle wrote that if you want to know how something is done, then ask someone who does it for a living. I didn't have to be as wise as Aristotle when I decided to put together a book on sports reporting and writing, though—it was obvious that I would need to rely on top people who do it for a living at some of the nation's top newspapers and magazines.

How to cover football? Ask Adam Schefter, beat writer at the *Denver Post* and a past president of the Pro Football Writers Association. The Olympics? Try Philip Hersh of the *Chicago Tribune,* who's been covering everything from luge to lacrosse for the past couple of decades.

Michelle Kaufman of *The Miami Herald* has covered lots of sports in her distinguished career, but as one of the nation's most prominent women sportswriters she had a thing or two to say about the progress of both women athletes and women journalists.

The acknowledgements section of any book is supposed to single out everyone, both in the public eye and behind the scenes, who made the work in question possible. A book such as this one, which is a collection of thoughtful, readable, and inspiring essays, is only as good as the quality of the contributors. Truly this is an "A" list.

Special thanks have to go to John Cherwa, who as president of the Associated Press Sports Editors recommended several of the writers who joined the project. Mentioning John's name was like dropping a $20 tip on a maitre d' at a fancy restaurant—you tend to get what you need in such circumstances. Howard Sinker of the Minneapolis *Star Tribune* was an early backer of this project. He was one of several people who wrote a sample chapter for the prospectus completely on faith, without guarantee of payment or even proof that the book would see the light of day. Other early contributors to the prospectus, which is what Indiana University Press committed to before the entire book was done, include Jeff Gordon, Bob Hammel, Dick Mittman, and Nelson Price. I hope their faith in me has been rewarded. Tim Franklin was helpful in recommending sports contacts.

A special thanks to Peter-John Leone, who supported this book as one of his early projects after coming to Bloomington to run IU Press. He was staking his reputation, in part, on me and the project. Tim Wheatley and Jim Lefko of *The Indianapolis Star* also provided useful tips. And a belated thanks to an old friend in Statesboro, Georgia. Hal Fulmer, a speech communications professor at Georgia Southern University, was highly supportive of an earlier book I wrote, *Real Feature Writing,* and made some recommendations for contributors to this one. But I failed to thank him properly in print before.

Abe Aamidor, September 2002

Real
Sports
Reporting

Introduction

Bob Hammel

Bob Hammel's journalism hero was William Allen White, who in the first half of the twentieth century felt no need to leave the *Emporia* (Kansas) *Gazette* to have a national impact. Hammel was sports editor of *The* (Bloomington) *Herald-Times* for 30 years (1966–1996), won a number of state and national awards, and wrote 10 books, including co-authoring *Knight: My Story,* the national best-selling autobiography of longtime Indiana University basketball coach Bob Knight.

We hear it frequently: sports is a microcosm of the world around it. Social issues, financial issues, drugs, sexual and gender issues, high-finance and business issues all sorts of topics more complex than "ball meeting bat" or "ball dropping through net" show up every day on the sports pages.

What that says is that there is considerably more to being a "sports-writer" these days than TV stereotypes such as Oscar Madison suggest.

Read it another way as well: a good sportswriter and a good general news reporter face the same challenges and requisites. One may be assigned to the ballpark and the other to the police beat or city hall or national politics, but the jobs are essentially the same: seek the news, find the news, print the news.

Over the 40-plus years that I did it, I heard thousands of times what an enviable "job" I had—the quotation marks I put around the word job essentially implied by the smile that accompanied use of it in re-lation to me. I heard, "You have the dream job." I heard, "I'd give anything to have your job." Sometimes said, sometimes too obvious to need saying, was, "Getting to go to all those games, getting the best seat in the house, and getting paid to do it. What a life!"

As my career was entering its final phase I talked to some sports-writers groups about this very common public image everyone in the room had come across. I didn't have to tell any of them the real work involved in being a sportswriter: the deadlines, the need to present readable coverage to people who had watched the event on television with replays the sportswriter didn't see, the deadlines, the challenge to sense and answer questions those viewers had after watching, the dead-lines, the late hours and time on the road and time alone in hotel rooms, the deadlines. . . .

What I did feel a need to tell my fellow sportswriters was: "You know what? In a good many ways, those envious people are absolutely right." We are lucky. At the end of our career, we have wonderfully rich memories few other careers can match.

They're wrong in considering sportswriting easy or frivolous or— as once again seemed implied in all the envy—so simple a job anyone could do it. Even the people in the newsroom, outside the cubicles that contain what the signs on the wall call the sports department and the sneers in the newsroom call the toy department—even those people with skills and learning that equip them to do their own jobs well are misled if they think anyone could do what a good sportswriter does.

Sportswriters would be equally wrong to think they could quite easily step in and replace a good political reporter or a good police reporter. To reach the "good" stage in any newspaper role requires experience and perspective, which are not functions so much of age as of alertness and diligence and unfailing attention to preparation before taking on an assignment or an interview. These are the areas of overlap among newspaper reporters of any kind: a proficient grasp of the En-glish language, an ability to concentrate under the most diverting dis-tractions, and an ability to see, not just to look at; to hear, not just to listen.

And, hardest of all, most vital of all—an ability to write. Writing effectively requires accomplishing the trickiest of all human challenges: taking a thought from the writer's brain and transferring it into the brain of a reader with all the nuances of meaning built into the word "understanding." In a newspaper sense, that means achieving that trans-fer to the brain of a man of 85 or a boy of 8, of a man or a woman, a girl or a boy, of a Ph.D. or an assembly-line worker, of a college grad-uate or a high school dropout.

Implicit in that process is using words and phrasing simple enough to be universally understood but not so simple that it's a turnoff to the erudite. The newspaper audience is all-inclusive—not all 85 or 8, not all men or women, but enough from all segments of society to justify a writer's frequent attention and consideration.

The difficulty of that job of transferring thought from brain to brain is at the heart of the parlor game in which a phrase or a comment is passed, one by one, by whisper into an ear all the way around a group until the last recipient tells what was communicated to him or her. Unfailingly, the end result is ludicrously different from the wording that started the communication chain.

Clarity thus becomes the first requisite. Simplicity is close behind, though clarity can survive a bit of complexity if the thought flow is clear. And brevity is the third requisite, but never at the risk of clarity.

There is a natural tendency to write in a cute way that other writers will notice and admire. When so tempted, it's time to recall Rule 1, the one that makes clarity paramount.

Michel de Montaigne, a French essayist of the 1500s, said things so clearly that his writing is a model to this day. He attacked the inclination toward cuteness with a few crisp words: *"Eloquence that diverts us to itself is unfair to the content."*

Think about that a minute. Think about the simplest application of it, in attributing a quoted statement: he said, she said.

We have a natural tendency to resist using the same wording over and over. We decide "said" isn't good enough. We look for ways to embellish. Maybe we mix in "shouted." Maybe "whispered" fits the situation well. Variations can help, but more often they intrude.

Don't overlook the good gray qualities of the word "said." The reading eye skips over it with bare notice and focuses instead on what *was* said. The impact, the color of the quoted comment, is all the more noticed if attention isn't distracted to "he said, in exasperation," or "she said, eerily," or "she screeched, in an annoying style peculiar to her." If the description is more important than the comment, describe away. If not? "Eloquence that diverts us to itself is unfair to the content."

Montaigne elaborated on what he sought in his writings: *"I want the substance to stand out, and so to fill the imagination of the listener that he will have no memory of the words. The speech I love is a simple, natural speech, the same on paper as in the mouth; a speech succulent and sinewy, brief and compressed, not so much dainty and well-combed as vehement and brisk."*

The eloquence of simple and natural speech can come in one-syllable words, in short sentences—short, *"succulent and sinewy, brief and compressed"* sentences. Within simplicity and clarity there is a grace that makes common words sparkle when they carry the intended message and *"fill the imagination of the listener."* Montaigne would have loved "we here highly resolve that these dead shall not have died in vain; that this nation, under God, shall have a new birth of freedom; and that government of the people, by the people, for the people, shall not perish from the earth." And "I have nothing to offer but blood, toil, tears and sweat," and "The only thing we have to fear is fear itself."

In the unidentified quotations above are 64 words so familiar and so powerful their speakers don't need identification. Fifty of those undying words—almost four of every five—had just one syllable. Within the 64 is only one word of more than two syllables: government (a four-letter word to some, but that's another topic).

The point of any writing rule is that it applies evenly to all writers—those with "sports" in front of the word or those with something else, or nothing else, there.

What makes the sportswriter's job especially challenging is the passion that many readers bring to the act of reading. What invariably comes with that passion is an assumption of personal expertise that produces opinions unlikely to be reshaped by one writer's views.

The sportswriter at an event becomes in a sense an umpire or a referee, forced by role to do a job everyone in the stands feels certain he or she could do better and considered to be right only when favorable to each fan's prejudices.

As with the umpire or referee, time provides the final judgment on the good or bad writer. One story rarely establishes worth, just as one call cannot do that for an official. Rather, it is the day-in, day-out consistency of high-quality work that elevates the writer, or official, in appreciation and recognition.

As sportswriters or as fans in the stand, we expect each baseball hitter to run out, at full effort, every ground ball, and every pop-up. As sportswriters, or as writers, we must demand from ourselves that same every-day, every-time all-out effort to be the best we can be—the clearest, the most accurate, the most informative, the most concise—in every story, bylined or not, long or short. When we insist from ourselves on discipline and excellence even with stories that aren't particularly big, we develop habits that make those qualities natural when a big story must be written with no time for revision. Habit prevails over pressure.

The self-discipline instilled by constantly trying for excellence avoids the worst pitfall of The Big Story—a temptation to overwrite. Your challenge then is the same as with your regular assignments: tell what happened, as clearly and quickly as possible. *"Eloquence that diverts us to itself is unfair to the content."* Always remember: the reader wants the spotlight on the event, not the writer.

In a now-gone era, Reggie Jackson earned the nickname "Mr. October" by his penchant for performing at his best in baseball's playoffs and World Series. It's not a bad reputation to gain, for it carries with it a suggestion of "dogging it"—going through the motions of effort, but essentially loafing—when the spotlight isn't on. My contention is that a writer isn't likely to be "Mr. October" if he or she isn't Mr. February, Mr. August, and Mr. December as well, Mr. or Ms. All-Year-Round in effort and performance.

I worked most of my career at a small-town newspaper that, because of Indiana University and (primarily) basketball coach Bob Knight, was involved regularly with major-league events. My newspaper's unwillingness to act small-town enabled me to cover 23 NCAA Final Fours, eight World Series, and five Olympic Games. These are among special events such as the Kentucky Derby, the Super Bowl, and the Masters that attract sportswriting's elite. It has been my treat to meet, to know, and to watch up-close many writers who were top-rated in the field I shared with them.

There's a fraternity at the top that is delightful. Two of the profession's giants are Blackie Sherrod of the *Dallas Morning News* and Hubert Mizell of the *St. Petersburg Times,* two friends whose paths cross frequently at major events. After the semifinal games at a Final Four college basketball event, Mizell finished his column, prepared to leave, and didn't quite make it before Sherrod—working beside him—glanced up and said, "It's amazing how fast you can write when you don't care."

Tales are swapped of experiences in covering sport's big names. Two Hall of Fame basketball writers, Dave Kindred and Dick Fenlon, once worked together at *The* (Louisville) *Courier-Journal.* Fenlon, to follow up a story, went to Adolph Rupp's house, where at the door he reintroduced himself to the legendary Kentucky basketball coach and got hit with this comment: "Hmm, Kindred and Fenlon. Fenlon and Kindred. One of you is a son of a bitch and the other is okay. Which one are you?"

Covering Bob Knight and traveling frequently with him have produced some experiences, obviously. Once, at a sold-out high school basketball game in Rochester, Indiana, folding chairs were set up at the end of the gym to accommodate a few special guests, namely college coaches there to watch a couple of top prospects playing in the game. Side by side sat Fred Schaus, the head coach at Purdue, and Knight, and I was on the other side of Knight. At halftime, kids came along to get autographs. One boy got Schaus, got Knight, and—still in front of Knight, who already was busy fulfilling another autograph request—looked over to me and said, "Are you anybody?"

Knight, without looking up, said, "No." The kid moved on.

At a service-club banquet when Knight knew I was there, someone asked the coach about the pre-season polls just out. "You know who makes up these polls: sportswriters," Knight said. "And we all know what sportswriters are. All of us learn to write in the second grade, but most of us go on to other things." Bob got the laughs he deserved and everlasting identification with what was a splendid putdown. I sent the quote to *Sports Illustrated* and I—not he—got $75 for supplying the Quote of the Week.

There is far more to gain from exposure to giants in sports and in sports journalism than a laugh or two, though.

Chances are you will be covering something sometime where someone you respect and admire is covering the same event. Use that opportunity to benefit from two completely different directions.

One is the obvious: watch what that acclaimed writer does with the very same story you're handling. Observe how he or she picked out something as a main focus and built a story or column around it—probably something you could have done, too, and maybe did. That's the other part of this opportunity I'm urging you to seize. Note that this esteemed writer didn't do anything you weren't capable of doing. Be careful with your prejudices but be honest: maybe on this one day you like what you did better than what The Great One did. Wonderful. Just keep it up. Every time.

I can assure you of another experience you will encounter. Self-doubt. Here I speak of doubt not of your ability to do your job well but of whether you should spend a professional lifetime watching and writing about games children can play. By far the best I have ever seen anyone deal with that kind of agonizing is Frank Deford's introduction to his book *The World's Tallest Midget.* The introduction explains the title: sportswriters in the general public's eyes somehow are not expected to be great writers, so the ones who are seem freakish for a sportswriter—like a tall midget, incongruous.

"As nearly as I can tell, sportswriting has always been disparaged," Deford wrote. "It is, surely, the only form of literature wherein the worst of the genre is accepted as representative of the whole. Any well-written article or book about sports is invariably praised by serious, patronizing critics as 'not really about sports' or 'different from sportswriting'— stuff like that. Sportswriting is assumed to be second-rate and, therefore, if any sportswriting is not second-rate, then, ergo, it must not be sportswriting."

Stereotyping, however, is not the source of the career crisis I mentioned. Rather, in Deford's words: "I can't imagine that any of us worth a dime doesn't go through a phase in which we question whether it is a fulfilled life in the toy shop. When it began to occur to me, seven or eight years into the profession, that I was beginning to look like a lifer, I did spend agonizing hours at the bar, staring into another disappointing bourbon or talking over the quandary with other sportswriters of like conflict. I could visualize grandchildren coming up to me in my dotage and saying, 'Big Daddy, what did you do during Vietnam?' And I would reply that I had been to the NBA playoffs. Or, 'Poppy, where you during the civil rights movement?' And I would explain that I missed that because of the Stanley Cup. But, finally, I resolved the issue with myself: that I am a writer, and that incidentally I write mostly about sports, and what is important is to write well, the topic be damned."

My good wishes to you, would-be midget. May you grow to be as tall as Frank.

Part I

Beat Coverage

1. Football

Adam Schefter

Adam Schefter, of *The Denver Post,* has covered the Denver Broncos since 1990, the longest continuous stretch of service of one reporter covering the team in franchise history. He served as president of the Pro Football Writers of America from 2000 to 2002 and is the author of two books, including Mike Shanahan's business-motivational book *Think Like a Champion* and Terrell Davis's autobiography, *TD: Dreams in Motion.*

When Colorado was awarded a Major League Baseball franchise back in 1991, the cub reporter wanted to cover the state's new baseball team as badly as he wanted his first job in sportswriting.

The newspaper said no.

When the same newspaper's long-time National Basketball Association writer debated exiting the beat that had become his professional home, the cub reporter wanted to take over the basketball beat as badly as he once wanted the baseball beat.

The newspaper said no.

The newspaper told the cub reporter to stay right where he was, on his assigned beat, not a hand-picked one. It left him on the Denver Broncos beat it had started him on back in 1990, when the cub reporter was greener than any football field.

To this day, there are only a handful of words the no-longer-cub reporter can express to the mean old nasty newspaper that refused to meet or honor any of his professional dreams and wishes.

Thank you, thank you, thank you.

Again and again and again.

Over the years, the cub reporter came to realize that his lack of qualifications for the baseball and basketball beats was matched only by his sheer stupidity.

Why anyone aspiring to any type of stable life would want to cover baseball or basketball or, for that matter, hockey—the type of sports beats in which a reporter spends more nights in Marriott beds than his own, in which dinners are not home-cooked but rather made in the press box, in which life is not beautiful—is purely beyond comprehension.

Perhaps it is simply because all the jobs in football reporting are taken.

Covering football lends itself to the most conventional lifestyle of any of the major sports. A reporter does not need to spend six weeks in Arizona or Florida at spring training, another 81 nights on the road, and another month on the road for the playoffs.

He does not need to work a night shift, filing close to deadline and filling his body with adrenaline that does not allow him to fall asleep until an hour when most others are getting ready to get up.

Football writers primarily work in their own city, oftentimes in their own homes, where they can eat dinner with friends or family, sleep in their own beds, and start the same routine all over again the next day. Such a lifestyle enables football reporters to last and their methods to endure.

There is a certain rhythm to the football season, a constant sense of knowing where you are. Summers are for training camp. Falls are for football's kickoffs. Winters are for playoffs. And springs are for unwinding and gearing up to do it all over again.

Of course, covering football is hardly an in-the-clear dash to the end zone. In this day and age, with the proliferation of media outlets and reporters, it presents increasingly difficult challenges that no other sport does.

As the country's most popular sport, it garners more attention, and subsequently more pressure, than any other sport. Sports editors expect their football coverage to mirror the intensity with which the fans cheer their teams. With free agency kicking off in February, and then a second wave of it again in June when more players are released for salary-cap purposes, there is next to no downtime in football. Labor Day—along with Thanksgiving, Christmas, and New Year's Day—is always celebrated by laboring. Off-seasons have gone the way of two-dimensional players—next to nonexistent.

And there is less access to football's players and coaches—basically, three mid-week 45-minute open-locker-room sessions—than there is in any other sport. When they do talk, coaches and players guard game plans and secrets in a manner this country's military would readily recognize.

Yet without question, football is the most civilized of the major sports beats. But then what did you expect? There are reasons U.S. president George W. Bush's national security adviser Condoleezza Rice is such a big football fan. Aside from protecting your own territories and advancing into those of your enemy, football is the commander-in-chief of sports, its president.

Which is why, when it comes to reporting on it, it takes so much work to do the job right.

During the spring of 2000, the Broncos were awaiting word on whether 49ers perennial Pro Bowl quarterback Steve Young would remain in San Francisco, retire from the game, or be willing to reunite in Denver with Broncos coach Mike Shanahan.

Young later decided to retire before the start of the upcoming season, but the story was a hot one from the moment it broke that winter. Yet it dragged on so long that it extended into June, the time most football writers usually use to recharge their batteries for the long season ahead.

My vacation already had been planned. And just before I left Denver, one of my editors called and asked me to leave telephone numbers of a couple of key people so other writers could find out the day's developments.

The editor talked as if this was one-stop shopping, as if, at the end of each workday, there were some secret code to punch in that would reveal all the answers.

Only there isn't. It is anything but. Here is football's secret code: developing sources, building relationships, gathering information, dispensing it, writing knowledgeably, studying competition, working hard.

Always working hard. It is, in reporting jobs from city hall to city's stadiums, the ultimate key. Every aspect of a reporter's job feeds off it.

If a football reporter works hard, he is able to develop a stable of sources that know the same information he is trying to track. These sources cannot be found overnight. They must be cultivated through the only means possible. Trust and time.

Like we learned in kindergarten, the way you treat people is the way you will be treated in return.

There was an instance in 1996 when I found out the Broncos were trying to trade their Pro Bowl kick returner, Glyn Milburn. His agent asked me to hold off on the story for a couple of days, that there were certain contract issues he needed to work out and without them there would be no trade anyway. So I listened to him. I trusted him. And two days later, he rewarded me, providing an exclusive story about his client's trade. Yet even more important than the story was this: A bond of trust had been developed. He knew he could trust me and I knew I could trust him.

If a football reporter works hard, he is able to build the types of relationships that endure way longer than any head coach's job. Amazing how an organization's gopher eventually can become a scout and then a personnel chief and then a general manager. Should you forge a bond with the person when he is at the bottom of the totem pole, he will remember you as he climbs to the top.

Look at future Hall of Fame tight end Shannon Sharpe. He joined the Broncos the year I began covering them, in 1990. He was an unknown seventh-round draft choice out of Savannah State. I was a cub reporter who was hoping to get onto the Rockies or Nuggets beats. Sharpe and I chatted regularly at his locker and formed a professional relationship; when his career began to blossom, he remembered who wrote about him when nobody knew him. During the winter of 2002, just before he rejoined Denver, Sharpe provided regular updates to me on the telephone about when he might re-sign with the Broncos. All because of a relationship that was more than a decade old.

If a football reporter works hard, he is able to gather the type of information that is his currency. The more information you have, the more anxious other agents and coaches and players are to speak with you. Then they will give you more information, and soon enough, there will be times you will know as much as any of the parties involved.

If a football reporter works hard, he is able to ask questions and write stories in a knowing and authoritative manner that sources respect as much as readers.

Sources do not want their valuable time wasted, just as readers would rather not bother with information they already knew. When you know your subject, others can easily discern it.

Sometimes they even give you credit for knowing things you don't. I can remember one time when a player told me about the arrest of one of his teammates, assuming I had known about it. I didn't at first, but after he blabbered away I did. Yet he never would have told me what he did if he hadn't expected me to know it anyway.

Let's look at a perfect example. In the days leading up to the 2000 NFL draft, certain Broncos sources let it slip to me that the team had brought in Southern Mississippi wide receiver Todd Pinkston for a visit. Denver needed a wide receiver and because Pinkston was the only player the Broncos flew in to their city, it was logical to assume the team would pick him.

Broncos officials said it was definitely possible. Pinkston's agent said it was more than possible. And so the day before the draft, I wrote an advance that said the Broncos were eyeing Pinkston. The only player who visited Denver. The receiver near the top of their ratings. The man expected to be available at Denver's turn at No. 15. Filed the story about 5:30 P.M., confirmed it with the office, and then ran out to pick up my date and attend the charity function I already was slightly late for.

At the function, I bumped into Broncos owner Pat Bowlen, who takes an active interest in knowing his team's affairs.

"So," I said, sidling up to him, "Todd Pinkston, huh?"

"Todd Pinkston?" Bowlen said, clearly surprised.

"No?"

"Nooo."

"Oh no."

Though I had been at the function for only 30 or so minutes, my time there essentially was over. I ran to the nearest pay phone, called the office, begged them to spike my story on Pinkston, and began making telephone calls to agents, scouts, coaches, players, anyone possible to ascertain whom Denver would draft.

I was on the phone from about 7 until 11:30. I missed my dinner, the entire event, and basically the whole night.

But by the time I left the function, I had dictated a story that ran in Saturday morning's *Denver Post* with the headline "Broncos want O'Neal."

And the next day, with the 15th overall selection, the Broncos selected California cornerback Deltha O'Neal.

I never had another date with the woman I escorted to the charity function. But I had the story.

Just as it is a more stable beat than the other major sports, football is unique in other ways, too. Baseball reporters file more than 100 game stories each year, and basketball and hockey writers file just under that total; football writers file about 25 game stories a year. This means that rather than the action finding the reporter, he must find it.

From Monday through Saturday, the burden is on the football writer

to produce a healthy mix of news, trends, profiles, and generally interesting pieces that other sportswriters might not have to be so enter-
prising to uncover.

Yet even with a lack of games, there is a certain uniformity during
football's regular season. Mondays are used for the best follow-up story
to emerge from the previous day's game, though breaking news obviously takes precedence. It also can be used to compile information for
Tuesday, which is the players' day off and a day beat writers often work
from home.

Wednesdays are often the week's most hectic day, featuring conference calls with the opposing head coach and an opposing player, not
to mention the weekly press conference of the head coach for the team
you cover. While they are bogged down in transcriptions, beat writers
also must focus on the package they are putting together for the Sunday paper, oftentimes a game advance, a notes column, and possibly a
takeout.

Thursdays are the day to catch up on everything that did not get
done on Wednesday. Fridays are the day to unwind, as Saturday papers
generally are the lightest papers of the week. And Saturday is a travel
day if the team you cover is playing out of town and an off day if the
team you cover is playing in town. In other words, Saturdays are the
day to catch your breath.

Maybe the most often asked question I get from people when they
find out I'm a football writer is, "What do you do in the off-season?"
Every time I hear it, I laugh. The off-season is the news season, a time
when football writers can distinguish themselves from their competition.

The off-season is the time when news springs from the strangest
of places. During the season, the events and stories are mildly predict-
able. During the off-season they are not. Teams do not hold daily press
conferences to update reporters on the status of players. They do what
they need to do behind closed doors. It is up to the reporter to find out
what is occurring behind those doors.

The best way is through the contacts he has developed with
coaches, players, and agents. Many reporters loathe dealing with agents,
who almost always are trying to increase their clients' salaries. Yet
agents are now as much a part of the game as injuries. In fact, many
of them are the true information brokers in the business.

They know their clients' every move. They know when a client wants out of a city or when he wants to sign a contract extension—both of which are newsworthy events.

Of course football-beat writers, like writers in other any other sport, are also always beholden to the news. This is critical to remember. After all, we write for newspapers, not feature papers. If the team's quarterback incurs a DUI arrest during a bye weekend—as has happened with the team I cover—it is up to the beat writer to gather facts, reaction, and all the pertinent information.

If anything happens, even at a time you thought you were going to be off, it is up to you to report on it. I remember arriving home from training camp in August 2000. I had spent the past three weeks living in a dorm room in Greeley, Colorado, about 65 miles northeast of Denver. I hadn't seen my friends in nearly a month, and we had long-standing reservations for a dinner party of 10.

To ensure I could make it, I awakened at 5 A.M. to pack up my dorm room and begin a busy day of work that included writing a training-camp wrap-up, another story on how the Broncos traded linebacker Nate Wayne to the Packers, and a notes package leading with a change at the team's cornerback position.

Three stories. A full day's work. A drive back to Denver, where it was time for a little break.

Just as I was about to walk out my front door, the phone rang. It was an agent calling to tell me that *Sports Illustrated* was running an item accusing Broncos linebacker Bill Romanowski of being a racist. A lofty charge and a significant story.

Knowing the amount of phone calls that had to be made and the work that lay ahead, I called my friends to inform them I would not be making the dinner.

Instead, I celebrated my return home from training camp on the phone, filing a story just before deadline, at 11 P.M., detailing a national magazine's allegations against one of the Broncos' most well-known players in the most balanced fashion possible.

Typical.

Really, when you look at it closely, the job of a beat writer in any sport really is not much different than a doctor's. We are on call 24 hours a day.

Only what we do is more widely critiqued but not nearly as significant.

It is no easy job, covering football. But then, no sportswriting job is. Yet so much of the job is so basic, so intertwined with the traits that dictate success in other fields. Acting professional. Treating others with respect. Being honest on expense reports. Showing up to work on time. Putting in the extra time that is mandatory if one is to get ahead.

But don't take my word for it. Take the word of others as well. Not long ago, I called around to some of the most respected reporters in the business, professionals I look up to. I asked them to describe the one skill a football reporter would need to succeed. Their responses were as varied as they should be valued.

Thomas George, *The New York Times:* "The one thing about covering pro football is the same thing about covering anything as a writer. Establishing relationships—with honesty and integrity."

Peter King, *Sports Illustrated:* "Learn the game. Too many people who come into the game don't believe it's necessary to know the inner-workings of why some teams play the 4-3 defense and why other teams play the 3-4. Where that manifests itself and hurts you is in relationships with players and coaches because soon enough they will see you're a lame brain and don't know the game and haven't worked at your craft. The best way to show readers and subjects that you should be respected and that they should give you the time of day is to know the game. Don't be somebody who just watches it."

John McClain, *Houston Chronicle:* "The key to covering pro football—or any other sport—is building the types of relationships that endure. When you can criticize someone, still be fair and still get stories, that means you're doing your job."

John Clayton, ESPN: "Networking. Being able to make enough contacts on stories that you can gain the trust of whoever is telling you the information. The NFL is probably the tightest league for getting information. Everyone is so regimented, so everyone is more prone not to talk than to talk. It really requires you to get everybody out of their realm of comfort to talk, to tell you what's going on. If you have a network of sources, you can do that."

Rick Gosselin, *The Dallas Morning News:* "Developing relationships with people and maintaining relationships with people is essential to covering football. When I was Kansas City in the '70s, I covered Jimmy Johnson and Dave Wannstedt at Oklahoma State. We became friends, maintained contact and lo and behold, 13 years later I'm covering the Cowboys coached by Jimmy Johnson and most of that staff I covered at Oklahoma State. Same thing in 1989. Bill Cowher was the Chiefs defensive coordinator and Tony Dungy was the Chiefs defensive backs coach. Now I cover the league they coach in."

Don Pierson, *Chicago Tribune:* "Most everybody gets into sports writing because they like sports. But it's real important to be able to define that line between being a reporter and being a fan, and to be objective in what is a subjective business. I remember somebody saying one time, 'There are two circles: the circle of team and the circle of our world.' You have to have one foot in one and one in the other. It's the tightrope idea. A lot of people fail in our business because they tend to become cheerleaders or fans or they get too close to a team or a player. It's important to establish that mindset not only with yourself but with the people you cover so they understand who you work for."

Ira Miller, *San Francisco Chronicle:* "The first thing to remember, particularly for young writers, is that football coaches and players are not your friends and they don't want to be your friends, either. They want to use you. But the important thing is to make them respect you through your work and the way you act—professionally."

So there they are, some suggestions for covering pro football. But there's one other thing, which might even be the most important for anybody aspiring to become a football writer or accountant or architect.

Do what you love and love what you do, even if it's something as crazy as covering baseball or basketball.

Your chances of succeeding then increase immensely.

SEEING THE LIGHT

December 9, 2001

The hits they have taken over the years are as different as the makeup of the two men.

Desmond Clark's hits have come on the football field, where he has developed into one of the Broncos' building blocks, among the best young tight ends in the game.

His father Paul's hits have come from crack cocaine pipes, in a maddening world only hard-core addicts can know.

The hits Paul Clark took on the streets of Lakeland, Fla., were an odd and disturbing juxtaposition. They were lively and deadly, at the same time. They cost him his savings, his marriage, his vision.

Even when his father was broken, little Desmond would wander Lakeland's streets, into its crack houses, just to visit the man who helped mold him.

Inside, they sat and talked and bonded, like any father and son. And eventually the conversation would come back to where they left off.

"He would tell me to hold that lighter right there for him," Desmond Clark said, sticking out his right hand and imitating the motion he used back in the day, from the time he was 12 years old until he was 15.

And young Desmond would. He would light the flame, touch it to his father's crack pipe and watch Paul Clark's eyes open wider and wider, as if he were being supplied a rush of oxygen.

"Then once he faded off," Desmond said, "I faded out. Got myself out of there."

Until the next time. Desmond would return to visit his father regularly, as much a fixture in Lakeland's crack houses as any drug dealer. But any time any one of those dealers ever tried to approach Desmond about joining their team, as they inevitably did, Paul Clark stepped right in.

"I told them, 'Get away from him,'" Paul said. "They were not going to get near him."

Paul Clark recognized talents in Desmond that other children did not have.

Desmond raced go-carts faster than anyone in the neighborhood, danced better than anyone not named Michael Jackson, worked harder than any person could expect. Which did not surprise his father.

Paul Clark always preached to his son what his grandfather had preached to him: If you don't work, you don't eat. So young Desmond would mow grass, lay tile, pick oranges, do anything to pad his pockets.

Eventually, part-time jobs turned into more regular ones. When Desmond advanced to Lakeland's Kathleen High School, he became a dishwasher in a Chinese restaurant, grasping the true meaning of overtime. When he enrolled at Wake Forest, he became a waiter in a steak house, with hands large enough to palm the restaurant's largest serving tray.

Desmond listened to his father, but he did not follow him. He did his own thing.

And the jobs he held formed the foundation of the work ethic he drew upon to become Denver's top pass-catching tight end, the successor to Shannon Sharpe.

"I knew that boy was going to be somebody, and I always told him that," Paul Clark said.

Paul Clark was right. It's just too bad he never got a chance to see it.

From the moment he put a pinch of crack cocaine in his cigarette and smoked it in November 1984, Paul Clark was an addict.

"Thought that was the best thing I ever did," Paul Clark said. "Best high ever. It was. Hooked right away. Wanted to feel that effect over and over."

The cost, as exorbitant as it turned out to be, did not matter. Paul Clark found something that became his sustenance.

At all hours of any day, Paul Clark could be found in Lakeland's crack houses, inhaling the fumes that made his mind dance and his body come alive. Paul Clark was so high for so long he couldn't see the world around him changing.

He couldn't see how his wife, Rena, had no choice but to end their marriage and fend for the couple's five children on her own in a fatherless household.

He couldn't see how the long hours he used to put in laying tile to make money slowly changed into wasteful hours in which he smoked his earnings

The last thing Paul Clark saw as he stood outside a crack house on Fifth Street in Lakeland on Oct. 17, 1989, in another altered and hazy state, was a series of pellets fired from a shotgun. He recognized the sight.

Twice before, while he was on a high or coming down from one, Paul Clark had been shot. The first time came in 1983 in the right hand. The second time came in 1986 in the right leg, left middle finger and groin area. Surgery was required to remove those bullets. The batch of BB's were fired from the gun of a man whose bicycle Paul Clark said he had borrowed without permission. The man retrieved the bike from the crack house and took it home to get his shotgun and revenge. Once the pellets began flying, most lodged themselves in Clark's right eye. Others ricocheted off a tree and lodged themselves in his left eye.

Clark fell to the ground, bleeding and blinded. He was rushed to a hospital in Lakeland, then transported by helicopter to an eye trauma center in Tampa. There the determination was made.

Paul Clark truly could not see. Nor would he ever again.

To Paul Clark, Desmond always will look the way he did the last time he saw him in 1989. Desmond was a 12-year-old, 5-foot-10, 150-pound boy, nowhere near the 6-foot-3, 250-pound man he is today.

But then, Paul Clark also is different these days, too. On June 6, 1994, Paul Clark smoked crack for the last time.

"Had made up my mind to quit," Paul Clark said. "Had to. It wasn't my willpower that did it. It was that I was desperate to do anything I could to stop."

Since then, he has begun work as a part-time counselor for Narcotics Anonymous, helping people as helpless as he once was. On a recent trip to Denver, Paul Clark delivered a lecture at the Narcotics Anonymous on the west side of the city. He has landed a job with Tropical Star, a seafood distribution company in Lakeland. During work days as regular as the one he once had when he was repairing homes and laying tile, Paul Clark makes boxes that transport the fish, always trying to ensure they are as sturdy as the life he believes he has rebuilt.

He remarried two years ago, settled into a new home in Lakeland, all while renewing a strong friendship with his former wife and her second husband.

"My problem is arrested," Paul Clark said. "But once an addict, always an addict. If I smoke that stuff again, I'll be out there again. That's why I go to meetings and try to give back. I give back so I can keep what I've got.

There is one other significant change in his life. His son has become a somebody, graduating to the NFL, giving Paul Clark a Sunday high better than any he ever has felt.

Each Sunday, Paul Clark is driven 15 miles to Plant City, Fla., to his father Edward Buchanan's home, which is equipped with Direct TV and the capability to see every Broncos game. While the gathering watches Desmond, Paul Clark—a former high school defensive end and kicker—listens to each game and visualizes it in his mind.

And after each game, he calls his son and their conversations are instant replays.

"How many catches?" Paul Clark will ask.

Then, "How many yards?"

Then, "How many touchdowns?"

Lately, there are more and more. Clark already has established career highs, with 45 catches for 529 yards and four touchdowns. Sometimes, Paul Clark does more than hear about it. He feels it.

Last Sunday, he sat in the fourth level of Miami's Pro Player Stadium as the Broncos and Dolphins squared off. Midway through the third quarter, Paul Clark felt his neighbors stand, his section shake and the cheers multiply. He didn't even have to ask his friends what had happened. He knew. Desmond had caught a 4-yard touchdown pass.

"Makes me feel good, just being in the stadium with him," Paul Clark said.

"Makes me feel good having him there with me," Desmond Clark said.

This is what makes their bond as strong as muscle. As different as their histories and dispositions are, their blood is the same. They talk about everything. They hold back nothing. They do it regularly.

"They're so close, they're more like brothers than father and son," said Desmond's wife, Denise, who struggles to imagine the pictures from her father-in-law's former life. "They're truly pals."

Desmond's pal always is looking out for him even if he can't look out at him.

For years, whenever Paul Clark would grab Desmond's arm to be walked around, he would always comment to his boy how little his arms felt.

Muscle up, he would instruct his son. Get bigger, he would order his boy.

Then last year, before another football season and during another visit in Denver, Paul Clark latched on to Desmond's arms and froze.

"Hold on," Paul Clark said, rubbing Desmond's biceps. "Your arms have a little size to them."

No doubt. The arms, not to mention the soul, are big enough to absorb any hit any defense dishes out.

CRITIQUE

My former writing professor at the University of Michigan, the great Don Kubit, always used to preach to me that there were three types of stories: A's, B' s and C's.

C's were the type that came up almost everyday—the throwaways. How a running back's hamstring was healing. How a defensive end was developing. A story on a slow news day. Like all stories, C's were to be taken seriously but were not serious enough to make the piece a front-page hit. It simply wasn't going to get there.

B's were the type that came up a bit more often—good solid features or news stories. A free-agent signing. A free-agent defection. A change in the starting lineup. B's were the type that required a little extra effort because more people would be reading them and more people would care about them.

But A's . . . A's were as rare as blue-chip players. They were moving features that had not been told. Or breaking news stories that could have a whole city talking. Maybe a half-dozen A stories come along in a given year, and when one did, it was incumbent upon the reporter to put everything he had into it. To make it the best story possible. An A story is to a writer what a championship game is to a player. The time to turn up the intensity.

The story on Denver tight end Desmond Clark was, I believe, a straight-A story. It might have been an A had it simply dealt with Desmond Clark's blind father. But introduce a blind father and former crack addict who had his tight-end son light his crack pipe for him, and it's an undisputed A.

How it came to be provides a lesson for aspiring beat writers. I regularly stay in the same hotel the Broncos do for their road games, a practice not all football writers observe. Some believe it more important to stockpile Marriott points; I believe it is the writer's job to be around the team.

Because I stayed in the team hotel, I happened to meet Paul Clark, Desmond's dad. I knew that at the appropriate time, once his son developed into the tight end the Broncos thought he would become, I would revisit Mr. Clark and his blindness.

And last season, once Desmond emerged as one of the top young tight ends in the game, I made arrangements for the story. Desmond agreed to talk with me on a Tuesday, the players' day off. We met at an agreed-upon location, and I was ready to hear all about his father's blindness.

But about 20 minutes into the conversation, Desmond began talking about how he would visit his father in a crack house and how his father was a former addict and how that was the way he lost his vision. Suddenly, I realized the story was completely different than the one I expected.

It was not about a blind father, but rather a blind father who was a former crack addict and shared a unique bond with his son. An A story.

The story was so powerful, so overwhelming, I struggled mightily to write it. I remember rushing through the 10 or so pieces I had to write for the *Denver Post* that week—including my Sunday game advance and notes column, typical B stories—just so I could devote as much time to my A story. And as is often the case with beat writers, I still did not have the time I would have liked to have had to craft it.

I sat at the desk in my home office a good three hours, and all I could come up with for a lead was what later turned out to be the second block of the story. I distinctly recall pausing and telling myself I was missing the point. As good a story as it was, football fans still would care more about Desmond Clark than his father.

Which is why I took the initial lead I had written, bumped it down to the full second section of the story, and wrote the new lead that meshed together father and son—what I believe was the essence of the piece.

Yet there are still mistakes I made. I should have called Paul Clark's former wife and asked her to describe her former husband's condition. I should have called some of Desmond's brothers and asked them to talk about the relationship that the Denver tight end had with his father. I should have flushed out the story better with other family members.

But this is the problem every beat writer faces. Time is in short supply. The words he must produce in a given week are not.

In the end, the story worked out well. But not as well as it could have if I had made some extra calls, blocked out some extra time, and put in a bit more extra effort that all A stories require.

2. Covering Hockey

Jeff Gordon

Jeff Gordon has been a sportswriter for the *St. Louis Post-Dispatch* since 1986. He is the author of the book *Keenan: The High Times and Misadventures of Hockey's Most Controversial Coach*. He is a 1979 graduate of University of Missouri-Columbia's School of Journalism.

I've written about most every conceivable sport during my 20-plus years of sportswriting at the *St. Joseph* (Mo.) *News-Press & Gazette, Kansas City Magazine, The Baltimore News American* and now the *St. Louis Post-Dispatch*. High school sports, college sports, Major League Baseball, the National Basketball Association, the National Football League, and auto racing all presented particular challenges and rewards. But I found that covering professional hockey was more difficult—yet more fun—than I could have imagined.

For many years, sports editors at major U.S. dailies regarded the National Hockey League as a proving ground for young writers. Women in particular have been funneled to the hockey beat because of the famed affability of NHL players. Females can have a tough go with the he-men in professional-sports locker rooms, but contrary to their on-ice image, hockey players have earned a reputation for politeness. In some cities, hockey players were just grateful to receive any meaningful coverage.

Also, hockey's popularity lagged far behind the other major sports. This allowed greenhorn scribes to learn on the job with less intense public scrutiny.

All that is changing. While writing for the *Post-Dispatch* and publications such as *The Sporting News, The Hockey News, Inside Sports, Inside Hockey, Goal, Rinkside, Hockey Stars, Hockey Digest,* and *In Your Face Hockey,* I've seen the NHL evolve into a true major-league beat. Expansion and franchise movement brought the NHL to key U.S. markets such as Denver, Dallas, and Atlanta. Minor-league hockey is flourishing too, especially with the largely independent leagues in the south and southwest.

Though hockey's television ratings still lag behind those of other major pro sports, the sport is back on network television and getting broad exposure through ESPN. Player salaries have soared to NBA levels. Pro hockey is no longer dominated by humble Canadian farm boys playing for the love of the game. When I started covering hockey in 1986, a top player earned between $300,000 and $400,000 per year. Today's superstars can command eight-figure salaries, and that sort of income buys an awful lot of insulation.

These guys are businessmen. The average NHL salary was $1.3 million in 1999, providing lifetime security for the journeyman player. In the old days, rudeness could get a player demoted or traded. Today's players are getting paid too much to worry about such matters. Some only grant interviews and make appearances when they feel like it.

The NHL, like the rest of pro sports, has been beset by strikes, lockouts, holdouts, free-agent migration, and franchise instability. Players are taking many of their cues from the NHL Players' Association instead of from their teams' management.

In that way, the NHL beat is like every other pro sports beat. But pro hockey offers special challenges too, like the international talent base. The superstars come not only from Canada but from the United States, Russia, Sweden, Finland, the Czech Republic, Slovakia, and Germany as well. Some of these imported players are easygoing and helpful; others are reticent or even resentful. Some are eloquent spokesman for their teams and the sport in general, while others can hardly speak English. Some make themselves available after every game, win or lose, while others sneak out back doors to avoid reporters altogether.

Most of these players did not grow up reading our newspapers or watching our television stations, so they are taken aback by the nature of media scrutiny in our culture. The top St. Louis Blues scorer in 1998–1989 was Pavol Demita, a publicity-shy Slovakian with a limited grasp of English. The top center was Pierre Turgeon, a soft-spoken French Canadian. The top young players came from Slovakia (Lubos Bartecko and Michal Handzus) and Germany (Jochen Hecht). The number-one goaltender for the Blues during 1999–2000, Roman Turek, hails from the Czech Republic. Defenseman Ricard Persson is a Swede. And so on. All these players are agreeable enough, but getting in-depth answers through the language barrier often proves difficult.

Player relations is the biggest concern for an aspiring sportswriter. Gaining the cooperation of pro athletes is the single greatest challenge in sports media today. My advice? Be friendly with the players without becoming friends, since a professional distance is essential. (If players think you're their buddy, they'll feel betrayed if you criticize them.) Chat with players when they are playing well so they will also talk to you when they are struggling. Make lots of small talk when you're not working on stories so you'll have a dialogue going when you do need some quotes. Get to know the players as people. This helps you work with them and it allows you to write better stories about them.

Learn to be both confident and tactful while interviewing the players. The same question will elicit all sorts of different answers, depending on how it's asked. From time to time, a confrontational tone may be necessary—but most of the top reporters I know get a lot farther by being evenhanded. Remain composed. Polite but direct questions usually work the best. Use a tape recorder as much as possible to eliminate any misunderstandings, particularly with players who wrestle with English. Be sure of what you write, because inaccuracies can put you in a hole you can't dig yourself out of.

You will be called on to describe the shortcomings of a player or team. Though columnists do the heavy lifting on this front, beat writers must probe negative topics and share their opinions as well. You are writing for an audience that spends a lot of consumer dollars on your sport, so readers don't want cheerleaders chronicling their teams.

For those times you do have to go on the offensive, document your case well and write without sarcasm. Most players can accept accurate criticism, but few will tolerate ridicule. Most NHL players read the newspapers, regardless of what they may say otherwise, and you can be sure their wives and girlfriends read every word as well. If a player does miss something pertinent, a teammate will be sure to point it out. So word choice is very important. Offhanded or throwaway phrases have gotten me in the most trouble over the years. You must weigh words very carefully.

A working relationship with the players is just a start. You must also build a professional relationship with the Players' Association, the agents, the coaches, the front-office staffers, and the various league executives. These people generally respect hardworking reporters who do their homework and demonstrate fairness in what they write.

NHL coaches have stunningly short professional life spans, so it behooves them to cooperate with the media. Each season, most coaches endure yet another disappointing year. Many teams fancy themselves contenders, but only one can capture the Stanley Cup.

Coaches can make easy scapegoats when their teams struggle. If they can win over the media, however, these same coaches can deflect some fan criticism and buy time for themselves. Coaches who battle reporters tend to get the axe more readily than the cooperative ones. Most coaches have figured this out, which is why they generally find time for reporters. (A notable exception has been the Detroit Red Wings coach Scotty Bowman, who has won so many Stanley Cups that he couldn't care less about public relations. He talks to reporters when he feels like it.)

A cooperative coach won't necessarily turn sportswriters into lapdogs, but they can help themselves by putting an optimistic spin on seemingly bleak developments. Conversely, sportswriters can't run a grumpy coach out of town—but they can arouse fan unrest with critical analyses.

General managers have less direct contact with reporters, but they are regularly called on to explain or comment on team developments. Some of these guys are terrific to work with; others are getting pretty good at playing hide-and-seek when times are tough. Ditto for the player agents. Some like to work the media, hoping for favorable coverage, and some absolutely never return a phone call. If varies from agent to agent. Public relations doesn't play a part in NHL contracts, so agents have increasingly shied away from the limelight.

The NHL front office has become far more media-friendly. Commissioner Gar Bettman came from the NBA, and he has worked hard to make himself and his charges more accessible. To facilitate trend stories and league features, the NHL offers weekly teleconferences with key performers. Reporters can ask questions during the conference call and later get a transcript of the group interview. At major events like the playoffs, all-star games, or the annual player draft, the league can intervene and make important folks available.

You must learn the economic side of the industry, both the working rules of the collective bargaining agreement as well as the revenue picture for the team and arena owners. The intricacies of the collective bargaining agreement dictate much of the player movement you see in the sport, so you had better know that document inside and out.

The game itself can be a challenge to cover. You must learn the nuances of hockey to become a capable analyst of strategy and performance. A lot of sportswriters (like me) come to the hockey beat without a true understanding of the sport itself.

If you haven't played or at least watched a lot of hockey, the game can seem a blur of confusion, even from high above in the press box. It may take time to develop a feel for the game and its unique rhythm.

Hockey is a terrific live spectacle, featuring lots of crowd-pleasing hits and the occasional scuffle between testy foes. But even seasoned fans can be left scratching their heads after a bang-bang scoring play. Sure, some goals result from the exciting end-to-end rushes and beautiful stick-to-stick passing that build anticipation before the climactic moment. But most goals result from broken plays. Hockey is a game of mistakes. An errant pass, a puck hopping over a stick, a funny bounce off the boards, a weird deflection in front of the goal . . . and the puck is in the net. What happened? Television replays are a beat writer's best friend, because you don't always have the time or opportunity to speak to the players involved in scoring plays before writing game stories. Also, you must quiz NHL scouts, NHL officials, official scorers, assistant coaches, and other front-office types who sit in the press box during games to fill in the blank spaces of your understanding of what's happening.

I survived my first year on the beat with the help of assistant Blues coach Doug MacLean, who also watched the games from the press box and was willing to explain what in the heck transpired. (MacLean remained a media favorite in subsequent jobs as assistant coach of the Washington Capitals, assistant· general manager of the Detroit Red Wings, head coach of the Florida Panthers, and president of the expansion Columbus Blue Jackets).

Writing game stories is not an easy task, given the tight deadlines facing you. Some newspapers will demand an early game story upon the conclusion of the game—or even an in-progress story for games in later time zones. Either way, you'll be writing "running" copy on the game as it occurs.

At best, you'll have a few minutes to quickly interview the coach and get several player comments before returning to the press box or press room to finish your story. This is not a novel you're writing; game stories should offer a clear, concise, and accurate assessment of what happened in the game and why.

Most newspapers want shorter game stories than our predecessors wrote. Most editors will expect you to sum up the significance and/or essence of the game in a few paragraphs, then expound on that.

Some papers ask their writers to file goal descriptions along with the scoring summary. This alleviates the need to describe the goals in the game stories and allows the writer more room to flesh out a clear story line for the game.

To write that story line, you need to be fully prepared. Every NHL team offers exhaustive pre-game notes that address every conceivable statistical trend for individuals and the team. This background material can be invaluable, though no writer wants to weigh down a story with too many numbers.

NHL teams don't allow reporters in the dressing rooms before games as Major League Baseball teams and the NFL do, but most hockey coaches do hold day-of-game skates around lunchtime. Reporters should always chat with coaches on game days to get a handle on lineup changes, strategies, and expectations for the game that night. You lose the opportunity with afternoon games, but you gain immeasurably more time to interview players and coaches after the game.

Though player access after games can be spotty, most can be trapped on practice days. Dressing rooms are typically opened 10 minutes after the last player leaves the ice. Though some players can flee the rink in record time, team publicists are generally good about arranging feature interviews.

How does each game you cover fit into the larger NHL picture? You must learn as much as possible about every team in the league in order to put the relative success or failure of your assigned team into perspective.

You must build a relationship with fellow beat writers so that you can trade information. You must also learn to use the Internet as a research tool, since more and more of your readers are surfing the Web for their own insights every day. Beat writers used to have a monopoly on information, particularly in a lightly covered sport such as hockey. But the information explosion has changed all that. Reporters must work extra hard to keep a step ahead.

A beat writer likely will get a high-powered laptop computer capable of storing background material, surfing the Web, perusing the home newspaper's archives, and tapping into the data bank established by the Professional Hockey Writers Association. Between this warehouse of information, which is filled by writers from each NHL city, and the Internet, the beat writer has the tools to compile a comprehensive notebook filled with anecdotes, pithy quotes, injury updates, and trade rumors. The work that was once done during tiresome conference calls with fellow scribes can now be done quickly and efficiently with your laptop.

There is no excuse not to offer your readers a tremendous package. Some team publicists even surf the Internet for their local media and distribute printouts of stories from other markets. But the beat writer must remember that not everything other media report is accurate. A lot of trade rumors are just that—rumors. This information should be used as discussion points as you check with players, coaches, general managers, agents, and so forth in the course of your work. You'll find that all these people are gossips who enjoy chatting with reporters who are truly plugged in.

Fans have a lot of other ways to get information these days, thanks to sports-highlight shows and the Internet. Your mandate as the beat writer is to present a "take" on your team—its players, its games, and the season as a whole—that fans will feel compelled to read.

You must do more than describe what's happening with your assigned team. You have to explain why good or bad things occur. You must constantly strive to put current events into the context of the bigger picture of the league and the industry. You must put today's triumphs and defeats into the context of the team's past and its hopes for the future.

Unlike your colleagues in other departments, you may wear many different hats in a given week: news reporter, feature writer, business reporter, columnist, and news-briefs editor. You might write a game story under a tight deadline, then come back with a sport feature the next day, work on a trend story for down the road, and compile a league-notes column for Sunday. This job demands versatility and judgment; you can't wear your columnist hat while writing a game story, nor can you get away with prose that is merely clear and concise for feature stories. So composing informative game stories is just the start of your job, the tip of the iceberg, as it were. You have to tell an interesting story repeatedly over the course of an entire season, weaving features, trend stories, analytical pieces, and NHL notebooks into the blend. All these elements work together to serve the readers, each of whom will test you in different ways.

Once the hockey writer has mastered all the key elements of his or her job—dealing with players, understanding the game itself, tapping into all the information sources, building a rapport with coaches, general managers, agents, and league officials—then the real fun begins. NHL games are seldom boring. There is always passion and conflict. A team may lose a game but start a war. Games turn into morality plays of good versus evil. There is lots of colorful action to describe, and the sport continues to attract more than its share of interesting characters. And though you may not have a broad audience for your stories, you'll have a fervent one. Hockey fans will hang on to every word they read in your stories.

YAP SHOTS: SOME OF HOCKEY'S BEST SHOTS COME OFF TONGUES, NOT STICKS

March 3, 1994

Todd "The Animal" Ewen never will forget his first attempt at yapping. Ewen, then a fledgling enforcer with the Blues, was sitting on the bench when Detroit Red Wings strongman Bob Probert triggered a scrum between the two benches.

National Hockey League rules forced Ewen to stay put, so he was restricted to a verbal response. But what would he yell? Unlike so many crafty veterans, he had no material at the tip of his tongue.

"I never used to say anything," Ewen said. "I was mute on the ice."

So now he was stuck. He opened his mouth but his mind had gone blank. He screamed anyway.

"PLAY FAIR!" were the words that roared out of his mouth.

"Their guys stopped fighting," Ewen said.

"Our guys stopped fighting. The linesmen stopped breaking it up. Everybody looked at me."

"Nothing Is Off-limits"

Ewen, now a member of the Anaheim Mighty Ducks, laughs at the memory of his lame salvo. He would have lots to learn about yapping, a traditional NHL exercise that serves many purposes.

At its best, yapping—commonly referred to in basketball as

"trash talking"—brings color and humor to a spirited sport. At its worst, it triggers small riots.

Players yap to fire themselves up, inspire their teammates and aggravate opponents. "It's a big part of some guys' game," Vancouver Canucks winger Sergio Momesso said.

"You hear some really funny things out there," Blues enforcer Basil McRae said. "Nothing is off-limits," Blues defenseman Rick Zombo said. "Anything you can do to get an edge, to get them thinking about what you are saying instead of what they are supposed to be doing."

Almost every team has players who are easily distracted or provoked. Yapping at them is like sticking a glove on their snout and giving them a sandpaper facial.

"When a guy starts worrying about what the bench is saying, he's not paying attention to what's happening on the ice," said Vancouver Canucks winger Tim Hunter, one of the game's great agitators.

Some players can even be intimidated orally. "I'm not saying who they are," Ducks enforcer Stu "The Grim Reaper" Grimson said. "Let's just say some players don't like to be physically harassed, and some players don't like being verbally harassed."

He Yaps, He Scores!

Coaches prepare for opponents by reviewing game videos. Fighters prepare for their rivals by studying highlights of their fights. And, yes, yappers prepare for their targets by developing fresh material.

"It's always good to have something at the ready," Grimson said. "I want to be prepared. I want to be quick."

But how do you prepare for European opponents? This challenge aggravates Red Wings pest Shawn Burr, one of the game's great motor mouths.

"It's hard to be a yapper now, because only half the guys can understand you," Burr said. "Now, to be a yapper, you have to be fluent in nine languages."

McRae said the great talkers earn their reputation on their comebacks, the oral equivalent of counterpunching. Anybody can construct a solid insult in advance, but the great ones can think on their feet.

He recalled how deftly defenseman Paul Coffey parried one

of his digs. McRae was riding Coffey about finishing second in the Norris Trophy voting, a slight he had complained about publicly.

"What's it like being No. 2?" McRae asked.

"What's it like being 484th?" Coffey answered.

Cha-ching! Hunter knows he has scored a hit when his flustered target offers a feeble comeback. "That's the best," he said.

Most of the really good rips are R-rated, and the players are reluctant to repeat them.

You can imagine the grief 1,000-point scorer Denis Savard got after marrying an exotic dancer. At least one volatile general manager was known to explore her vocational history during press box tirades.

Ragtime Chin Music

Players speak fondly of the great orators, those clever guys who can get their targets—and teammates of their targets—laughing at a razor-sharp quip.

Grimson became an instant McRae admirer when he came into the league. "Basil is pretty good, pretty funny," he said. "He had me going pretty good. He kept telling me, 'Save your meal money, save your meal money,' because he didn't think I'd be staying in the league too long."

An early role model for McRae was former Edmonton Oilers goon Dave "The Skating Bear" Semenko, who wielded a sharp tongue and heavy fists. You didn't rush the stage when he had the mike.

Ex-Blue Garth Butcher may be the grand master. His gravelly voice, machine-gun delivery and perpetual smirk has made him a Hall of Fame agitator.

He once fired this salvo at Grimson: "What's wrong, Stu? Couldn't your parents spell Stupid?"

And then there was this shot at ex-Blackhawk Rob Brown, who had one of the worst hair weaves in recorded history: "You were offside by a hair, but don't worry, it wasn't yours."

Not every tough guy is clever. Longtime Flyers enforcer Dave Brown once got a stand-up comedy gig while serving a 15-game suspension for trying to remove Tomas Sandstrom's head from his neck with his stick. But Brown bombed on stage.

"Actually, Dave Brown would be a guy who doesn't say too

much," McRae said. "When he would say, 'I'm going to rip your head off,' he wasn't being sarcastic. He was pretty much to the point."

Another class of yapper is the career pest, the little, in-your-face forwards who get paid to buzz skilled players. Ex-Blue Doug Evans, now in Peoria, is an annoying chatterbox. So is venerable Keith Acton.

"You could always tell when Keith was really into the game," McRae said. "He'd be getting the rest of the guys inspired. He's really vocal."

Blues hit man Kelly Chase sometimes gets orally involved to make certain he gets physically involved. Why does he rag guys in warm-ups? "Then I know I'm going to have to go out and do what I'm paid to do," he said.

"Consider The Source"

Sometimes the yapping can yield nasty results. After Chicago Blackhawks defenseman Neil Wilkinson leveled Los Angeles Kings winger Tony Granato with a crushing body check, he stood over him and added insult to injury. Enraged, Granato got to his feet and poleaxed Wilkinson over the head with his stick. That left Wilkinson with a mild concussion and Granato with a 15-game NHL suspension.

Granato couldn't recall what Wilkinson said or explain why he snapped. "A person couldn't say enough for me to respond that way," he said. "But it happened, and I have to deal with it."

Coaches can get involved, too. In 1991, Tom Webster was coaching the Kings and ex-Blue Doug Gilmour was playing for the Calgary Flames. When Webster launched into a tirade against Gilmour—probably touching on the scandal that forced him out of St. Louis—all heck broke loose.

Gilmour got in Webster's face, and Webster smacked him. "He said something personal to me, something that shouldn't be written in the paper," Webster explained.

Tony McKegney was one of a handful of black players who had an extended NHL career. That gave opponents ample opportunity to prick him with racial barbs that he learned to shrug off.

When McKegney was with the Blues, then-Red Wings enforcer Joey Kocur earned a gross misconduct penalty for uttering a racial slur against him. McKegney got a written apology from then-NHL President John Ziegler after the episode.

"In a situation like with Joey Kocur, I consider the source," McKegney said. "It didn't mean too much. I played with the Stastnys in Quebec, and they called them commies. I played with Dino Ciccarelli in Minnesota, and they called him a wop."

Hunter said there is a code of honor among top yappers. "One thing I try to do is not make it personal, stay out of a guy's family life, stuff away from the game," he said.

You don't have to get personal to set somebody off. A good example was provided by Montreal Canadiens defenseman Lyle Odelein.

On Feb. 5, Odelein found the time during a game against Ottawa to lecture the Senators' bench about a few matters. When Bill Huard raised a voice of objection, Odelein cut him off. "Shut up," he said. "I've already beaten you."

Huard, whose nose was broken by Odelein earlier this season, was incensed. "I don't have respect for a guy who talks like that," he said. "He thinks he's one of the league's heavyweights, but I've never heard of him. We can square off at center ice and see who the toughest guy is."

Odelein knew his yapping had worked. Huard seems rattled, primed to do something stupid—something that could give the Canadians a nice advantage when they play Ottawa later this month.

Zombo tips his helmet to the effective yappers, but he said he won't ever be a good one himself. "Either you're Don Rickles," he said, "or you're not."

CRITIQUE

I liked this story because it captured some of the colorful aggression that makes hockey unique. Also, it drew material from all the sources available to the hockey writer: personal observation, interviews with players on several teams, archived material from his own newspaper, and a few stories written in other markets.

Gathering information for this particular feature was not difficult. Any beat writer accumulates anecdotes and insights along the trail that can be developed into bigger pieces. The good beat writer looks past the nuts-and-bolts stuff—the game stories and injury updates—and tries to bring his team and his sport to life in the newspaper. This story is just one example of how a reporter can put a reader right into the fray.

After you gather a ton of material, then what? Personally, I like to type everything into a file, organizing it into an outline as I go. Move a block here, move a block there . . . in time, the story starts to take its rough shape. In this case, a beginning anecdote emerged.

So did a closing quip. The challenge then became to get the reader from point A to point Z.

What I tried to write was a breezy story that moved quickly, provided a bit of insight, and gave the readers some fun as well. This was a general feature, something of an issue story, but it came from the local angle. I used more quotes that I normally would for a story of this nature, but then again this story *is* about talking.

I opened with an anecdote shared by a former Blues player, Todd Ewen. I loved the story because it was a comically bad example of yapping. I wrote the anecdote pretty much as Todd shared it. I liked how he set it up himself.

My editors chose to put a sub-headline right after this anecdote, before the readers could get to the summary paragraphs. I disagreed with this. I think anecdote leads work, but you can't wait too long to explain what your story is about and why readers should stick with it.

In retrospect, I would take out those first quotes by Sergio Momesso and Basil McRae. Neither comment added anything and should have been paraphrased. As I noted, this story had an unusual number of quotes—so some should have been eliminated to increase the effect of the more pithy comments in the piece.

Reporters often use too many quotes just to prove to readers (and editors) that he did a lot of work on the story. We should hone our ability to write narrative passages and *never* use quotes as a crutch.

Conversely, I really liked what the later McRae comments and recollections added to the story. He, Tim Hunter, and Stu Grimson were the stars of this story. All three players spoke expansively on this topic during one-on-one interviews after the team practiced in St. Louis before games there. They weren't sitting on a roundtable, but the structure of the story almost made it seem like they were.

A story like this wouldn't work without highlighting some actual insults used during games. I particularly like Garth Butcher's greatest hits, lines that got repeated for years in the Blues dressing room.

If I were to trim the story today, I would have removed the references to the talking skills of Dave Semenko, Doug Evans, and Keith Acton. I didn't provide supporting material behind the first two players, and the Acton stuff wasn't strong. At a few points in the story, I got caught merely cataloguing information to prove I knew my stuff.

On the other hand, I'm glad I provided actual examples of how talking can lead to violence. The Tony Granato-Neil Wilkinson story was a widely covered news story of that season and a natural item to incorporate into a story like this. The Tom Webster-Doug Gilmour episode came from the *Post-Dispatch* archives. It was a famous incident that illustrated most dramatically how yapping can make competitors lose their minds. I never mind going a few years back to illustrate trend or issue stories if the incidents in question were big enough.

I got the McKegney anecdote and quote while doing a story a few years earlier about racism in hockey. I thought it was a relevant piece of background to use in this story.

The Odelein-Huard anecdote was a nice tangible example of the cause-and-effect of yapping. This more current story, discovered in wire reports while gathering material for a midweek notes column, helps flesh out the story.

I liked the final Rick Zombo quote because it was a nice quip and it tied back to Ewen's futile stab at yapping in the story lead. However, I didn't do much to set up the final quote, and the story sort of ended with a thud. We needed another summary-type paragraph to tie the story together before letting Zombo take the reader out. Without that summary-type paragraph, the story reads like it took an editing bite to wedge the story into a layout hole. In my own haste to make the story fit, I did it a real disservice at the end.

3. Soccer

Scott French

Scott French, Senior Editor at *Soccer America* magazine, has been writing about soccer (and other sports) since his high school days in Garden Grove, California. He spent nearly 20 years in a variety of capacities at the *Long Beach Press-Telegram*—doing everything from sports slot/copy editor to high school sports editor to rock/jazz/film critic—before moving to Berkeley-based *Soccer America* in January 1999. He has won nearly a dozen awards, and his work has appeared in *The Village Voice, The Washington Post, The Miami Herald, USA Today,* nearly every soccer magazine in North America, and in Major League Soccer (MLS) and Women's United Soccer Association (WUSA) publications.

Forget everything you've ever read by lazy sports columnists who think it's cool to hate the world's second-most-loved activity. Forget the stereotypes—"nil-nil" snoozefests starring one-named, short-pantsed foreigners who can't use their hands but fall down at the least provocation amid rioting in the stands—and forget the idea that it's a game best left for children who will soon go on to better things.

What has passed for soccer coverage in much of American mainstream media isn't going to get the job done anymore. Those assigned to the soccer beat—and more and more newspapers have such a beat—had better know what's going on, on and off the field, and how to accurately assess it, or they're going to fail their readership and get blistered by competitors who do understand. Soccer won't conform to expectations tempered by American sports. It has its own rhythms, its own idiosyncrasies, and if it appears chaotic to the uninitiated, its charms will be revealed to those willing to invest some time and effort.

The core of the game is simple. Teams, 11 players per, try to advance a ball over a field of varying size (120 by 75 yards is ideal) into an 8-by-24-foot goal defended by their opponents. They are governed by 17 "laws," including one that forbids players—aside from goal-keepers—from guiding the ball with their shoulders, arms, or hands. The team that scores the most goals in 90 minutes, divided into two halves, wins.

We call it "soccer," but most of the world knows it as "football," or some variant thereof—futbol, futebol, fussball, voetbal, fotboll, calcio, pallo, boldspil. There are dozens of names. It's a game of territory, of space and time, of tactics and teamwork and individual skill, of gamesmanship. Analogies can be drawn to chess or war—or ballet. It is "the simplest game" and the "beautiful game," as rich in its variety as is the world.

Soccer is, by a considerable margin, the world's No. 1 sport, dominant over most of the globe—on every continent except Australia and North America. With roots reaching back millennia, the sport's often-violent ancestors can be found in nearly every culture. It is called football not because the ball is played primarily with the feet, but to distinguish it, long ago, from games played on horseback.

The modern game is a product of the English. Its birth dates to 1863, with the publication of the London Football Association's rules. It separated "association football" (from which the term "soccer" comes) from "rugby football" (American football's grandfather), solving the heated debate about whether players should be allowed to carry the ball in their arms or hands. The game grew in popularity in the British Isles, especially among the working classes, and was exported to the rest of Europe and the world by British workers. This legacy can be seen in the names of some of the hundreds of clubs that sprouted around the world in the late nineteenth century and the years before World War I, clubs such as Santiago Wanderers in Chile and Liverpool in Uruguay. It's why it's "AC Milan" rather than "AC Milano."

The rise of professional (and semiprofessional) soccer, especially in Europe (and most especially in Britain), mirrors that of baseball in this country. International competition dates to the 1870s, and the sport was part of the Olympic Games as early as 1900. FIFA, the Zurich-based world governing body for the sport, was established in 1904—it grew in prestige and to immense power over the final 30 years of the twentieth century. South America instituted a nations championship in 1917, and the World Cup—a quadrennial tournament that has grown into the world's biggest and most popular sporting event—debuted in 1930. England, considering the tournament an affront to its sense of superiority, refused to take part, and Uruguay, the host, won the trophy.

Soccer, or its predecessors, has been played in the United States since well before there was a United States. There is evidence of a similar game in Virginia in 1609, and some form of football is believed to have followed the first Thanksgiving meal a few years later. Immigration to the northeast spurred the growth of the modern game, and ethnic clubs and company teams provided the foundation for amateur leagues and a series of "professional" leagues beginning in 1894.

The American Soccer League, formed in 1933, lasted until the 1980s. Tours by foreign clubs over more than a half-century drew large crowds—46,000 gathered at the Polo Grounds in 1926 to watch Vienna's Hakoah lose to a U.S. all-star team; Pele's American debut, in 1965, lured more than 25,000 to New York's Downing Stadium. The establishment of two national leagues in 1967 led to the North American Soccer League's debut a year later. The outfit grew in popularity by importing some of the world's most celebrated players, including Pele, Franz Beckenbauer, Johan Cruyff, Eusebio, and George Best. At their peak, the New York Cosmos outdrew the Yankees per game. Unwise expansion led to the league's demise in 1985, but other outfits—including several indoor leagues—kept the pro game alive in the years that followed.

A boom in youth soccer that began in the 1970s, fueled in part by the North American Soccer League's popularity, continues today and has led to a soccer subculture throughout America. This has spurred the United States to unprecedented international success in women's soccer and led to its growth worldwide. The men's national team has played in four successive World Cups, reaching the quarterfinals in 2002; the women's national team has won two World Cup titles and Olympic gold and silver medals. American players can be found on the rosters of top foreign clubs, and several play pivotal roles for their teams.

The hugely successful 1994 World Cup, held in the United States, brought greater soccer consciousness to these shores and led to the formation of Major League Soccer, which kicked off in 1996. The celebrated U.S. women's team's success at the Atlanta Olympics in 1996 and at the 1999 Women's World Cup—when more than 90,000 packed into the Rose Bowl for the final—resulted in uncommon attention for the sport and the creation of the Women's United Soccer Association, the world's first fully professional women's league, which played its inaugural season in 2001. Several American players—Mia Hamm, Brandi Chastain, Landon Donovan, and Alexi Lalas—have become national (and international) celebrities.

Internationally, the game is centered in Europe and, to a lesser extent, South America. The "major leagues" of soccer are Europe's elite leagues: England's F.A. Premiership, Italy's Serie A, Spain's "La Liga," Germany's Bundesliga and—fifth among the five—France's Division 1. These leagues, and others in Europe, have attracted the best players from throughout Europe, South America, and Africa, the continents that have supplied the majority of the sport's best talent. There are many legendary clubs, including Spain's Real Madrid and Barcelona; Germany's Bayern Munich; Italy's Juventus; England's Manchester United, Arsenal, and Liverpool; and the Netherlands' Ajax Amsterdam. The leagues in Argentina, Brazil, and Mexico also are of substantial quality.

Soccer is a multibillion-dollar business, with myriad championships of every sort involving club and national teams from throughout the world. The sport's government is hierarchical, with FIFA at the top. There are six continental "confederations," one for each continent and Oceania. The most prominent are UEFA (Europe) and CONMEBOL (South America). The United States is a member of CONCACAF, sometimes called The Football Association, a New York–based body governing the sport in North and Central America and the Caribbean.

National associations, all members of various confederations, govern the sport in each country, overseeing professional, amateur, and youth soccer. More than 200 are affiliated with FIFA. The U.S. Soccer Federation, or U.S. Soccer, runs things in this country. The Federation is, among other things, responsible for organizing and funding national teams (men's, women's and several at youth levels). Under U.S. Soccer are state associations, and the national youth soccer associations also are affiliated with the Federation.

There is a world club championship—two of them, actually—but the greatest club competitions are the European Champions League and the Copa Libertadores (South America's club championship). The oldest and most storied tournament, the F.A. Cup, is solely for English clubs. Each confederation also stages national-teams championships.

The European Championship, a quadrennial event dating from 1960, is the most prestigious. South America's Copa America is held every two years, and the championships in Africa and Asia have gained in importance.

The CONCACAF Gold Cup, usually held every two years or so in Southern California (and sometimes South Florida), is the regional championship in this part of the globe. Mexico traditionally is the region's strongest power, although the United States has twice won the competition (1991 and 2002) and has been challenging Mexican superiority since the early 1990s. Costa Rica and Honduras are considered the strongest Central American nations; Jamaica and Trinidad & Tobago have been the most successful from the Caribbean.

Qualifying for the World Cup, which now is a 32-nation competition, is a two-year process carried out within the confederations. Brazil, which in 2002 won a record fifth World Cup crown, is the only nation to have played in all 17 final tournaments (as of 2002). It became the dominant nation in the late 1950s with the emergence of a golden generation headed by Pele. Three-time champions Germany and Italy have been the most consistently powerful European nations. The 17 titles have been captured by just seven countries: Uruguay, Italy, (West) Germany, Brazil, England, Argentina and France.

Soccer has its own terminology, too. Not just corner kicks, penalty kicks, and yellow cards, but also "off-the-ball runs," "diagonal balls," "spot kicks," "strikers," "sweepers," "50-50 balls," "second balls," "through balls," "professional fouls." You'll need to be familiar with all of these, and quite a few more.

Another one is "friendly." A friendly is a match with nothing at stake, an exhibition of sorts. Coaches use friendlies, particularly nearing big events, to test players and tactical ideas and to build chemistry. Often the primary aim in these games is something other than victory. Your coverage of such events should make clear what that aim is.

A term you will hear often in international soccer is "caps": A player has X "caps." He's been "capped" X times. The word means "international appearances," the number of times he or she has played for his or her national team against another national team. They're called "caps" because the old custom, going back many decades, was to give each player a cap—a hat—every time he saw international action. American players, men and women, tend to have more "caps" than players from other countries because the U.S. teams' international schedules have been more extensive.

And "international," in soccer, is reserved for national teams; an "international" can be a game between two national teams or a player who plays for his national team.

The essentials of covering soccer are the same as with any sport. You cover games, write advances and player profiles, and report news while delivering cogent analysis. You deal with players and coaches, general managers, scouts and agents, and league and team officials of various stripes. You must be prepared to write about economics, law, labor strife, medicine, and crime—it's the same as covering basketball or football or baseball.

Assignments vary greatly. You may be asked to cover the local high schools, or clubs, or the college team in town. You could be assigned to write about a pro team, whether men or women, outdoor or indoor, at the top level—MLS or WUSA—or with one of the minor leagues spread across the country. You may write about the national teams, possibly in great depth, and you may do a column touching on goings-on around the country and internationally. You may be a general-assignment reporter who covers occasional events, such as a professional exhibition or national-team match that takes place in your coverage area. You may write profiles about significant local athletes, some of them soccer players.

Many papers handle soccer coverage, especially the national teams and World Cups, through their international/Olympic beats, which deal with everything from figure skating to track and field to gymnastics. There are a few general soccer writers who cover all aspects of the sport. These positions are a luxury at most newspapers and often are accompanied by regular desk shifts. Those who fill such roles usually have a deeper involvement in the game. Magazine reporters may deal with soccer on a regular basis, usually while covering other sports as well, or face the occasional soccer assignment. Beats at soccer publications are narrower. You could be asked to cover Major League Soccer or women's soccer or youth national teams or Europe.

Editors often will assign young reporters to cover soccer; it can be a proving ground that leads to more prestigious beats covering sports that are more popular. There also are "soccer" people, many of whom write for specialized publications and Web sites. The quality of their work varies greatly, from quite good to truly awful. I got into soccer writing, in part, because I grew up playing the sport. When the newspaper for which I worked, the *Long Beach (Calif.) Press-Telegram,* needed a soccer story, I got the assignment because I knew what was going on. I coordinated, from Long Beach, our coverage of the 1990 World Cup in Italy—getting yelled at when the phrase "Ugly Irish," a reference to Ireland's less-than-attractive style of play, was used in a hed, angering the Irish news editor. I also watched Yugoslavia lose in the quarterfinals with a crowd from San Pedro's Serbian community, writing an atmosphere piece common to American World Cup coverage.

As Long Beach's Latino population exploded, my editors thought stronger soccer coverage might improve circulation in the city's Mexican and Central American communities. I was given a weekly quarter-page (later a half-page) and the freedom to write about whatever caught my fancy. The page featured news and commentary and included scores and standings from around the world. It proved popular but didn't draw the intended audience, which, naturally, patronized Spanish-language media. Our soccer coverage grew quickly. The U.S. national team—in preparation for the 1994 World Cup—took up residence in nearby Mission Viejo. I covered the team, and the '94 Cup, and the birth of MLS (and, for three seasons, the Los Angeles Galaxy), and went to France (on crutches with a broken leg that effectively ended my playing career) for the '98 World Cup.

I also wrote about local indoor and outdoor teams, high school playoffs, and UCLA's powerhouse men's team in the NCAA Tournament, all the while working three or four desk shifts a week. I was, primarily, a sports slot and copy editor, putting out the newspaper night after night. In 1999, I joined the staff of *Soccer America* magazine, the country's oldest and most prestigious soccer magazine. I had freelanced for *Soccer America* since '91, and the opportunity to do nothing but write (and edit) soccer—and an ownership change in Long Beach—lured me to the Bay Area.

There are two guidelines that will dictate how a soccer reporter covers his assignment: the sophistication of the audience and the demands of the editors.

A sophisticated audience allows a reporter considerable freedom in deciding how to approach a story. Greater tactical analysis is possible, and the game can be presented as something more than a chronological description of goals interspersed with quotes from the coaches and goal-scorers. In Long Beach, my audience was a mixture of very knowledgeable soccer fans, players, coaches and neophytes whose eyes would glaze at mere mention of a 4-4-2. (Note: 4-4-2 refers to a team's alignment, always listed as defenders-midfielders-forwards: 4 defenders, 4 midfielders, 2 forwards. Other common formations are 3-5-2, 5-3-2, 4-3-3, 3-4-3, 4-5-1, 5-4-1, 4-2-2-2, 4-3-1-2, 4-1-3-2. . . .)

Rather than dumbing down the coverage, I tried to explain in simple terms the most important tactical concepts and emphasized context within my stories. The why was as important as the how. My goal, accomplished on occasion, was to illuminate the game for the uninitiated while giving the hard-core fans what they'd expect. I was given decent space and the freedom to cover the sport as I believed it should be covered. Some reporters will find they have very limited space—a couple inches for an advance, 15 inches for a player profile (long on personality, short on technical info), and maybe 10 inches for a game story written to a readership that understands goals but could care less what tactics made the goals possible.

At *Soccer America,* my audience is very sophisticated. So much that would have to be explained to a general audience—certain rules or customs or references to players and previous events—is accepted as common knowledge. Tactics is important subject matter. My approach to a story is entirely different. For instance, had I covered the first WUSA championship, in August 2001, for a daily newspaper, my story would have focused on the game's drama, its key moments, the chief personalities, and the atmosphere surrounding the event. My *Soccer America* story dealt almost exclusively with the Bay Area CyberRays, the winning team, depicting their evolution and concentrating on a midseason tactical change and the two unsung players who filled critical roles that enabled those around them to succeed. The game's events were secondary and were mentioned only in passing.

Dealing with American soccer players, coaches, and officials, in general, is a dream. They are starved for media attention and will do whatever they can, within reason, to help. They are patient, courteous, and usually willing to explain why or how something occurred, and a good number of them—especially the women—are very well-spoken. The communications departments of U.S. Soccer, MLS, and the WUSA are unusually helpful, and most of the top clubs and several of the minor-league teams also employ very capable press officers who will help you get what you need. MLS organizes weekly teleconferences with media during the season. U.S. Soccer does so before big events.

Good sources can come from anywhere. I've had general managers, players, trainers and more than a few press officers who kept me informed on what was happening behind the scenes. There have been league and U.S. Soccer officials who, once convinced I knew what was what in the soccer world, granted me deeper understanding of how things worked. Building a network of sources can take time, but gaining the trust of those in the game will pay great dividends. This will likely require more effort than is needed to fulfill the requirements of most newspapers' soccer beats. Talk to the team general manager, the president, the vice presidents—introduce yourself, say hello every time you see them. When you need them, a rapport already will exist. Meet the local college coaches and the guys who, seemingly with nothing to do with the team, attend practice each day. Some will be former players or friends of the coach; some will provide great insight.

Get to know the other writers on the beat, whether from the big newspaper or the little soccer Web site. Most will be helpful. Read the fan Web sites, or the postings on BigSoccer.com and *Soccer America*'s chat page. Some of the posters are very plugged in, and it's a good way to keep up with circulating rumors. An impressive number of them turn out to be true; many are far-fetched.

To do your beat justice, you'll need to know about the other teams in the league, the players in the league, the best players in feeder leagues. It's good to have a decent knowledge of the college game, which remains the primary supplier of talent to American pro soccer. Keep up with the national team, certainly, but also with the youth national teams. Landon Donovan's "sudden" emergence wasn't a surprise to those who followed his exploits with the under-17 team. Danielle Slaton's was a familiar name to dedicated women's soccer watchers well before she was a No. 1 WUSA draft choice.

Have at least a general idea of what's going on internationally. Nobody can know every player on every team, but keeping up with the biggest leagues—in England and Spain and Italy and so forth—and with the European Champions League and with the major national-teams competitions can only help. You should know who George Weah or Lilian Thuram are before they are signed by the team you cover.

The world soccer-talent market works somewhat like free agency in baseball. Instead of trades between clubs, players are sold or loaned from one team to another. These sales, called "transfers," can be for tens of millions of dollars. This is one route by which the club you cover may acquire players.

Both MLS and the WUSA have single-entity structures in which league offices have more power than individual clubs. Team "owners" invest in the leagues, for which they receive operating rights to a team. The leagues negotiate contracts and sign players, and teams operate under a somewhat strict salary cap. Neither league's officials will talk specifically about financial subjects, and player salaries and transfer fees are not divulged. Contract clauses bar players from reporting what they are paid. Some players and agents, and even league officials, will provide a general idea of a salary or transfer fee; a few will be more specific.

Transfer fees are regularly reported in the foreign press. If MLS sells a player to, say, an English club, the figure can be found in English football coverage. The Internet and cable television has made following international soccer as simple as keeping up with the NFL. It's a good idea keep up with other sports, the business world, international politics, and popular culture and to have a good grasp of world geography. It's good to know that Lamar Hunt, one of soccer's most passionate backers, and Robert Kraft have NFL ties. It's worth noting how the stock market is treating Discovery, WUSA founder John Hendricks's company. As Philip Anschutz—he bankrolls MLS, among other things—lost billions during Qwest's nosedive, the league's health naturally came into question. Other soccer bigwigs have interests elsewhere. The profitability of those interests may determine how long they're willing to lose money in soccer.

Soccer impacts, and is impacted by, what's going on in the world. Wars have started, and gone into cease-fire, because of soccer. Knowing the political situation in Spain or Italy or Africa can enhance your ability to write about the sport. If you'd had an opportunity to speak with Chung Mong Joon, the key figure in South Korea's efforts in hosting the 2002 World Cup, knowledge of his background (his family owns Hyundai) and aspirations (he's a good bet to become his country's president) would have aided you in the interview. Understanding the role of immigration in France provided telling insight into the greater meaning of France's 1998 World Cup title. Awareness of the role witch doctors play in African tribal culture could prove valuable when writing about African soccer.

When I covered the national team in Mission Viejo and during my three seasons as a Galaxy beat writer, I found that being at practice at least three days a week was essential. I got to know the players and the coaches, developed a deeper understanding of the teams' tactical aims, and could see things brewing within the squad before they spilled over. The players and coaches saw that I was serious about giving them serious coverage.

One player who had received minimal attention in the local press during a spell in which he hadn't played up to par refused to speak to other reporters following a game in which he'd performed brilliantly. He talked to me because, he said, "You'll talk to me whether I'm playing well or not."

A language barrier will exist with at least some foreign players. Although many, if not most, foreigners who choose to play soccer in the United States possess at least a rudimentary understanding of English, there are some who do not. It is invaluable on the soccer beat to speak a second language—Spanish would be great, French or Italian worthwhile. I, sad to say, am stuck with English, although I have learned to read some Spanish from years of perusing *La Opinion,* a Spanish-language daily in Los Angeles. A Spanish-English and French-English dictionary are always at hand and several translation Web sites are among my Internet bookmarks.

When I covered the Galaxy and, before that, the L.A. Salsa, I found developing relationships with the foreign players was critical. Most foreign players in America play pivotal roles for their teams, and you will need to talk to them. The media's relationship with soccer players in other countries is not as amicable as in the United States, and some foreign players have a natural distrust of the press. By developing a working relationship from the start, demonstrating that you do not subscribe to the manners of the vicious tabloid press elsewhere, you will benefit yourself and your readers. Getting a translator to speak with a foreign player is simple. The club's press officer should be able to arrange it. (You can always say hello without a translator.) Getting good translation is another matter. Some translators will give you every nuance of a reply; some will listen to 45 seconds of emotional commentary and offer, "He says he's happy to score goal." If you are not getting adequate translation, let the team know.

For deadline game stories (and for any sort of issue piece), I found it worthwhile to have go-to guys—players who are well-spoken, honest, analytical, and perhaps a little emotional—to grab immediately after the action. Sometimes you have 15 minutes, or less, to gather quotes and still make your deadline. Rather than waste the dwindling seconds with some big star who had little to say, I'd go straight to Dan Calichman, Robin Fraser, and Danny Pena—all defensive players—when I covered the Galaxy. They were going to say something smart, something entertaining, and something illuminating. Not that you shouldn't talk to the game's heroes, of course. A 90th-minute winning goal deserves comment. Sometimes the player who sets up the goal or a nearby teammate who sees it happen will provide a better response than the scorer. Sometimes not.

At some point, a soccer writer may be asked to do player ratings. This is uncommon in the United States—*Soccer America* does them, *USA Today* used to—but it is a regular feature everywhere else. A 1-to-10 scale is most often utilized, but only rarely does one see a player rated above 8 or below 3. A 5 is, naturally, average. A 7 or 8 is a very fine performance. A 3 is quite poor.

I'm aware of two 10s, although I'm certain there have been others. The first one I awarded back in 1993, when Joe-Max Moore scored five goals (four of them counted; the fifth slipped through a hole in the netting and wasn't allowed) in a U.S. national team rout of a young El Salvador squad at the Los Angeles Coliseum. An editor at *Soccer America* changed Moore's grade to a 9. "There's no such thing as a 10," he told me. Five years later, the same editor awarded a 10 to Kasey Keller, the U.S. goalkeeper, after an astonishing performance to beat Brazil, also at the Coliseum. So 10s do exist—you may see them once or twice a lifetime.

Properly done, ratings offer readers insight into matches. It's important to be fair, and if a player stinks it up, you've got to have the backbone to say so. Doing ratings can be difficult, especially for unsophisticated viewers. Let's say a striker goes all game without touching the ball, without causing any danger: an invisible showing. Perhaps he's a 3 or a 4; perhaps he went without the ball because the opponent's defensive plan isolated him from his teammates or because his teammates provided no decent service. Is the goalkeeper or his defense to blame when too many goals have been surrendered? Did the back line err or was it overloaded because the midfielders or forwards weren't doing their job defensively?

It takes an understanding of what's happening on the field to be effective doing ratings, and even then you're going to miss things. I try to get a general impression of each player. Are they solid with the ball or do they give it away with ill-advised passes? Do they make defensive plays or are they continually beaten by opposing players? What role, if any, do they play in the game's most important moments? Are they making off-the-ball runs to open space for teammates? Are they creative? Do they neutralize the opponent's best players?

The biggest assignment for a soccer reporter is the World Cup; it is both exhilarating and draining—a month-long marathon of trains, games, press-center food, early mornings, and late nights. Over the course of 33 days in France in 1998, I had one day off. I slept in, then did laundry. There's not much time for sight-seeing, although atmosphere and lifestyle pieces are part of the assignment. Should you cover a World Cup, your primary assignment likely will be the U.S. national team. It will play at least three games (more should it advance from the first stage), taking the field every four or five days. Your access to the players and coaches will be limited. Most practices will be closed, but several players likely will be made available at the team hotel every day. Each coach has a different way of doing things, and this will determine the amount of access you receive. No coach is going to tip his hand during the competition, so expect that you will learn about injuries or lineup changes only through diligent reporting—or luck. If you suspect a player isn't 100 percent, ask him, and ask if he'll be ready for the next game. Many won't lie. Listen for hints in the coach's answers. The better you know how he communicates, the better you can interpret what he's saying.

Your World Cup game stories, and advances, should display an understanding of tactics and the influence of any (or every) player on the field. This is the one soccer event for which every American publication will require strong analysis. If the team does poorly, the coach likely will be fired. There may be, as there was in '98, rancor among the players. Be prepared.

Secondary assignments will likely deal with the competition as a whole—surprise teams, interesting personalities, on-field drama—and the atmosphere surrounding the tournament. You will probably tackle more serious concerns, such as economics, hooliganism, or doping. You may cover certain teams, either live or from a press-center TV, that have large appeal to your readership. A New England reporter may pay extra attention to Italy, Ireland, or Portugal. California and Texas newspaper readers will want more news on Mexico.

Possessing a credential doesn't guarantee a seat in the "press tribune" or a mixed-zone pass, although if you are a U.S. writer, you can expect priority at U.S. games. Postgame access takes place in the mixed zone. (You'll never see the inside of a World Cup locker room; locker-room media access seems to be a purely American custom.) There will be a press conference with both coaches and possibly a player or two. All players and coaches must walk a serpentine path through the media—who are sequestered behind barricades—to get to their team buses. None has to stop to talk; most will.

Positioning is a critical element of successful mixed-zone reporting. You must be aggressive but accommodating. Typically it will be crowded, and you won't be able to put your tape recorder within earshot of every interview you want to hear. A good strategy is to group with other U.S. reporters and ask the press officers to bring you specific people. A corner position, one in which players can be stationed on both sides, could be perfect. Be ready to switch positions, maneuvering into space to listen to one coach, player, or official, then into another to speak with somebody else. If you are overly aggressive, you're going to piss people off. The Brazilian media has an international reputation for trouble: There are so many of them, all seemingly armed with cell phones to broadcast interviews back to Brazil (and over the airwaves). Too many of them lack manners. During the 1994 World Cup, one cell phone–carrying assailant thrust his arm past my head—well, through my head, actually—while pushing into space that didn't exist. I found that pushing the end button on his phone did wonders.

Things were so bad with the Brazilian media that even the Brazilians didn't want to deal with them. Just before the championship game, a press conference was arranged with Brazil's star forwards Romario and Bebeto. It was top secret—the Brazilian media wasn't invited, and the rest of us, no matter what our nationality was, weren't about to tip them off. It turned out to be a stunning success: We were quietly led around the back of the hotel and into a conference room while Brazil's media patrolled the hotel lobby looking for someone to thrust their phones at.

Every team in a World Cup, or similar international event, will provide some access to its players and coaches. There will be occasional press conferences, a few will be made available after practices, and occasionally a small group of media will get an hour with the players around their hotel pool. Sometimes these events will take place in remote locations, accessible only by car. Your primary home during the World Cup, or nearly any other large international event, will be the Main Press Center or one of its satellites. There are places to work, watch game videos, eat, socialize, shop, exchange money, buy magazines and newspapers, or surf the organizers' vast computer files. Quotes will be made available from each mixed zone and press conference. Sometimes these will be the only quotes available to you. There's a strong rapport among soccer writers in America. It's not uncommon to see groups of reporters huddling together and sharing quotes after the mixed zone empties. If you need help, ask somebody; if asked for help, provide it. This is essentially how it works at all international events, from the Women's World Cup to the Olympics to a confederation championship. Standards often aren't to American expectations, and things we take for granted—such as no smoking or cheering in the press box—aren't observed everywhere else.

If you are going to cover a World Cup or some similar event, it's best to assemble materials on the teams as early as you can. I start collecting printouts of stories and match reports during the qualifying process and keep files on each team and its players throughout the buildup. The Internet is an invaluable resource; so is *Soccer America* and a number of foreign soccer magazines. *World Soccer,* an English monthly, is must-read for any soccer reporter who will deal with the international game. During such tournaments, I try to keep up with the media output, which is impossible. I've found the British broadsheets— *The Times, The Observer,* and the' like—invaluable; the Italian and Spanish sports dailies, too, are worthwhile. And during the '98 Cup, *L'Equipe*—a French sports daily—was a must-peruse.

To write about soccer, you've got to understand the game; many soccer reporters in this country don't, and their copy is little more than descriptions of goals and assumptions based on match statistics. More so than any other sport, stats mean virtually nothing in soccer. A player gets off six shots—so what? One team outfouls another, 16-10. Big deal. It doesn't mean anything. Just because a team possesses the ball two-thirds of the time doesn't mean it was the dominant side. Some teams would rather their opponents have the ball; they lure them toward their net, then destroy them by counterattacking. Huge differences in shots or corner kicks, or if there were 50 fouls and eight yellow cards, may indeed be worth mentioning. You should know when a statistic is meaningful and how to use such statistics to support your analysis.

A good game story also is a well-constructed critique of the game. It should explain how and why a result was achieved and what the result means in a larger context. It should describe the match's pivotal elements—whether that be one team taking charge in midfield, straitjacketing an opposing playmaker, carving up a foe with an impressive possession game, or using aerial dominance to create scoring chances. And it should provide insight into the impact certain tactics and/or individual performances played on the outcome. Sometimes teamwork and tactics will determine the final score, and other times it will be some stunning piece of work by a particular player.

Your story should be able to answer a few simple questions. What happened? Why did it happen—what factors enabled it to happen? Did one team succeed or another team fail? Did the teams play well? Were there any major shifts in momentum? What spurred these shifts? How, if at all, did substitutions or the referee's decisions impact the match? How did each team play? What style of soccer did each employ? Use detail and quotes to illustrate the answers. Goal descriptions are valuable when writing "running" for first-run stories. They are not as important, generally, in "chase" copy, which should contain more analysis. I've written many game stories in which the scoring was dealt with in a paragraph or less. You may lead with the winning goal and revisit it in greater detail; rarely will every goal require the same attention.

When writing profiles of soccer players, be specific when explaining what makes the player special. If he or she is a forward, are they a creator or a finisher, technically gifted or an opportunist, better with his or her back to the goal or facing defenders, strong in the air or better on the ground, a good off-the-ball runner or dominant in the air? If a defender, are they a strong tackler or an outstanding organizer or superb at attacking out of the back? If a goalkeeper, are they strong on crosses or stopping shots or playing with the ball at their feet or organizing their defense? Talk to teammates, coaches (current and former), and opposing coaches and players to get a grasp of the player's abilities, his or her strengths and weaknesses.

A strong soccer library can be a huge asset but a major expense. The one book every soccer writer should read is *The Simplest Game,* a wonderful overview dealing with tactics and history by Paul Gardner, an English-born New Yorker who writes columns for *Soccer America* and other soccer publications. This is the first stop en route to tactical understanding. If you are going to cover, or follow, the international game, there are several invaluable annuals. The best is the *Annuario del Calcio Mondiale,* an Italian almanac published each December. It's in Italian, but that's not a problem. The majority of the book consists of lists, charts, and statistical records, which are very easy to follow.

Also important are *Rothmans Football Yearbook,* which is an exhaustive guide to British clubs and national teams, and *European Football Yearbook,* which has rosters and stats for every club on the continent. The Spanish *A-Z del Futbol Europeo* contains information and career records for every player in Europe; another volume covers South America–based players.

In addition, the season previews from several magazines—*Kicker* (Germany), *France Football* (France), *Guerin Sportivo* (Italy), *Four Four Two* (England), and *Voetbal International* (Holland)—are indispensable but difficult to find unless you have access to an international newsstand. If you have access to a Spanish-language daily newspaper—or, better yet, to the Mexico City–based sports daily *Esto*—following Mexican soccer will be a cinch.

A good soccer encyclopedia is worth owning—there are several, mostly British—as is Colin Jose's *NASL: A Complete Record of the North American Soccer League.* And U.S. Soccer's annual media guide is must-own. A better understanding and appreciation of soccer can be gained by reading the sport's classics. There are dozens of must-read titles: soccer, like baseball, has inspired a wealth of literature. I'd especially recommend *The Miracle of Castel di Sangro* by Joe McGinniss (a great tale of an American in Italy), *Football in Sun and Shadow* by Eduardo Galeano (poetic observations on soccer by a Uruguayan author), *Fever Pitch* by Nick Hornby (a diary told through Arsenal flashbacks), *Brilliant Orange* by David Winner (investigation of Dutch soccer), *All Played Out* by Pete Davies and *Football Against the Enemy* by Simon Kuper (World Cup tales), and *The Story of the World Cup* by Brian Glanville (World Cup history). Good luck finding any of these (although you might find *Fever Pitch*) at Barnes and Noble.

Your best bet (and for the annuals, too) is on-line bookstores. I often use www.soccer-books.co.uk or www.sportspages.com. The latter is the Web arm of a wonderful London bookstore (Sports Pages, off Charing Cross Road near Leicester Square) that I visit every time I'm in London (usually dropping 150–200 pounds sterling). Other American soccer writers do, too: I've run into several of them digging through the shelves.

SPAIN WEEPS WITH RAUL

History intertwines with the pageantry of a grand event such as Euro 2000. We invariably wonder if things will continue as they have or if this is the year they change. For now, Spain remains the master of the tragic fall.— *Soccer America* ed.

If one takes hyperbole as fact, the whole of Spain—its Catalans and Basques aside, perhaps—wept with Raul. He'd gone Roberto Baggio one further, sending his penalty kick not just well over the crossbar but a good deal past the left post, too.

When the Spaniards disappoint, as they always do, they do so with flair. And so it was again: Among the favorites to win the European Championship, based wholly on form and not at all history, Spain offered uninspired soccer, reached the quarter-finals anyway, then fell to the world champions when its star forward shanked the biggest penalty of his life.

"I learned not to dramatize soccer a long time ago. And I would recommend you do the same," Jose Antonio Camacho, the Spaniards' bulldog of a coach, told sports daily AS after France's 2-1 victory at Jan Breydel Stadium in Bruges. "The team went as far as it could and played with total commitment. If the opposition was better, or luckier, well, that's soccer."

Camacho, capped 81 times for Spain and thus familiar with its tendency to fail when it counts—isn't one to get too riled up about anything. He believes in strength, in honesty, in common sense. Raul's miss—a grotesque blast in the 90th minute when proper placement probably would mean overtime—was "just one of those things," Camacho said. "The penalty . . . was not our only chance."

It goes like this, he knows. Someone screws up, usually a goalkeeper. Next thing you know, a plane to Madrid.

"You know what always happens," Camacho confided before

the tournament. "We win all the qualifying matches, we fail to respect the opposition, and then it all goes wrong."

Deviation from Script

Camacho made certain Spain deviated from the script somewhat this time. He came aboard after the '98 flop—when Spain, considered a contender, dropped out after the first round—was followed by a 3-2 loss to Cyprus in the Euro 2000 qualifying opener.

His revolution was on a simple scale, like Robert Waseige's with Belgium: He boosted morale that had sagged under his predecessor, the dour Javier Clemente, and encouraged players to play to their strengths and attack, creating an atmosphere in which there was room to thrive.

Spain won its last seven qualifiers, scoring 40 goals in the process (albeit against weak competition), and the dominance of Spanish clubs in the European Cup during the spring lent credence to the idea that Camacho's squad was likeliest to triumph in the Low Countries should France and the Netherlands fall.

There was no disrespect to its foes, but reality arrived quickly, in a 1-0 loss to Norway in Rotterdam and an uninspiring 2-1 win over Slovenia in Amsterdam. The Spaniards looked ordinary in both matches.

They were thoroughly frustrated by the Norwegians' constrictive approach and took to launching long balls to their forwards, a plan that had no hope of success. Norway, limited to five shots, got the only chance it needed a little after an hour when goalkeeper Francisco Molina, a surprise starter, raced off his line in pursuit of a long punt by his counterpart, Thomas Myhre. He never got there, and Steffen Iversen's header looped into an empty net.

Something Extraordinary

Spain got the result it needed against the Slovenes, with Joseba Exteberria answering Zlatko Zahovic's equalizer within seconds, then pulled off something extraordinary, rallying from three deficits and scoring twice deep into stoppage time—in the 94th and 95th minutes, the first a penalty kick—to beat Yugoslavia, 4-3, in Bruges and collect a trip to the quarterfinals.

Once there, they gave a superior French team a fight, battling back from a sublime Zinedine Zidane free kick as Gaizka Mendieta converted his second PK in as many games, but falling behind again when Youri Djorkaeff finished from a long Patrick Vieira run just before halftime.

It was France's game from start to finish, dominated by the lofty Zidane, but the Spaniards wouldn't go away. Roger Lemerre, the French coach, had gambled by playing in Emmanuel Petit's absence (with a knee injury) just two holding midfielders—Vieira and Didier Deschamps—behind Zidane. The French defense isn't what it was two years ago, and goalkeeper Fabien Barthez found himself under growing pressure as time wore down.

"Of all the internationals I have played, this was probably the most difficult," reported Djorkaeff. "We knew that the Spanish players would be very good technically, but we didn't expect that they would be as strong physically."

The chance to tie arrived in the 90th minute, when Abelardo ran onto a ball Barthez fumbled to the left of the French goal. Although Abelardo was well-covered, Barthez leapt at his feet, and the Spaniard didn't try to stay upright. It was a foolish challenge by the French keeper, and referee Pierluigi Collina of Italy pointed to the spot.

Mendieta, the usual penalty-taker, had departed in favor of Ismael Urzaiz 12 minutes into the second half, so Raul—who had missed two of his previous five penalties—stepped up. There was no need for a golden goal.

Raul Was Inconsolable

"I cried on the field, in the locker room and in the hotel," he said. "When I saw the ball go over the bar, the whole world crashed around me."

And around his countrymen, hyperbole and all.

"Raul made Spain cry," declared *Marca,* another Spanish sports daily. "It wasn't quite what we expected from Raul. It was the last thing we expected from Raul."

Short memories, perhaps. The Spaniards always fail, usually spectacularly. Why?

Said Camacho: "I cannot tell you why Spain makes it difficult for themselves."

"There is not the same feeling for the national team," said former Spanish international Julio Salinas. "June comes around and everybody will be interested, but it is not the same as in the other big soccer countries. They would rather Barcelona win the league than the national team win a championship."

Spain lacks the swagger of champions, the attitude with which France and the Netherlands have cavorted through the competition. The Spaniards may have superb technique and a strong fighting sense, but they lack the backbone possessed by the few who share the spoils over and over again.

"The distance [between Spain and the champions] has maybe been one minute sometimes," says playmaker Pep Guardiola. "Soccer is not always black and white. Sometimes it is gray."

No Regrets

Camacho, for one, said he has no regrets, that he plans to soldier on "as long as they don't fire me." He acknowledged some key players—Raul, Guardiola, Molina and fellow keeper Santiago Canizares—hadn't performed as he'd hoped, but he put little emphasis on that.

"You select a group of players based on how they have performed during the year, but when you get to the tournament, some of them don't live up to your expectations, and others aren't on form," Camacho told AS. "The problem is that by the end of the season, players are exhausted, both physically and mentally. It's not easy to focus in a tournament when you've just won the European Cup, or the league, or perhaps after having won nothing."

And that's that.

"There is nothing to say," Camacho offered. "We tried to win the match, we couldn't do it, and now we're on the plane back home. . . . I feel sad, but at least now the players can have a vacation."

4. Basketball

Tim Povtak

Tim Povtak has covered the National Basketball Association for the *Orlando Sentinel* since 1989, the year the Magic began play. He has been with the *Sentinel* sports department since 1979. Among the events he has covered are the NBA Finals, the World Series, the Super Bowl, the NCAA Final Four, the Indianapolis 500, and the Rose Bowl. He graduated from Ohio University in 1979 with a master's degree in sports administration and a bachelor's degree in journalism.

Imagine trying to maintain your professionalism as a sportswriter when Shaquille O'Neal—at 7'1", 350 pounds, the world's strongest, most powerful basketball player—grabs you under the armpits, then lifts you high up over his head, almost giving you a haircut with the ceiling fan.

"Now do you understand what I'm talking about?" he asked me with a straight face.

I nodded yes, and he put me down.

I had asked a question O'Neal didn't particularly like. That was just his way of letting me know, of flexing his muscle, in his own playful way back in the early stages of his NBA career.

I didn't take it too seriously. We both chuckled, changed the subject, and finished a more serious interview. Nothing else was ever said about the incident. Although he left the Orlando Magic two seasons after that meeting, joined the Los Angeles Lakers, and started winning championships, O'Neal still makes it a point now to say hello when our paths cross a few times every year. I still work at the *Orlando*

Sentinel, where I have been since 1979, covering the NBA since 1989. As the first beat writer who covered O'Neal in the NBA—the Magic drafted him in 1992—I praised him to the highest at times, and I criticized him repeatedly when he deserved it. We had our rocky moments, but overall we got along fine. More than most, I understand where he has been, and how he has changed, in his career.

Rule No. 1: Don't take yourself, your job, or the people you write about too seriously. Have fun with it. And we both did in O'Neal's early years, which is how I survived them.

So much has changed since I first started covering the NBA, and so much will continue to change as the league evolves through the first decade of the twenty-first century. The players are getting younger, coming into the league more athletic but less fundamentally sound; they have less understanding of what a reporter does, too. Young players today can do things that the stars 20 years ago could only dream about, yet they need on-the-job training both on and off the court. They can make your job tougher and more aggravating, but their foolishness often can make it more interesting, more exciting, and give it more flavor. These are not the athletes your father grew up watching. The world has changed, and the NBA has changed dramatically.

Game stories may be the bread and butter of any sports beat, including the NBA, but the games often are overshadowed by today's thirst for more unusual story lines and more breaking news. In an 82-game regular season, it's hard to remember one particular victory or loss. But in one year alone, it's easy to remember the other stories I covered. Here is just a sampling of other kinds of stories I and other staffers wrote about during the 2001–2002 season alone:

When NBA veteran Patrick Ewing joined the Magic the summer before the season began, our readers got a taste of the lifestyle that rich athletes often live. We covered Ewing's testimony at the federal tax evasion trial of an alleged gangster who owned and operated an adult strip club in Atlanta. Ewing, a patron at the club, provided a glimpse of how he was laundering money. His testimony, as expected, often was steamy and graphic, unfit for a family newspaper.

We also wrote about the disappointment Ewing felt when he was credited with the first DNP-CD (did not play, coach's decision) in his 17-year NBA career. It shocked him, but the future Hall of Famer player tried to take it in stride. "I'm going to have to keep a copy of this box score," he said, waving it around. "And save it as a reminder."

Grant Hill, once one of the league's marquee players, struggled through another huge disappointment when his twice surgically repaired left ankle failed him again after 14 games, requiring a third ankle surgery that threatened to end his career. It was devastating for him, and a huge story for us. He had signed a seven-year, $93 million contract, but he never came close to earning it, which bothered him tremendously. I spent a year and a half chasing surgeons who knew something about bad ankles in general and Hill's bad ankle in particular. Hill is one of the nice guys of sports who was saddled with incredibly bad luck.

In the summer before the season, we wrote about rising star Tracy McGrady and his attempt to handle the fame, learning to be a leader by taking a leadership class at Rollins College. We also wrote about O'Neal leaving Los Angeles at midseason, returning to his Orlando home to rest his arthritic big toe, only to be seen cruising down the Florida turnpike on his new Harley-Davidson motorcycle while his Lakers were losing in Milwaukee.

We wrote about the tattoos that have become so commonplace around the league. In New York, I wrote about officials at Madison Square Garden announcing their 430th consecutive sellout, yet I wondered in print why 5,000 of the 19,763 people there strangely resembled empty seats.

We wrote about McGrady's battle with the league's fashion police, who deemed his gangster-style shorts too long, violating the NBA uniform code. We wrote about him stealing the show at the NBA All-Star Game. I wrote about McGrady's fight with New Jersey forward Kenyon Martin, his frustration with teammates who just didn't play up to his hopes. I wrote about his new shoe contract, which guaranteed him income well beyond his playing days. I wrote about his "guarantee of victory" in the playoffs that he failed to back up.

There was the night in Chicago when Coach Doc Rivers diverted the team bus on the way to the airport, treating everyone to a late-night dinner at White Castle, the greasy burger joint which was his favorite stop growing up in the Windy City. It seemed innocent enough until everyone got indigestion the next day, which made for a few comical moments.

These are all examples of away-from-the-game stories, which editors now prefer. Frankly, there are many more examples from one season alone.

Although covering the NBA was once just an eight-month job, it has become a year-round venture in recent years. The summertime chase and signing of free agents has become as important as any game

After the NBA Finals end in June, there are the college and high school drafts, free agency, summer camps, and contract negotiations that go right up until training camp opens again in October.

The mid-season firing of coaches is always a possibility, and an interesting story, unless your team is winning championships. The trade talks, always an interesting read, grow considerably in the month before the trading deadline each February.

In covering the NBA, often you are dealing with athletes, coaches, and front-office people who would prefer doing anything but talking to reporters. Access to people you need has grown more difficult through the years, creating an almost adversarial relationship with teams. When I first started covering the league in 1989, it was easier dealing with the athletes, and they were considerably more accessible. Practices and locker rooms then were open to the media. Teams flew on the same commercial flights as reporters. They stayed in the same hotels. There were opportunities to see players in informal settings, giving you chances to know them as people and them chances to see you as a regular person.

Today's NBA, though, is more sterile. Teams fly on luxurious private jets and stay only in five-star hotels. They are isolated from fans and from reporters. Usually after games, instead of returning to hotels, where a reporter could often find them, they fly to the next city, while the reporters must wait until the next morning to catch a commercial jet.

Travel has grown considerably tougher, and covering the NBA includes the most grueling travel schedule among the professional sports leagues. Baseball plays twice as many road games as the NBA, but baseball writers get to unpack their bags and often play four consecutive games in a visiting city. NFL writers usually travel only on the weekends, and their season is short by comparison. With the NBA, it's one game and move to the next city. Five games in eight nights, in five different cities, is not uncommon. You can wake up in the morning and forget where you are until you read the local newspaper that is outside your hotel-room door. And I can't count the number of times I have put a key into the door of a hotel room only to discover it was the wrong room. The number of the door was the one from the night before in a different city.

It may sound trivial, but learn to pack light so you don't ever have to check baggage, even on those long trips. Going through airports, with the new security measures, is a bigger hassle than ever before. And remember, with a new city every day or two, no one remembers what you last wore. Find a travel agent you trust; one who knows what you like. Park in the same spot at the airport every time, eliminating the stress of returning home and having no clue where your car is. Join every hotel and airline frequent travel club you can so that you feel like there is something gained personally with every trip. Otherwise the grind of the road will run you off the beat.

When it comes to covering the team, don't become close friends with those you write about because it causes problems when you have to write a critical story. Most athletes and coaches and general managers can handle criticism if you do it correctly. Stick to the facts. Then they have no argument. Let the columnists deliver the snide remarks or take the cheap shots. If the team sucks, say they suck, but use numbers to back up your statements. If they were wonderful, say they were wonderful, again backing up it up with facts.

Don't become too big a sports fan if you can help it. Too many times I've read and heard remarks by writers and editors that sound almost bitter and hurtful when their teams fail. That's what happens when you take those losses and the games too seriously. Remember, it's just a sporting event. These are games. No one loses on purpose, and there's no reason to get personal in your criticism.

If you have family at home waiting for your return, use the time on the road to work the extra hours this beat requires. Use that downtime in hotel rooms to make all those extra phone calls to sports agents, scouts, and personnel managers you need to talk to. Use all that travel time well. Use your laptop to write on the airplane instead of making idle chatter to the guy next to you who will never be seen again.

Try to budget time every day to go through a few of those sports Web sites that specialize in the sport you are covering. It's amazing how much garbage you will find on the Internet but also how many good ideas you also may discover for future stories.

If writing on tight deadlines is not your idea of fun, then you had better look elsewhere for a sportswriting beat. Typically during an 82-game regular season, at least 75 of those games are going to be at night; you'll be facing the pressure of deadline every time. On game nights, in addition to any daily news on the beat, most newspapers use a daily notebook that will include a variety of odds and ends, tidbits, or upcoming notes. Most should be gathered before the game and submitted by halftime.

Although the NBA still has that 45-minute open-locker-room policy before the game to help the writers with early stories and feature angles, it has become tougher to make good use of that time. Players often avoid the locker room during that period, leaving a gaggle of writers to stand around and talk to themselves. Often, quick interviews are done on the run, talking to players as they walk from locker room to the court for warm-ups.

NBA players often are available on the mornings of games when the teams do hour-long shootarounds at the arena, but it makes for a long workday for the writers, particularly if they live any distance from the arena. Often players who won't talk to reporters before the game make themselves available briefly after those morning workouts.

Most NBA games start at 7:30 P.M. local time with first-edition deadlines ranging from 10 P.M. (about the time the games end) to 11. Then most papers want a rewritten story, a more analytical piece for the final edition.

And don't write about your problems as a reporter. If players are refusing to talk to you for whatever reason, the readers don't care. They also don't care about the press room food or your conversations with other writers. Readers don't have any sympathy for your problems. Don't hold grudges, either.

Massage your editors like you would your sources. Most editors, like players, have inflated opinions of themselves and what they do, so let them have their say. Your life as a beat writer will be a lot easier if you aren't constantly butting heads with the editors. Work with them.

And lastly, keep your ego in check. It's a fun job if you don't take it too seriously. Your best story probably wasn't as good as you thought it was, and your worst probably wasn't as bad as you thought, either.

ONCE-PROUD KNICKS CRUMBLING AT FOUNDATION: POOR DRAFTS AND EVEN WORSE CONTRACTS HAVE DOOMED NEW YORK TO A FATE FILLED WITH LOSSES

March 31, 2002

They have too many point guards, no center worth playing, a checkered-past star who wants to make personnel decisions and a recycled coach working for a general manager who probably will be fired this summer. The New York Knicks—once a proud and arrogant franchise—are an incredible mess.

And the cleanup isn't going to be pretty. They have the league's highest payroll, the priciest tickets and the largest cable-television contract, but the once-feared Knicks have fallen to the bottom of the Eastern Conference, left to grovel with the Chicago Bulls, Cleveland Cavaliers and Atlanta Hawks.

"People in New York are accustomed to having a dominant team," said Magic center Patrick Ewing, who spent 15 seasons anchoring the Knicks. "They were good for so long, but there comes a time when change happens. It's going to be rough on them."

The Knicks (27-44) are in town today to play the Magic (39-33) at TD Waterhouse Centre, a game that NBC dropped from its original schedule because basketball turned sour in the league's biggest television market.

The Knicks have reached the NBA Finals twice in the past eight years—more than anyone else from the Eastern Conference outside of Michael Jordan's Bulls.

Yet they will miss the playoffs next month for the first time in 15 seasons, victims of bad management, poor drafting, dumb trades and overpriced role players.

Banking on draft-lottery hopes may work in many cities, but the fans at storied Madison Square Garden—where some pay $1,600 a night for a courtside seat—are not exactly the most patient customers.

Although the Knicks still brag about their league-high sellout streak (428 games) and their 7,000-name waiting list for season tickets, there are 1,000 empty seats now every night at the Garden.

Those that come often have booed this season. Even their own public-address announcer has poked fun, playing Fat Albert's theme song last week after a dunk by bulky Knicks forward Clarence Weatherspoon.

"I'm just kind of wondering what's going to happen here," said guard/forward Latrell Sprewell, the Knicks' best all-around player. "I really don't know. I don't know how much I should say, or what I should say. I expect something to happen [this summer]."

The Knicks have lost 15 times this season after blowing double-digit leads. Twice they have blown 20-point leads—and lost. Last week at home, they led the lowly Denver Nuggets by 19 points—and lost.

"I see a team in disarray," said Utah's John Starks, who played for eight seasons in New York, reaching the NBA Finals once. "Their spirits are down. You could tell when a team makes a run against them, they just kind of stop playing. The team I used to play with [in New York], we would fight back. But now you don't see that fight anymore."

When General Manager Scott Layden tried to explain during a recent news conference that the Knicks were a team in "transition," one New York columnist concurred: "Must be a transition from bad to worse."

Although many teams eventually go through a down cycle, then rebuild through free agency and the draft, the situation in New York has been compounded by unbelievable salary-cap problems that will make major changes difficult and costly.

The Knicks have a payroll of $86 million, more than double the NBA salary cap, which will make it impossible to seriously bid for the best free agents. And they aren't quite bad enough—six teams still have worse records—to get the inside track on a franchise center such as Yao Ming of China.

Like many teams, the Knicks are desperate for a big man. They had hoped to land Dikembe Mutombo last season before he was traded from Atlanta to Philadelphia. They made a weak effort last summer to lure free agent Chris Webber out of Sacramento, but they never came close. They talked to Denver about Raef LaFrentz before he was traded to Dallas, but nothing went beyond the preliminary stages.

The Knicks are smothered by a sea of bad contracts, which has made personnel moves next to impossible.

To re-sign Allan Houston, 30, last summer, they gave him a seven-year $100 million deal, even though no other team was offering anything close for the two-time all-star. They signed Weatherspoon, 31, to a five-year $27 million contract even though he hasn't averaged more than 12 points a game in four seasons.

They traded last summer for point guard Howard Eisley (seven years, $41 million) and swingman Shandon Anderson (six years, $42 million) even though the Knicks already were secure at those positions, making them high-priced reserves.

When forward Larry Johnson and center Luc Longley retired before this season—both with back troubles and long-term contracts—and oft-injured center Marcus Camby came up lame, it stripped the Knicks of any real hope before the first game.

Coach Jeff Van Gundy, who took the Knicks to the 1999 NBA Finals, resigned less than six weeks into the season, knowing he was headed for nothing but headaches.

"For New Yorkers, I'm sure it's a difficult season," said Magic Coach Doc Rivers, who played in New York for 2½ seasons. "The Knicks are supposed to be good all the time, aren't they? It's a proud franchise. I don't know exactly what happened there, but it looked like a snowball effect. Once it got rolling, it's a bear to get it stopped."

Don Chaney, who was elevated from assistant to head coach and was signed through next season, is wondering about his future. Layden, who brought in many of the current players, is expected to be replaced this summer if ownership decides on major changes.

There is daily speculation in New York about where the Knicks are heading. They have two outstanding players in Sprewell, 31, and Houston, but one will have to be traded this summer to land an experienced frontcourt player.

At point guard, they already have Mark Jackson, Eisley and Charlie Ward, all making big money and all unhappy with the three-headed rotation at their position.

Power forward Kurt Thomas has been a bright spot in the second half of the season, but he is out of position at center, where Felton Spencer and Travis Knight are buried down the bench.

Just three years ago, the Knicks were starting a playoff run that ended in the NBA Finals. They won 50 games two seasons ago, reaching the conference final. And last season they won 48 games before falling in the first round of the playoffs.

Today, there are five players on the Knicks' roster who were part of the team that played in the 1999 Finals. Yet they don't feel the same. They still wear Knicks uniforms, but they don't look like the Knicks anymore.

They lost by 21 points in Minnesota on Friday. They lost by 29 in Atlanta two weeks before and lost by 22 at New Jersey last month.

"No one is happy with the record we have now," said Layden. "What is the plan? That's a much-asked question now. Just from a strategy standpoint, we won't lay out the plan. But clearly we'll use everything at our disposal to make this team better."

CRITIQUE

This is an example of turning a simple game-day, regular-season advance story into a readable feature with some insight. The key was planning ahead, taking a look at the schedule, and talking to people about the Knicks long before they came to town.

It helped that Patrick Ewing and Doc Rivers were with the Magic as former Knicks players. They were happy to talk about their former team and how things had fallen apart. I also got other players like John Starks when his current team was playing the Magic.

This also is a story that you can do if there is a second person on the beat, a league-wide story that really helps your coverage, freeing up the primary beat writer from the daily coverage.

People don't want to read the same "how are the Magic playing" story that we too often do as an advance. There are 82 regular season games, and it's hard to come up with 82 different ways to say they are playing tonight.

But with some planning ahead, gathering information long before you have to write it, it's not that difficult to give the readers some insight into what else is happening around the league.

5. Auto Racing

Dick Mittman

Dick Mittman, currently Senior Editor, Indianapolis Motor Speedway/Indy Racing League, learned to operate a lino-type and press as a teenager. He began his newspaper career as a copy boy at the former *Indianapolis Times* in 1950 and was sports editor when it folded in 1965. He later spent 31 years at *The Indianapolis News* and *The Indianapolis Star,* and his story on the 1988 Daytona 500 NASCAR race was voted story of the year by the Associated Press Sports Editors.

As a rookie sportswriter assigned to cover the Indianapolis 500 Mile Race for the first time, nothing can be more unsettling than to walk out into the pits during practice seeking a driver to observe or interview.

Looking to your right, it seems the pits stretch on forever. And there are more pits to your left. Is Helio Castroneves up there? Is he down there? What color is his car? What is the major sponsor's name emblazoned on the side of it? What color is his helmet? What is his team's name?

This isn't baseball or football. There aren't two teams and two dressing rooms. There isn't a manager or coach for each side. The referees don't wear striped shirts.

Auto racing is a simple yet complex sport. The winner is the driver and car that crosses the finish line first. It's like a 100-yard dash stretched over many miles. At Indy on Memorial Day each year the distance is 500 miles, but at Charlotte on the same day the stock car drivers race 600 miles.

This is where it starts getting complicated. At Indianapolis and elsewhere in both the Indy Racing League and CART (Championship Auto Racing Teams) events, they race open-wheel cars (meaning no fenders) and attain speeds of 225 mph. The suspension parts are exposed, too, and the drivers sit low to the ground in open cockpits.

At Charlotte and elsewhere on the NASCAR circuit, the stock cars resemble something you might have driven to the track yourself—a Ford Taurus or Chevy Monte Carlo, for example, except that the Chevy, Ford, or Pontiac reaches nearly 200 mph. Truly, the similarities are only skin deep—the racing cars have custom-made tubular frames and the only way to get inside is to crawl through the driver's-side window opening.

Racing has its big leagues and minor leagues. And it has more types of vehicles than one can imagine.

There are world-famous tracks like the Indianapolis Motor Speedway and Daytona International Speedway. Then there are little dirt tracks like Paragon Speedway in Indiana that run Saturday-night shows and Saturday-night warriors, men—and a few women—who work 40-hour-a-week jobs and race on the weekends in souped-up jalopies more for the fun of it than for the few bucks they can win. But the crowds they attract—maybe only a few hundred fans at a time—add up. They are like little rivulets that, taken together, combine to create a major stream of auto-racing revenue.

There are barely enough letters in the alphabet to handle all of the sanctioning-organization initials: NASCAR, IRL, CART, USAC, SCCA, and F-1 are just a few.

The sports has its czars like Tony George, president of the Indianapolis Motor Speedway and founder of the Indy Racing League; Bill France Jr., who rules NASCAR; and Bernie Ecclestone, the majordomo of Formula One, the great European-based racing series.

There is the mechanical end of things to consider, too. There are a chassis, wheels, and an engine. Mechanics and engineers are constantly trying to find the perfect combination that will make the car go faster than the other cars. There are terms like "loose," "push," "tight," and "neutral" that refer to the way a car handles.

It doesn't stop there. There are automotive chieftains and small-town garage owners, television honchos and celebrities, sponsors and public relations people, rules infractions and lawsuits, huge crowds and dramatic finishes, crashes, and, yes, death.

Covering auto racing means being prepared to be an all-round journalist, one who can jump from one beat to another in an instant. It's a sport, but one that has more facets that can be imagined.

Mostly, like every other sport, it is about people. The race car is a tool—like a bat or puck—and it is the story of the people who make the car go that you want to tell.

Finding those stories is your job.

First, let's discuss writing a race story itself. One driver wins, and as many as 42 can lose in the same race.

Remember, in today's world of instant communication, the nuts and bolts—yes, a pun—of the race already have circled the globe before you have plugged in your laptop. Thus, the old Associated Press hard lead stating who won and by how much becomes unacceptable.

Even for morning dailies, a feature lead probably is best. Your goal, after the smell of the racing fuel and smoking tires have dissipated, after you've completed your interviews, is to pick out from your notes the most interesting angle involving the winner and how he accomplished the victory and weave this into your lead. It could be that it was on Father's Day and Dad beat son, as happened in 1984 when Mario Andretti nipped son Michael in an Indy car race.

It could be a driver returning from serious injuries or a fan favorite like the late Dale Earnhardt winning the Daytona 500 in his 20th start. Maybe it's Jeff Gordon winning the first Brickyard 400 at the Indianapolis Motor Speedway only a few miles from where he cut his racing teeth, or Al Unser Sr. winning the 500 Mile Race in a show car retrieved from a hotel lobby.

Sometimes there is more to the story than is apparent. It was a heartwarming tale in 1988 when Bobby Allison beat son Davey to the checkered flag to win the Daytona 500. When father and son arrived for the post-race interview, standing to the side basking in the glow of the moment was Judy Allison, wife and mother of the two drivers.

An interview with her brought out a touching side to the race that was overlooked by the other writers. Her comments made for a story that decidedly was not just another race summary. The Associated Press Sports Editors must have felt the same way, because they voted it the best sports news story of the year, possibly the only time an auto-racing story has been so honored.

Following is that story.

FAMILY AFFAIR

February 15, 1988

DAYTONA BEACH, Fla.—One day after Davey Allison was born on Feb. 25, 1961, father Bobby Allison drove in his first Daytona 500 and won $200.

Sunday, 26 years later, Bobby Allison won his third Daytona 500 and earned $202,940. Chasing him across the finish line by 1½ car lengths was that now grown up son Davey.

It was one of those heartwarming family affairs that only auto racing can provide. Indy car racing in recent years has seen Al Unser beat son Al Jr. at Phoenix and Mario Andretti nip son Michael at Portland.

The victory in his Miller High Life Buick also was applauded by the Geritol set. Bobby Allison is 50 years old, has a paunch, wrinkles and gray hair. Yet in four days he drove 925 miles and won three races on the high-banked Daytona oval—Thursday's 125-mile qualifier and Saturday's 300-mile grand national race before out-running 41 determined competitors Sunday to add the final plum of the Speed Weeks competition.

Ironically, another 50-year-old, King Richard Petty, provided the other excitement of Sunday's race. He got sideways coming out of the fourth turn, was banged in the rear and his car went flying through six barrel rolls against the fence and was smacked again when it returned to the pavement. Miraculously, he escaped with only a sore ankle and slight concussion.

Last time a father-son finished 1-2 in a NASCAR race was July 10, 1960, at Heidelberg Speedway in Pittsburgh, Pa., when Lee Petty beat that same Richard Petty.

Judy Allison, Bobby's wife and Davey's mother, still vividly remembers that weekend more than a quarter-century ago when Bobby drove and Davey arrived.

"He (Bobby) was running an old car that belonged to my brother-in-law," she related. "I went in the hospital (in Hollywood, Fla.) on Friday. My sister got the message to him and the police got him home."

However, the Allisons were told the baby wouldn't arrive until after the race so he returned to the track. Instead, Davey showed up on Saturday and Bobby, who started 36th and finished 31st, saw his first son late the next day.

"I think he was really proud," Judy said. "Davey was a nice-looking baby."

They named him David after a close friend, Dave Juhan, who attended Sunday's race. Judy said there already were five Bobbys in the Allison family so the baby was not going to become Bobby Jr.

"It's intensifying," she said of the competition between father and son, "and also kind of neat."

The senior Allison, who led seven times for 70 laps and averaged 137.531 miles per hour, said George Blanda, who played pro football until he was 48, always had been an inspiration to him.

"I never felt anyone should step aside," he commented about looking at older drivers when he was 25. I admired them and wanted to learn from them.

"I wanted to race side by side with them. If they retired, I'd never get that opportunity." Allison intends to continue his short-track racing (he's driven several times in Indianapolis not only at the Speedway, but at IRP and the Speedrome) in addition to driving a full Winston Cup schedule this season.

"When I feel like it becomes a real chore, that's the key to when I'll quit," he said.

"I know I can't stand serious injuries as well as I did when I was younger. I did recover from the last one pretty quickly.

"Age is not a number you can put on everybody. You can look at one person who may be past his talents and prime at 40 and at others who go on and on."

Davey grew up at Bobby's Hueytown, Ala., work bench. When he was 16 and willing to work with the uncompetitive Matador, Bobby said he knew his son was going to be a race driver.

"I love the challenge," Davey said. "Dad showed me all the hard points and then showed me the rewards."

Darrell Waltrip's Tide Chevrolet and Bobby's Buick seemed to be the class of Sunday's field. On two occasions, Waltrip held leads of 35 plus seconds.

But 15 laps from the finish, Waltrip suddenly slipped backwards and by the checkered flag had faded to a disappointing 11th.

"I heard a noise (in the engine) and then we started heading towards the back," Waltrip sadly explained.

Another who faded at the end was defending NASCAR champion Dale Earnhardt. He never led, but rode as high as second. A cut tire near the end sent him to the pits and back to 10th.

Bobby Allison snatched the lead from Phil Parsons after a restart on lap 183 in a duel with Waltrip.

Davey hooked up with his dad, but couldn't get around him on the last lap. Eight cars finished within nine-tenths of a second at the finish.

"Would you really have passed me if I had let you?" Bobby Allison asked Davey when he arrived for the post-race press conference. "Without a doubt," Davey exclaimed.

CRITIQUE

This article told the story of the race. But it also told the story of a racing family. It took a little curiosity and reportorial feeling that the wife and mother of these two men would have something valuable to contribute. She made the story.

This is what being a reporter is all about. Auto racing is no different than any other sport. It is made up of people, and asking that extra question or finding that one more person to interview turns an ordinary story into one that is special.

There could have been no sweeter day for the Allison family.

But when you cover auto racing, days of victories and tears of joy can quickly turn into days of tragedy and tears of sadness. That must be covered, too.

Bobby Allison later crashed at Pocono Raceway, was severely injured, and when he recovered had lost much of his memory. Younger son Clifford was killed in a racing accident at Michigan Speedway and, Davey, a rising superstar, was killed in a helicopter accident trying to land at Talladega Superspeedway not far from his Hueytown, Alabama, home. These tragedies ripped apart Bobby and Judy's marriage. *Sports Illustrated* writer Ed Hinton later wrote a beautifully moving story about Bobby living with his aging mother.

Despite the occasional violence of the sport, race drivers—the good ones—tend to stay around much longer than other athletes. For instance, A. J. Foyt drove in 35 Indianapolis 500s and Mario Andretti drove in 29. Reporters who cover the sport on a regular basis become friendly with many of them and fear the worst whenever they are involved in an accident.

Yet as a reporter, you must take a detached approach and report the accident and injuries, if they occur, as a viewer from the press box rather than as a personal friend. One of the toughest race assignments I had was reporting and writing about Foyt's crippling crash at Road America in Elkhart Lake, Wisconsin, on September 23, 1990. On the other hand, his determination to regain the use of his legs and drive in the next Indy 500 made for several inspirational stories.

The secret to covering auto racing is no different than for any other sport. Make friends with the drivers, mechanics, owners, and officials. Not necessarily the type friends you hang out with, but the kind that know who you are, respect you, and will talk to you when you walk into their garage or call on the phone.

I've always had a policy to interview every driver, whether winner or back marker, at some time. In fact, when I traveled the Championship Auto Racing Teams circuit I tried to regularly attend the post-race press conferences of the podium finishers in the major support race. What this did was acquaint me with them and vice versa. And a year or two later when they came to Indy as rookies, it was easy to approach them because they remembered and appreciated those earlier media encounters. It pays off.

Here are two examples of how friendship paid off in an exclusive story: In 1993, Formula One world champion Nigel Mansell came to America to drive on the CART series as Mario Andretti's teammate. He crashed at Phoenix and had to undergo surgery before showing up late at Indy. His participation at Indy had worldwide interest, and many foreign journalists came to the track to report back to their fans.

Mansell was due to arrive at the track on Wednesday of the first week of practice, and a press conference had been set up. However, the Newman-Haas team manager was a close friend, and he alerted me that Mansell would be in the team garage Tuesday evening to be fitted for a seat. They brought me and our photographer into the garage, where we conducted an interview and took pictures. The story and photograph dominated the front sports page of *The News* the next day and made a lot of journalists, American and foreign, irate because they had been scooped.

Another time, General Motors was holding a private test session at the Indianapolis Motor Speedway for its NASCAR drivers, including the late champion Dale Earnhardt. The media weren't invited, but I went out anyway, and a guard who knew me allowed me to enter the garages. When I approached Earnhardt, he said, "Dick, you know I don't do interviews during testing." He paused, then added, "Now, what do you want to know?"

Again, that interview was obtained because I had covered so many of his races and had met him at various times over the years.

Another tip. Don't forget the janitor. You'd be amazed how much he might know. I always chatted with the press room janitor at the Indianapolis Motor Speedway when others didn't give him the time of day. He repaid me in kind when he called my office to inform me the old wooden garages were to be replaced by modern concrete buildings. It provided another opportunity to beat the opposition.

Unless you are mechanically minded, writing about cars can be tough. The best advice here is, don't try to be an expert. Quote mechanics, engineers, and team managers, but let them put very technical information into simple terms. Remember, a majority of your readers aren't mechanical geniuses, either. They understand there is a chassis, an engine, and four tires. Beyond that, they don't care to read a dissertation on how the car functions internally to make it race at 200 mph.

However, there is a place for technical writers. There are many racing and automotive magazines that specialize in the car more than the driver. This provides a writing opportunity for the person who not only understands what makes a race car go fast but can put it down on paper. It doesn't have to be so plainly presented because the readers more readily comprehend the technical nature of the article.

It does pay for any motorsports writer to understand that a normally aspirated engine uses the air as is, while a turbocharged engine reuses the air in a compressed state. Turbocharging gives the engine more horsepower.

Races at the major speedways receive the most attention. But autoracing writers also must cover other, lesser forms of the sport. These are the weekly events held around the country on the small pavement and dirt tracks that abound, many of which are off the beaten track.

It is here that young drivers learn their trade driving sprints, midgets, stock cars and what have you. Every driver who has won the Indy 500 or Daytona 500 was pushing on the throttle at some obscure track trying to make a name for himself at one time. Some do; many don't.

Still, this type of racing provides an abundance of stories for the aspiring motorsports writer. It gives him the chance to learn the sport, the triumphs and travails, just as the driver is doing the same. There are drivers and mechanics, officials and cars, rules and crashes. If the writer shows a knack for covering the sport, then one day he could be at Indy representing his media outlet writing about a competitor he watched come up through the ranks.

Jeff Gordon, now a NASCAR star, is a perfect example of a driver who made it from the boondocks to the big time. His family moved from California to the tiny central Indiana town of Pittsboro when he was a teenager so he could get a USAC racing license and compete against tough drivers on the circuit. It was like going to college when he was 15, and he quickly showed a special talent behind the wheel.

One year after he had moved on to the Busch Grand National series, he raced on the road course at Watkins Glen, New York, then flew back to Indiana to run a sprint car that night at Indianapolis Raceway Park. Approaching the small nearby airport, the plane flew over the track and the crowd cheered. They applauded even louder as his mother dropped him off at the track and he ran by the grandstands, helmet in hand. His car was running when he arrived in the pits. He jumped into the cockpit, dashed out, and set the track qualifying record. What a story! It's one that's repeated regularly around the country and makes for good reading. It's a story that has high drama and nothing technical about it. It's a story that the casual sports reader might pick up and read to the very end, rather than just skip over the headline.

Sponsors: Motorsports probably have more of these than any other sport in the world. Some of the tracks have sponsor names, the cars are plastered with sponsor decals, and the drivers wear uniforms that often look like walking billboards—and they usually mention all of them, particularly in television interviews. Most media outlets determine how they want to handle the sponsor names. Some, like Associated Press, don't use any at all. Most papers allow the primary name of the car to be mentioned on first reference and the same for the name of the race. Often some teams make the car name too unwieldy by listing too many sponsors. The advice there is to use the first one.

Along with sponsors come public-relations representatives. Each team with a decent budget has one, and at each race there is a competition among them to get their driver's story told. But among the top teams, sometimes the PR person works in reverse and limits access to the driver since he or she usually is besieged with interview requests. Working with and around the PR people is an important skill for any young writer to learn.

Never let the PR person dictate what you should write. They want everything to sound hunky-dory, and quite often it isn't.

Today, media press conferences are the norm. The drivers on a whole are extremely articulate. At the 1999 Indy 500, for instance, 22 of the 33 starters had some college education. One had a master's degree, and another was working on his. The press conference gives everyone an equal opportunity for an interview. But it also provides everyone with the same quotes. Each reporter interprets and writes his story in a different way, but still it is best to try to get a quote or two that are exclusive. That makes your story better and special.

It takes an excellent reporter to cover auto racing. There is a need for the sports reporter, the business reporter, the police reporter. And just like the news in general, sports coverage can be divided into various subspecialties. Motorsports is one of them. It has all the drama, intrigue, and action that you will find in any other sport; perhaps more. The only real difference is that in auto racing, it's who crosses the finish line first that wins.

Well, most of the time.

In 1995, Scott Goodyear crossed the finish line first at the Indianapolis 500 but didn't win. He had passed the pace car on a restart late in the race and was penalized 14 spots.

6. Golf

Melanie Hauser

An award-winning columnist and feature writer, Melanie Hauser has covered everything from golf to swimming to the NFL in her 27-year career as a sportswriter. She spent the first 20 years as a writer for the *Austin American-Statesman* and a writer/columnist for *The Houston Post*. She is currently secretary-treasurer of the Golf Writers Association of America, a Houston-based freelance writer/ author, and a teacher of sports reporting at her alma mater, the University of Texas. She collaborated with Hall of Famer Ben Crenshaw on his autobiography, *A Feel for the Game: To Brookline and Back*.

There would be no discussion. No wiggle room. No way to say, "Thanks, but no thanks. Haven't done it. Don't want it. Can't you find someone else?"

Golf?

When the sports editor handed me the beat in my first year—my rookie year, period—at the *Austin American-Statesman,* all I could think was, "That's no sport." Sure, top golfers such as Ben Crenshaw and Tom Kite were big in the city. I'd met them when we were all students at UT-Austin. Even had a class with Crenshaw. But write about them and that game my parents played every weekend? Ha. I was dead set on covering football, thank you very much. And the NFL as soon as possible. I had Super Bowls in my future. And columns. Not golf.

Grudgingly, I accepted the sports editor's edict and soon headed over to Morris Williams Golf Course to do a story on two of the best high school golf teams in the state—Austin High and LBJ.

Talk about fate.

I expected the worst and got, well, the best.

The kids were great. They took me—for a couple of months at least—under their wings. They made sure I understood the terms. They demanded, as only kids can, that if I was going to write about them, I should at least know how to putt. So they pulled me onto the putting green and taught me about lines and breaks and speed and . . . well, how to love a game I'd sworn to hate.

Twenty-eight years, innumerable golf lessons, and God knows how many major championships later, golf isn't just a beat anymore. It's a career.

The NFL, Super Bowls, NBA Finals, Major League Baseball, the Olympics? Been there, done all of that. And covered golf at the same time. One minute I was at a Super Bowl, plowing through a crowded locker room, the next I was sitting on the upstairs veranda at Augusta National chatting with Gene Sarazen and watching Jack Nicklaus tee off in a practice round.

Rough duty? Your friends won't think so. Neither will your colleagues. They'll whine on and on about walking with Jack or Tiger Woods at the Masters or flying to Scotland to watch Tiger become only the fifth man in history to win all four majors. Or they'll remind you golf doesn't have triple overtimes that force you to write on the worst of slam-it-as-fast-as-you-can deadlines and that when you're covering, say, the British Open, you have a six-to-nine-hour time cushion.

But let's just say covering golf—whether it's an NCAA Championship or Tiger's Slam in 2000–2001—isn't the cushy job everyone else seems to think it is. To begin with, golf is the only sport where the action doesn't unfold in front of you—or in four quarters, two halves, or three sets. There's no court or field, but rather 18 holes, a driving range, a putting green, a locker room, and, more often than you'd think, a parking lot where learning everything you need to know for the day can and will take place. We're talking acres and acres here, somewhere between 90 and 156 players, half of whom either haven't started to play or have just finished, for four days of pressure and no closed-circuit TV.

So how can you be everywhere at once? And be expected to write about shots you never saw? And never will, because they weren't captured on video in the first place?

We do it every day. Take the 1989 U.S. Open at Oak Hill Country Club in Rochester, New York. It was the second back-to-back Open for Curtis Strange, which a lot of people saw, and the year of the "Four

Aces," which most reporters never saw. But write about it? Most definitely.

The aces all happened at the 159-yard sixth hole in a 110-minute span—from 8:15 A.M. to 10:05 A.M.—in the second round. First Doug Weaver, then Mark Weibe, Jerry Pate, and Nick Price. The last two in back-to-back groups.

Now, Thursday and Friday at the Open just happen to be the two longest days in sport. Although they did test the split-tee theory for the first time at the 2002 U.S. Open, ordinarily the first tee times are around 7 A.M., the last close to 4 P.M. Can-'til-can't days. The action finishes at sunset, but the reporters are still working at 11 P.M. So not many make a full day of it, considering that even arriving at 10 A.M. makes for more than a 12-hour day.

I'd actually gotten there early that day—just after the second ace—and several of us headed out to the hole. We heard the eruption for the third and were almost there when Price's went in. Bad luck? We weren't alone. Undaunted, we started interviewing the marshals and the woman who was calling in the scores. We knew it would be hours before we could talk to a player.

Back in the press room, a Boston columnist called a Harvard mathematics professor to get the odds on four aces on one hole in the same day—1.89 quadrillion to one, he said. We rolled our sleeves up and pitched in, making calls to the National Golf Foundation, *Golf Digest,* and who knows who else to get their odds, which ranged from 8.7 million to 1 to 332 thousand to 1. By then, the players were finished and we surrounded them, asking each one to describe his shot, his feelings, the scene.

Put it together and you've got a great 20-inch story about something you never saw. One of at least two or three articles—plus a notebook or a column—you'll write in one day alone. Get the picture?

Golf is the only sport where you might walk 18 holes with a player and never use a thing about his round in that day's story. Or where you spend two hours standing behind the 18th green during the final round of a major championship and never see a shot. You're talking to players while others are finishing. You're looking for notes. You watch the leader board—if you can find one—just to know where whoever stands for the day. And about those four straight birdies that gave some guy a top-10 finish? The player is coming off the 18th right now. Wait for him to sign his card and listen in. He might be the top item in your daily notebook.

You might think covering golf today is all about Tiger. It isn't. It wasn't just about Jack Nicklaus or Arnie Palmer, either. They're all extraordinary players—the best of their times—but they're not the entire job.

Golf isn't just birdies, bogeys, and world rankings. Sure, you need to know the basics—all the terms, how far most players can hit a 3-iron or wedge, and a hook from a slice—but you also have to deal with technology issues such as the design of golf balls and clubs, plus sponsorships, purses, course design, PGA and LPGA TOUR regulations, and just about anything else you can think of surrounding the game. And playing the game—or at least attempting to—is another must.

Seriously, though, golf is basically about the players—who they are as well as what they do. Tiger does amazing things with a golf ball, but there's been as much—if not more—written about his heritage, his parents, and his love life. David Duval's 59 in the final round of the 1999 Bob Hope Chrysler Classic was incredible. So is his penchant for snowboarding. And Phil Mickelson? What makes his close calls at winning majors even more compelling is that he was willing to sacrifice a chance to win one by announcing he would walk off the course no matter what if he received a page announcing that his very pregnant wife had gone into labor.

Yes, you can pick up some of this in mass interviews. But not everything. In football, you have 48 players on a roster, a coaching staff, a training staff, and a front-office staff to get to know. And you see them every day during the season.

In golf? Well, try forging relationships with players from all over the world, some of whom you might see no more than four or five times a year. No one, save the Associated Press writer and magazine writers, goes to many more than 10 tournaments a year, so getting to know players means a lot of one-on-one time when you can get it. And you can't force it. Sometimes it takes years to get to know the players. And don't forget about the caddies and teachers and tournament directors. They're some of the best sources for anecdotes and stories, period.

Crenshaw's Masters caddie, Carl Jackson, was my man behind the scenes at the 1995 Masters, sharing tidbits with me all week that I could weave into columns and stories. And in 1993, the inside story came from CBS's Jim Nantz and 2000 Presidents Cup assistant captain Paul Marchand. Nantz, Marchand, and TOUR player Blaine McCallister had been suitemates with Fred Couples at the University of Houston—and I had written about them back then. They spent hours talking about their career dreams, even about Couples winning the Masters and Nantz being there to describe it, and all of them dreamed of the day one would win the Masters. After Couples did win the Masters with, among other shots, a tee shot at the famous par-3 12th hole which magically stuck to a steep bank instead of rolling into the water, Nantz told me about throwing his script into the air when the broadcast went to a break before he could see what had happened to Couples's shot. Marchand told me that, to add to the story, after the cameras stopped rolling in the Butler Cabin (where the green jacket is presented to the winner) and the telecast was over, Couples buried his head on Nantz's shoulder and the two cried. The insights made for a great column on Couples's win.

As with covering any other sport, it's all about trust. Whether you're talking to a caddie or a player, you have to respect them and they have to respect you. And that doesn't come easily. Strong relationships take years to forge, not just one interview. Or even one week.

Golf is a game of longevity, and many of the strongest relationships between writers and golfers date back to covering college and junior tournaments. Some relationships last 30, 40, maybe even 50 years instead of the three to 10 years for football, basketball, or baseball players and those beat writers. And sometimes the stories you tell are as much about the golfer when he was 14 as when he is 44 or even 54.

For example, I met Payne Stewart his junior year at SMU. He was only a few years younger than I and very cocky. I was amused. We spent years watching each other mature in our respective careers—and picking on each other. The day he died in a plane crash in 1999, I cried on the shoulder of another player. I wasn't the only reporter who shed tears. I also wrote some of the best columns of my career that week, using those twentysomething years to put a tragedy, a surreal week where golf became incidental, and a man I admired so much into perspective.

As a group, golfers are among the most accessible athletes in professional sports. But a word of caution. You don't try to interview them before a round like you might in a Major League Baseball clubhouse or NBA locker room. They're focusing and it's no time for chatting. And don't think they all rush into the locker room after a round. They may head to the putting green, the practice tee, or straight to the parking lot—they've sent their caddies for street shoes from the locker in order to make a quick exit. When you're on the beat, you learn who gets to the course two hours before a round or who breezes in an hour before his/her tee time. You know which players spend their lives on the range and which players you had better catch at a locker or risk not talking to until the next day. All of us have found out the hard way, too, almost getting caught in a locker when a player slams it or getting blown off verbally—and not always politely—after a player has had a bad day.

Most players will stop after signing their cards at the end of the round and usually will field questions near the scoring trailer. But the leaders are generally taken to the press room for a bigger interview. Both places are great for your basic daily quotes, although there are opportunities, at times, to get players by themselves in those situations, too.

Of course, there are exceptions. Just two months after winning his first Masters in a runaway, Tiger Woods teed off in his first U.S. Open as a professional. He shot 74; he was hot and he blew off a large group of reporters waiting for him outside the scoring area. As the pool re-porter assigned for just such situations, I went after him. Twenty-five minutes, a stop in the fitness trailer, a stride-for-stride walk to his car, and a slam-dunk of his Discman later, he stopped and gave me cursory answers to share with the other reporters. I also had to describe his mood and moves.

The next day's papers were filled with columns ripping Woods. Nicklaus and Palmer—among others—always stopped, no matter what they shot. Sometimes they asked for a few minutes to cool down, but they knew the importance of answering a few quick questions because everyone wanted to read what they had to say. Even about a 78. Tiger learned from that day and a year later apologized to the Golf Writers Association of America at their annual dinner where he was honored as Player of the Year.

Now, about trudging the course: Covering golf doesn't mean walk-ing all 18 holes of a final round with Tiger or whoever has the lead and writing down every club hit and face made. Anything can and will happen—usually somewhere where you aren't. That said, it's best to walk the course during practice rounds and get a feel for it so when players describe their second shot—around a tree and over water, or to the par-5 whatever hole—you can visualize it and describe it.

Unless you know that—no matter what happens—you're writing about a certain player, it makes no sense to walk all 18 the final day, in particular at a major. You'll find most veteran golf writers will walk a bit in the morning to get used to where the pins are and watch some golf. They might even walk the front nine with the leaders or someone they just like to watch. But come the back nine? Everyone's glued to the television monitors because, frankly, that's the only way to see every shot and know, at the end of the round, which ones were key to the outcome.

Often, the story isn't about who won as much as it is about who lost. Like the 1996 Masters, when Greg Norman went into a slow, agonizing meltdown, losing a six-shot lead and the tournament to Nick Faldo. Or the 1995 Shell Houston Open when Scott Hoch lost a seven-shot lead with 13 holes to play and, when chased into the parking lot, called it like it was—"You can print it now," he said. "Hoch as in choke."

And when it's close? Take the 1986 Masters. I walked the front nine with Seve Ballesteros and Kite, who happened to be playing behind Nicklaus. I came in after watching Nicklaus birdie the ninth and . . . the press hut (it was an old tin Quonset hut at the time) spent the next 2½ hours watching Nicklaus win his sixth Masters and everyone else fall back.

The mental aspect was as huge as anything that day. Until Tiger came along, no one focused as well as Nicklaus, and that mental side is something you must understand to cover the game. We've all played it—many of us rather poorly—but anyone who has ever picked up a club understands the incredible focus a player has to have to play the game at a high level, let alone win.

The next time you marvel at a clutch three-pointer with three seconds left in a basketball game, remember that the player just won a game that's now over. A clutch putt like the lag putt Ben Crenshaw made at the 14th hole on the Friday of the 1995 Masters might get your attention, but remember that Crenshaw still had two-and-a-half days and 40 holes of golf left before he won his second Masters. And he was playing in the long shadows of his longtime teacher Harvey Penick, whom he had helped bury Wednesday of that week.

Or think about Tiger's first Masters or the 2000 U.S. Open. Both times he was playing not against the field but rather against himself— and a number in a record book. The shots were incredible; the focus mind-boggling. And then there was the British Open, when he joined Ben Hogan, Nicklaus, Gary Player, and Gene Sarazen as the only men to win all four of the game's majors. This is how I described it for *GolfWeb:*

We ain't seen nothing yet.

A Grand Slam? How about four of them, maybe more. Three runaway major wins? He'll hardly stop there. A place in the history books before he turns 25 and his automobile insurance rates come back to earth? Wait 'til we're talking 62 and Medicare.

The best player ever to play the game?

Move over Jack. Tiger Woods just took the lead—with decades of majors in front of him.

Incredibly, Woods completed his slam at St. Andrews, the cradle of golf. Which brings us to another important thing about this game—there is no James Naismith in golf. In fact, no one knows exactly when golf was invented. It could have come from Scandinavia, but the roots are in Scotland where, in 1567, Mary Queen of Scots hit golf balls in a field after her husband, Lord Darnley, had died. The British Open—The Open Championship in golf-ese—dates back to 1860 and is the oldest of the majors, followed by the U.S. Open, which began in 1895. And when you cover the game, the history smacks you in the face at every turn.

It's a montage of Hogan, Nelson, Nicklaus, Tiger, Francis Ouimet, Babe Zaharias, Nancy Lopez, and a cast of thousands. Football looks back when records are broken. Golf looks back daily. The PGA TOUR stops at Riviera Country Club in Los Angeles and Colonial Country Club in Fort Worth, where both cities remember how Hogan won each of those two events five times. The U.S. Open goes back to Tulsa and Southern Hills, where Tommy Bolt won an Open and threw a club or two. The British Open goes to St. Andrews, the mecca of the game. And there's the Masters, which came of age when Sarazen holed out from the fairway for a double eagle in 1935.

All you need do is follow Jack around at Augusta—even during a practice round—or watch the crowds Lopez still draws on the LPGA Tour to see just how easily the past and future of golf blends together.

The game? It's so much more. It's Tiger. It's Justin Leonard capping an improbable comeback—for himself and the U.S.—at the 1999 Ryder Cup. It's Lopez's smile and the Babe's theatrics. It's Crenshaw, the Ryder Cup captain, shaking a finger at an assembled press room on the eve of the Ryder Cup singles matches and saying, "I'm a big believer in fate. I have a good feeling about this." It's Jack winning his sixth green jacket and Arnie walking up the 18th hole at St. Andrews or Augusta for the final time.

Golf? It's most definitely a sport. It's also a game of longevity—for both players and reporters.

LOATHE HIM OR LOVE HIM, MONTY KEEPS ROLLING

Sept. 25, 1999

BROOKLINE, Mass.—He spent much of the day acting like a petulant child.

Lower lip stuck out. Arms folded. Evil eye trained on the crowd. Daring someone to snap a photo or say something to set him off.

It didn't matter if it came while he was lumbering down the fairway, lining up a putt or stalking across a green. He was asking the crowds to bring it on. And when it came? He loved it.

Colin Montgomerie may huff and puff and threaten to take himself straight to the Concorde when someone riles him, but it's all a game.

Monty lives for events like this and moments like Saturday morning at the sixth hole when he let that glare last through a rain delay and two backaways—he just stood there glaring and refused to putt—before he drained a 6-footer to halve the hole. Or late that night when he peered out the locker room door and, upon seeing a small group of reporters waiting for him, ducked back in and refused to come out until his courtesy car had driven up and the doors had been opened so he could jump right in.

He doesn't wonder why he's the one America loves to hate. He figures out ways to make it worse. Take Saturday night. The third-ranked player in the world, the best player in Europe and maybe the best player in these 33rd Ryder Cup Matches refused to hold a civil conversation with reporters about one of the best matches of the week and Europe's 10-6 lead. Instead, he sent these thoughts along on a quote sheet: "You know we've won, don't you?," he said, not mentioning if he meant the day or the three-day matches. "It's silent. Great and that's the best thing we can do—silence the crowd by outplaying them."

We asked for the Full Monty and we're getting it. He's rung this one up with four points to go. He's said it's in the bag even though there are still 12 points left to divvy up.

Is he nuts?

Maybe he's tiring of being simply the best player in Europe. Maybe he looks at this mini war as a new challenge. And it just may be every bit a war Sunday when he faces America's most vocal player—Payne Stewart—in the singles at 12:26 p.m.

Stewart didn't play well Saturday, but the guy is tough. He hates to lose. And he hates to be told it's over—especially when it's not.

Yes, the Europeans have outplayed the Americans to this point. And, yes, the red-white-and-blue has an uphill battle. But talk about waving a red flag in front of a bull.

Maybe this Full Monty is his way of tell us to take a hike. Maybe he's bound and determined to end his career as the best European Ryder Cup player ever—no matter what America thinks. Maybe he wants us to concentrate on his 2-1-1 record this week and stop reminding him he hasn't won a major. Maybe he wants to take the flak for the team.

Whatever his plan, it seems to be working.

The Rock—as he's known in Europe—is rolling.

Yes, he and Paul Lawrie lost to Hal Sutton and Jeff Maggert in the morning foursome, but in the afternoon, Monty—teamed with Lawrie again—stole a huge match away from Tiger Woods and Steve Pate, 2-and-1. It didn't take much, mind you. Just a two-putt par at the 14th for birdie to halve the hole and keep the match square and stiffed a 7-iron—to a foot—at the 15th to go one up in the match.

But it was devastating.

Woods was on two at the 14th and had a 7-footer for eagle to win the match and send the United States up by one. When he missed, you could see the gleam in Monty's eye.

"I couldn't reach (the green) with two drivers and he got up there with a 4-iron," Monty said. "A hell of an advantage. But he missed and gave me confidence and from then on, I thought we were going to win."

And, since he's such a team player, Monty let Lawrie put them up by two at the 16th when he stiffed a tee shot to 24 inches. But Monty ended it with a two-putt par at the 17th.

Monty was brilliant in the afternoon. He hit great shots and holed putts. He upstaged Tiger. And after grabbing the top spot, he refused to let go.

Just to add insult to injury, Monty commandeered the last courtesy van in line and made Tiger wait 10 minutes in the chilly air for the next available ride to the team hotel.

Seve we loved—even when he'd jingle change in his pocket, cough or question the honesty of a U.S. player. Monty we barely tolerate.

He can hear a pairing sheet drop at 50 yards. He can see a camera lens two fairways to his right. He has a grumpy look for every situation. We can't wait for Mrs. Doubtfire himself, Robin Williams, to play Monty in a made-for-tv movie.

He sees that glare of his as knee-knocking fearsome. We see it as a reason—profane, uncalled for comments not condoned— to bring it on.

"For me, I take jeering as a compliment," he said, "because I am a threat."

What Monty doesn't get is this: He's a threat because he's a brilliant player, not because he's a grump. Given the chance, we'd love to see him shed those silly stares and sensitive ears. We'd like to see him take that focus and apply it to his game. We think he's shown moments of brilliance for years now, and we dare him to stop this silly posturing and concentrate on what he could become.

He left the course with one of those smirks of his across his face. He didn't acknowledge the reporters who would have loved to hear his thoughts on that afternoon match—not simply read them. He waved to the fans that cheered him and didn't give Tiger and his girlfriend who stood shivering on the curb a second thought.

He was relishing the silence. The four-point lead. The brilliance of his own words.

He was asking the United States to bring it on and they will.

We wonder if he can handle it.

CRITIQUE

This column was written following the second day of play at the 1999 Ryder Cup. At that point, the United States trailed the European team by four points and most writers were tackling one of two subjects: the fact that no team had ever rallied from a four-point deficit to win the Matches or that Captain Ben Crenshaw seemed lost and a bit crazy when, in a formal interview in the media center, he abruptly ended his interview by saying he was leaving the press with one thought—that he believed in fate and he had a good feeling about the final day, which was 12 singles matches.

I had been in a group of reporters near the clubhouse trying to talk with a few players that second night, including Colin Montgomerie. He didn't even acknowledge us, but a quote sheet was distributed in the press room with his comment about "You know we've won, don't you?"

Montgomerie had borne the brunt of the crowd's jeers that week, in part because of his petulant demeanor. Having observed Monty for much of his career—I first wrote about him when he played college golf for Houston Baptist University—I had often thought about how much better he plays when the crowd seems against him. He was a thought in the back of my mind, but nothing was decided until we pulled everyone together after play and the captains' interviews were over. At that point, we decided I should tackle Monty and the red cape he seemed to be waving at the United States in a column. And since the red-cape quote did not attach a day/week value to his statement, we tried to find the official who talked with him but could not. So most of us added that disclaimer to the stories/columns.

What could I have done differently? Not much except jump a guardrail, tackle Monty, and make him try to talk to me. Of course, if I had done that, Brookline's finest would have arrested me. So that's a moot point. The Ryder Cup itself is an emotional week for both sides and has, over the years, drawn more than a few comparisons to war. That week, at least, there is no love lost between players. And Monty's attitude seemed to epitomize that.

We couldn't speak with any of the European players—and many of the U.S. players—that night and thus were left with what we were handed. Things like that happen more often than you would think, and you're left to write a sidebar/column off a quote sheet.

I did have the added edge of having observed Monty that night when he stuck his head outside the door and jumped in front of Tiger in the courtesy-car line. Those details added to the column and helped make the decision that I should write that. We divided up the other stories with three others working with me to provide a complete look at the day—and set the stage for the final day.

In hindsight, the column proved a bit prescient. The next day, the United States came from four points down to win the Ryder Cup. And, yes, Monty's comments were mentioned. Over and over. The United States capped the comeback when Justin Leonard made an improbable putt at 17 and triggered a controversial celebration which is still being debated to this day. And Monty? He was heckled by the crowds all day, although many of the comments were crude, rude, and totally inexcusable.

That final day I wrote about Leonard, another player I've known for a long time. I was able to get up onto the lawn with the team— usually off-limits, but several reporters were brought up there by players or their families—and observe the celebration firsthand. At that point, I found out that Leonard was in tears when he was four down in his match and that Davis Love III had calmed him down. Another day, more tidbits for a better column.

Reporting a big event like this is all about being in the right place at the right time. Or at least about working every angle—which doesn't necessarily mean walking 18 holes. Even though we knew the chances of talking to players were slim, there was a group of reporters who were at the clubhouse late both of the first two nights. We wanted to be there just in case, which often pays off. A number of U.S. players did stop to talk with us because they knew the assembled group of reporters and respected the job we were trying to do.

Sometimes you know what you're writing—as I did with Leonard that final day. We had made that decision when the putt went in. Other times, you don't, like that second day when Monty was a last-minute decision. I can't tell you how many times that happens too. So I collected what I had and wrote, while everyone was coming by asking me if Crenshaw had totally lost it. Funny, but that would have been a good column too, because I've covered Crenshaw's entire career. Instead, I helped Crenshaw write his autobiography, which has a number of chapters devoted to Ryder Cup week.

7. The Olympics and International Sports

Philip Hersh

Philip Hersh has been the Olympic and international sports specialist of the *Chicago Tribune* since 1987. He has been recognized by the German sports newsletter *SportIntern* as one of the 125 most influential people in world sport for each of the past six years. He's also been nominated for the Pulitzer Prize four times. Hersh is a 1968 graduate of Yale University, where he majored in French.

It was the day after the 1991 World Figure Skating Championships in Munich, Germany, where U.S. skaters Kristi Yamaguchi, Tonya Harding, and Nancy Kerrigan had finished 1-2-3, the first time women from one country had swept the medals. With less than a year before the next Winter Olympics, the story had been big back in the States, page one in most sports sections, even if Tonya Harding had yet to become TONYA HARDING.

With several hours to kill on a perfect spring day before a flight to Geneva, a colleague and I went to lunch at an outdoor café on Munich's historic square, the Königsplatz. After a beer or two and a couple of sausages, my colleague said, "You know, the guys at spring training couldn't begin to understand why we would rather be here."

For most sportswriters, being miles from mainstream "ball" games would be unbearable. For the handful of us who concentrate on what can loosely be called "international sport"—minus tennis, golf, and auto racing—it is exactly that distance that makes this beat so appealing. And so what if the water in St. Petersburg, Russia's, grand old hotel came out purple, if Italy's phone system for the 1990 World Cup defied the Tandy computer modems we all used at the time, if an East German hotel charged $300 for a 20-minute phone call to Chicago, if the 1991 Gulf War broke out while you were in Cuba, one of the few nations still in a cold war against the United States?

When the sun sets over the 4,500-year-old ruins of Persepolis, Iran, or the moon rises full over the White Ring arena in Nagano, Japan, the hazards of a sportswriting life without Marriotts or Baby Bells seem pretty insignificant. In fact, covering international sport is like being a foreign correspondent without having the risk of being shot at. Sporting clichés may incorporate a lot of militaristic terminology, but death and the world's games overlap only rarely, when soccer hooligans run amok.

The worst part of the beat is its perceived insignificance. It also is one of the best parts of the beat. A writer covering another nonball sport (hockey) summed it up as the 1983 World Series between the Phillies and the Orioles was being played at Philadelphia's Veterans Stadium. In the tabloid *Philadelphia Daily News,* in which the sports section begins on the back page and runs inward, the World Series coverage began on, let's say, page 140 and filled the next 30 pages. So it was that hockey writer Jay Greenberg began his story, "It's lonely back here on page 106. Everyone else has gone to the Vet, and we're guarding the Flyers beat. Time hangs heavy on hands."

For the international sportswriter, most of life passes back there on page 106. Only during an Olympics, a World Cup, and the odd world championship do the stories regularly creep out to the first page of the sports section or the front page of the newspaper. Some of the time, you are considered expendable. Then an Olympic skating scandal comes along, and every media outlet wishes it had a reporter with the Palm Pilot entries of the few specialists.

"When steroids become a big story in a mainstream sport, like baseball, papers immediately turned to their Olympic writer, the only one who knew about steroids because the Olympic writer had been writing about them for years," says Amy Shipley, *The Washington Post*'s Olympic writer.

The Olympic/international specialist is like a fireman trained to put out only fires caused by earthquakes. No one else on your staff, including your editors, really knows what you do. That is a bad thing only if your ego needs constant stroking.

"If you need constant buzz or the adrenaline of being on page 1 all the time, the Olympics is not for you," says Selena Roberts, who began a stint as *The New York Times*'s Olympic writer in 2000.

Better that your senses get stroked, as they do from the unexpected joys of travel associated with this beat. One night in 1979, during my first of four journalistic trips to our embargoed Caribbean neighbor, Cuba, I ate dinner at one of Hemingway's favorite restaurants, the Bodeguita del Medio. After feasting on Cuban Creole hash and more than one mojito, a potent rum drink, I tried in vain to get a cab back to the hotel. Knowing the hotel was on the waterfront and figuring it could be only a two- or three-mile walk, I set out on foot along the malecon, Havana's seawall. For 40 minutes, on a perfect tropical night, the only sounds I heard were my footfalls, save for the few minutes when singing from a freighter at anchor drifted my way.

Cuba has been just one of the fascinating stops on my magical mystery tour. I have written about women's sports in Iran, where women face incredible cultural restrictions. About Tonya Harding's picaresque background and the shack in which Sammy Sosa's grandmother continued to live as her fabulously wealthy grandson and Mark McGwire battled to break Roger Maris's record in 1998 (it might be baseball, but if it's a foreign country, the international writer usually gets the call). About how newly independent East Timor marked its place on the world stage by sending a few athletes to the 2000 Olympics. About doping scandals and Olympic-bid scandals and judging scandals.

An international writer has to know the difference between a lutz and a flutz as well as the historical and political differences between Catalonia and Spain that explain why fans in Barcelona, the Spanish city that was the 1992 Olympic host, booed the king of Spain when the Olympic stadium opened in 1989. I have listened to Tutsi athletes at the 1996 Olympics describe massacres of their families by Hutus in Rwanda. I have seen an Aboriginal athlete all but deified by a country, Australia, that made slaves of her ancestors. I have reported on how cyclist Lance Armstrong won the Tour de France, the most physically demanding event in sports, three years after he was given a 50-50 chance to live because of cancer.

I have, for a story honored by its inclusion in the book *Best Sports Stories,* drunk licorice-flavored pastis and eaten local olives and cherries while learning how the sport of boules—the French version of bocce—reflects life in Provence, the south of France.

"To a visitor," I wrote, "a boules tournament does not seem to generate much heated competition. The major impression a spectator has is of groups of people mainly standing around, gesturing, talking and drinking. And that, of course, is what the players are doing. These are the Provencal passions, and these are games of boules a la Provencal."

Try to find that at the Bears' training camp in Bourbonnais, Illinois, where the only thing French is the town's name.

So what does it take to get—and do—a job like this?

One: Get management interested. Other than *The New York Times*, no U.S. papers had reporters assigned to Olympic- and international-beat reporting, even on a part-time basis, for the three decades after World War II. The near-total absence of Olympic Games from North America during that period diminished editors' interest in the Olympics. The 1960 Squaw Valley Winter Games were more a curiosity than anything else, remembered mainly for being the first televised live in the United States, with Walter Cronkite as the anchor.

A confluence of events, both geopolitical and Olympic, changed editors' attitudes. From 1976 through 1988, there were four Olympics— two Summer and two Winter Games—in North America. One, in 1984 in Los Angeles, would be the first Summer Olympics in the United States for 52 years. Even more significant, the 1984 Olympics came with particular financial and political baggage, making them more than just a sports story.

First, the 1976 Montreal Summer Games were such a financial disaster that Los Angeles would be the only candidate for the 1984 Games when they were awarded in 1978. That meant Los Angeles could establish new rules for Olympic financing, making the 1984 Olympics the first to be funded privately (save for government support services, such as police and fire) and run like a moneymaking enterprise (they left a $225 million surplus, which provided the funding for the Amateur Athletic Foundation of Los Angeles and the U.S. Olympic Foundation).

Their eventually stunning success, both financial and competitive, was seen as highly unlikely when the Soviet-bloc nations announced a tit-for-tat boycott. The Soviets were retaliating for the U.S.-led boycott of the 1980 Moscow Games, President Jimmy Carter's reprisal for the Soviet invasion of Afghanistan.

Despite insistence by Olympic pooh-bahs of separation between sport and state, the Olympics and politics long have been intricately intertwined. Yet never was the linkage so obvious than in the period from 1968 to 1984, when three Summer Games (1976, 1980, 1984) were boycotted, one (1972) remembered for the massacre of 11 Israelis by Arab terrorists, and another (1968) marked by the gloved-hand protest of African-American athletes and the Mexican government's murderous crackdown on student protestors 10 days before the opening ceremonies.

With issues of such complexity becoming part of the Olympic scene, covering them required more than occasional attention. Starting with *The Los Angeles Times,* newspapers created Olympic beats. By the late 1980s, *USA Today,* the *Chicago Tribune, The Boston Globe, The Washington Post,* and *The Dallas Morning News* had joined *The Los Angeles Times* and *The New York Times* as papers with reporters whose primary responsibility was covering the Olympics and related matters. Other papers, like *The Miami Herald,* the *Detroit Free Press,* and *The Denver Post,* assigned someone to keep up with if not concentrate on the Olympic world. Nearly 20 years later, that coverage continues.

Two: Have an expanded idea of what sports are important and interesting. In his book *A Year in the Sun, New York Times* columnist George Vecsey paid me and one of my colleagues, Randy Harvey of *The Los Angeles Times,* perhaps the nicest compliment we could ever receive. Among the qualities of the ideal sportswriter, Vecsey wrote, would be the "international vision of Phil Hersh or Randy Harvey." Who are, respectively, a guy from a blue-collar suburb of Boston and a guy from East Texas.

What we share, however, is a sense that the World Cup soccer final or the Olympic 100-meter final are a lot more meaningful to most of the world than the Super Bowl or the seventh game of the World Series. With that feeling comes the desire to inform, but not lecture, our readers about the global significance of such big events and the reason why just having your flag seen in an Olympic opening ceremony is an event of tremendous national significance for most of the world's smaller nations.

You need to understand something about Japan, and its respect for personal property, to know why the U.S. hockey players' trashing of rooms at the 1998 Olympics was not just boys being boys but an act of tremendous cultural insensitivity. That is among the things a writer with international vision can bring to a newspaper.

Acquiring that scope of knowledge is a factor mainly of curiosity, of wanting to know as much about the meaning of the 200-kilometer

Elfstedentocht speed skating race to the 11 cities of Friesland as the meaning of the Packers to Green Bay. Being open-minded enough to realize that the world is bigger than baseball and U.S. football does not mean one has to disdain the sports most popular in the United States. It means what it says: being open-minded.

Three: Be female. Although most of the first Olympic beat writers were men—because there were far fewer women in sports departments 20 years ago—the majority now is female. At the time of this writing, women were the Olympic writers at *USA Today, The New York Times, The Washington Post, The Miami Herald,* the *Detroit Free Press,* and *The Dallas Morning News,* and the beat was split between a man and woman at *The Los Angeles Times.*

Some female Olympic writers feel that stereotyping has caused that imbalance.

"Sports editors and people who make assignments historically have seen the Olympics as a 'female beat,' partly because there women's sports are so important in the Olympics," says *The New York Times*'s Roberts. "This is particularly true of sports editors at small and mid-size papers. There is an attitude of, 'If it's a hard-core beat, you have to have a guy.' A lot of male writers think the Olympics is not as high-profile and sexy as other beats."

The Washington Post's Amy Shipley agrees. "It's not that you can't do the Olympics if you're a man. It's a matter of what man would want it," she says. "Men are not beating the door down to get it. For women, there is the added dimension of possibly feeling more comfortable with the Olympics. Some women may think, 'I'm not a baseball encyclopedia, maybe I can't compete there.'"

Skilled, dogged reporters like Roberts or Shipley have, of course, competed anywhere, and they have been beat reporters of great distinction on men's professional sports. I covered every men's pro sport for major newspapers and chose to switch to the Olympics because, quite frankly, I was fed up with the greed, arrogance, and poor manners of most U.S. professional athletes and the lamentable intellectual level of most so-called student-athletes. I have a gut feeling that there is more to the disproportion of women covering the Olympics than stereotyping. Because many women sportswriters thankfully were spared the youthful indoctrination that provides encyclopedic knowledge of mainstream sports trivia, they are more open to embracing sports that use different frames of reference.

Four: Don't worry about the language barrier. Nearly all the best

Olympic writers of my generation knew only a few words in any language other than English. That did not stop the likes of Shipley or Roberts or Randy Harvey or Jere Longman of *The New York Times* or Vicki Michaelis of *USA Today* from doing their jobs exceptionally well. First of all, English is, more than ever, the world's lingua franca. Not only do Alitalia pilots flying into Rome speak English to the control tower, Russian figure skaters in St. Petersburg will speak English to a reporter. English predominance is even more evident in the Olympics; because it is one of the official languages, every formal interview has an English translation. That such translations are becoming unnecessary was evident at the 1994 Olympics, when the pairs-skating podium included four native Russian-speakers, a native French-speaker and a native English-speaker. In the 30-minute, post-event press conference, every question and answer was in untranslated English.

Speaking a foreign language has its advantages. The reclusive French sprinter, Marie-Jose Perec, was much more at ease when she knew she could lapse into her native tongue, if necessary, during our lengthy interview, because I speak French. When doing event coverage abroad, it helps to be able to read coverage of the event in foreign newspapers. But one can always find a foreign colleague to help with translation. At least one U.S. phone company has an excellent, if expensive, conference-call–type interpreter service that allows one to do telephone interviews in the interviewee's language. Any reporter who lives near a university can generally find a foreign student or teacher who will do translation for more reasonable prices. Using the Internet to contact various German universities, I found the graduate student with whom I worked on a weeklong visit to report on the status of sports in the former East Germany 10 years after German reunification.

Many foreign athletes, especially soccer players, will give U.S. reporters access they deny the beat reporters from their own country. We generally are interested in personality and background more than in why they played so poorly in the previous game. A different line of questioning often is just what the athlete needs to open up. Italian soccer star Roberto Baggio promised 15 minutes for an interview before the 1994 World Cup. An hour later, he still was talking.

Five: Learn something about the history and culture of places you will be visiting—and how a particular sport fits into that culture. While on vacation in France during the 1982 soccer World Cup, my wife and I went to a bar in the Provencal city of Carpentras to watch a first-round match between France and England. Given the historic rivalry between France and England, we figured the bar would be pulsating. In fact, only two more people would come to the bar to watch. Carpentras, we learned, is in a part of France where rugby is more popular, and the French, we learned, are famous for jumping on the bandwagon. No Frenchman was willing to invest any energy on a first-round match of a team that had advanced past the first round just once since World War II.

And while soccer may be the most popular sport in France, to kids in the poor suburbs of Paris where many recent immigrants live, basketball was becoming just as big until the French soccer team took on a more multicthnic look in 1998.

One thing any U.S. reporter needs to learn immediately is the extent of the pressure on stars in smaller countries. First of all, Americans show relatively little passion for U.S. national teams in any sport, and when we do, it is short-lived. The Miracle on Ice U.S. Olympic hockey team of 1980 did not lead to blanket coverage of its Olympic successor in 1984. Interest in the U.S. national soccer team was considerable for two weeks during the 2002 World Cup, then nonexistent afterward. In sports, we are a nation of city-states. We care about teams from Chicago or New York or Dallas or a favorite college. (Foreign universities do not indulge in the folly of big-time spectator sports.) And while a soccer-loving Munich fan will worry about the Bayern Munich team, a traditional powerhouse in the German league, he will think equally about the German national team, a traditional powerhouse on the world scene.

In the United States, we have hundreds of star athletes, but rarely do we feel that our national pride depends on Michael Jordan or Tiger Woods or Andre Agassi. Many nations have one or two superstar athletes, which places often-suffocating pressure on them, as Steffi Graf or Perec or Cathy Freeman or Hermann Maier will attest. If U.S. athletes feel it is tough playing for the New York Yankees, they should consider what it would be like playing for the U.S. Yankees—or, even more, playing in a place like England, where facts-be-damned tabloid journalism leaves athletes to live with printed rumor and innuendo that wouldn't get into any decent U.S. paper.

Six: Keep your passport up to date. I dropped everything to leave for France as Armstrong was about to win his first Tour. Then I put the physical demands in this perspective: "Armstrong began riding the Tour de France as his countrymen were celebrating the 4th of July weekend and kept at it for three weeks. He covered an average daily distance that is roughly equal to a trip from Milwaukee to the Indiana border. He rode the race's prologue and 20 stages in weather that included nearly freezing rain, hail, scorching sun and temperatures of more than 100 degrees. He flew across flats to win the prologue and two time-trial stages. He won a stage that climbed over a mountain pass at 8,675 feet above sea level, descended at breakneck speeds, then finished at 6,626 feet. On France's independence day, he was fifth in a stage that ended with eight miles of climbing through 21 switchbacks up a 7.9 percent grade."

That journey is a lot harder than anything an Olympic writer will do. But in a way, it sums up the job—here, there, and everywhere, with a different challenge every day.

8. Tennis

Mark Ambrogi

Mark Ambrogi has covered tennis for *The Indianapolis Star* since 1988. He has written about all aspects of the Central Indiana tennis scene, including coverage of the RCA Championships, a major ATP Tour event. He appreciated John McEnroe's shot-making and the showmanship of Jimmy Connors and Boris Becker on the court.

Shortly after ATP Tour chief executive officer Mark Miles took over in 1990, he expounded on his wishes for media coverage of the tour. The Indianapolis native told this writer he hoped the media would one day cover the tour much like the PGA Tour had been covered in those days when there was more focus on the tour events themselves and not the golfers. Miles hoped the media wouldn't be caught up with who was or wasn't entered at each tournament, always a sticking point with tennis officials.

It didn't take long for Miles to realize that the focus on personality wasn't about to change, though. He learned that media coverage and fan interest in the tennis world will always be focused on the personalities, especially in the United States.

In the United States, so many sports are competing for space in newspapers. Without the colorfulness and controversy of Jimmy Connors or John McEnroe, tennis coverage has moved farther back into the sports section.

Typically, only the largest U.S. dailies cover the two-week Grand Slam events, with the U.S. Open obviously drawing the most coverage. My newspaper, *The Indianapolis Star,* frequently covers three of pro golf's majors but does not cover any of the Grand Slams. Several newspapers have reporters that cover tennis as a beat, but only a few of those reporters have it as their primary beat. Nevertheless there are many opportunities for sports reporters to write about tennis at the high school, college, and professional levels.

Women's tennis is drawing more press attention in the United States now than men's because of the play of strong Americans like the Williams sisters and Jennifer Capriati and because personalities, including Martina Hingis and Monica Seles, are stronger.

Women's tennis began growing when Billie Jean King beat tennis hustler Bobby Riggs in the Battle of the Sexes in 1973. The long rivalry between Martina Navratilova and Chris Evert strengthened the women's prominence in coverage.

At all levels the best tennis stories typically focus on the players and refrain from including too much match detail. Tennis play-by-play is often dry or tedious to read. In a tight match, there is usually a key turning point, perhaps a service break, the writer should focus on or develop. Too many details about tennis scoring or players trading volleys can be confusing to the readers.

The challenge for writers covering professional men's and women's tennis tournaments is getting time with those personalities to develop compelling feature stories.

My first introduction to a major men's tournament came in 1984 when I covered the ATP Championship near Cincinnati, now a Tennis Masters Series event, for *The Cincinnati Post.* I was ill-prepared for the short interview sessions, often with shy Swedish players, and the need to balance sparse quotes with the match coverage. I've covered the RCA Championships, an ATP event, in Indianapolis each year since 1988. Since 1990, I have gone to an ATP event near Cincinnati the week before the Indianapolis event primarily to gather features for the RCA special section.

Often I get the interviews during post-match sessions, and occasionally I'm able to get one-on-one interviews. For instance, I was able to obtain a 15-minute private interview with Stefan Edberg during his farewell year on the tour in 1996 since he was playing in Indianapolis.

A few weeks before he won the U.S. Open, I got a few minutes alone with Marat Safin to talk with him about spending several weeks in Indianapolis on a visit with a Russian tennis contingent. It would have been boring to other reporters but was a good angle for me before his first RCA Championships appearance.

Through the years, access to players has improved, but it still pales in comparison to other sports.

The post-match interviews are conducted in press-conference settings, where various reporters are seeking different angles. These sessions can be from as short as 5 to 10 minutes to as long as a half-hour depending on the player's willingness to stay and the tour media-relations representative's willingness to allow it to continue.

Depending on the player's mood, these sessions can be entertaining. I've watched players such as John McEnroe, Pete Sampras, and Andre Agassi become more comfortable in these sessions through the years.

Once McEnroe couldn't wait to end interview sessions and was often short-tempered. But by his last two visits to Indianapolis, including a run to the 1989 title, he would hold court in the interview room on tennis subjects for as long as there were questions.

Sampras reveals a humorous side in media conferences that may not produce a sound bite or a key quote but shows he is more at ease than many expect.

Agassi has always understood the importance of image but has become more analytical and given better quotes through the years. He had nothing to say, however, after he was defaulted from the RCAs in 1996 for verbal profanity toward a chair umpire. He took a fine for not showing up to the media conference.

Opportunities for one-on-one interviews with the most prominent players are infrequent. Even with the lower-ranked players, these interviews can be difficult to arrange, given their practice sessions and the fact you are relying on the on-site personnel.

There is no open-locker-room setting where reporters can wait for players, such in the NFL, NBA, NHL, or Major League Baseball.

Two of my most engaging one-on-one interviews with tennis superstars were with McEnroe and Martina Navratilova. Unfortunately, it was after both had retired from the main tours and were playing in senior events!

If you are able to arrange a private interview, it is important that you have an angle prepared and are ready to get to the point quickly. Also remember that many of the top players hail from countries like Brazil, Spain, Russia, Germany, and Croatia. Most speak English—some much better than others. My suggestion is to get as much background as possible through the tour Web site, tennis magazines, and the tour representatives. Periodically throughout the year, and especially prior to the Grand Slams, the ATP Tour will conduct media teleconferences. Participating in or reviewing the transcripts of these teleconferences will give you ideas of which storylines to pursue. If you participate in the call, those quotes will help flesh out a future story or help with background materials.

Since 1990, I have written the lead coverage story for the RCA Championships. Most pro tennis tournaments have afternoon and evening sessions through the week. On a typical tournament week, I will arrive an hour before the matches begin. I study the matchups and tour notes to seek interesting story subjects. I then evaluate which matches should be considered for the main story, which are sidebar possibilities, which are notes, and which are of little interest to the average fan. Often the main story will change throughout the day as upsets happen. You have to be flexible because the stories keep evolving. Some busy days, a match that seemed like a good focal point at 11 A.M. might end up barely a note by the time the matches are all concluded.

I write one wrap-up story on both the afternoon and evening sessions, but I attempt to focus on no more than two or three matches. Usually there can be a summary paragraph or two about key upsets or upcoming pairings. Here is the first portion of a story I wrote on the 1994 RCA tournament, which was filled with upsets. I focused the first few paragraphs on the tourney overview before beginning to focus on the biggest surprise.

NO-NAMES ARE BEST AFTER EDBERG UPSET

August 20, 1994

Stefan Edberg had no legs. Alex Corretja had no mercy. The RCA Championships now has no names.

Big names, that is. Although Corretja might be making a name for himself. The giant-killer exploited a tired Edberg to move into today's semifinals at the Indianapolis Tennis Center. Corretja, who previously dispatched defending champ Jim Courier, edged the third-seeded Edberg 1-6, 6-2, 6-4 Friday afternoon.

The Spaniard will now face seventh-seeded South African Wayne Ferreira, the only remaining seed, in today's noon semifinal. The second semifinal pits France's Olivier Delaitre against Germany's Bernd Karbacher. The survivors battle for a $152,500 winner's check Sunday.

It's the first time no Americans have played in the semifinals here since they paved the clay courts in '88.

Fittingly, clay courter Corretja is the big story.

"I think it is the greatest week of my life," said the 20-year-old Corretja. "I just came here to play a little bit on hardcourt and practice and now I am in the semifinals. I beat Courier. I beat (Andrea) Gaudenzi, too. He is 25th (in the rankings). Now I beat Edberg."

Corretja, ranked 43rd and the youngest player in the field, is playing his first hardcourts tournament of '94.

"I began playing very slowly like on clay," he said. "Now I am playing a little more aggressive and I like it. When you win, you always like it even if is on grass or ice, it doesn't matter."

When you're covering a men's or women's pro tournament, it's important to remember that the fans always want to know which stars are left in the field. Here are the first several paragraphs of a 1999 story, when injuries were the tourney's hot topic. The top of the story might be loaded with too many facts, but I felt it was important to set the stage before moving on to the matches.

HURTING SAMPRAS LEAVES UNFINISHED BUSINESS

August 21, 1999

Pete Sampras felt a twinge in his hip on an overhead. Not too long after, RCA Championships tournament director Rod Davis would feel his heart sink.

The top-seeded Sampras pulled out of the RCAs with a right hip flexor strain after splitting sets with Vincent Spadea at the Indianapolis Tennis Center on Friday afternoon.

Thursday, second-seeded Patrick Rafter withdrew from Friday's scheduled quarterfinal match with Jan Siemerink because of a right shoulder injury.

Third-seeded Gustavo Kuerten and fourth-seeded Carlos Moya bowed out in more conventional fashion on Friday. Kuerten lost to Sebastien Grosjean 6-4, 6-3, and Moya was whipped by No. 11 seed Nicolas Lapentti 6-1, 6-2 before 7,203 fans in the evening session.

So today's semifinals will feature three unseeded players and Lapentti. Spadea and Grosjean will meet at 11 a.m., followed by the Lapentti-Siemerink duel.

During the year, much of my coverage centers on who has committed to play in that year's event or the tournament's marketing efforts. If most of your coverage of tennis is at the high school, junior-age group, or local levels, I would suggest seeking out the best tennis instructors in your area. Often the player's personal coach can help you analyze a player's strengths and weaknesses much better than their high school coach. The personal coach's comments are often more insightful because they have spent more time working with the players and have a better knowledge of the game unless the high school coach is also a teaching pro.

Coverage of high school tennis in most areas is relegated to the same space as softball, soccer, and cross-country. There are some areas of the country, like Florida or California, where college tennis is covered more heavily. Also, in tennis hotbeds such as California and Florida, a tennis-beat writer will have several professionals to follow on the tour. In the Midwest, on the other hand, the number of players advancing to the elite professional level is smaller.

Your coverage of area players often ends with their college careers. But if a player does move on, you might be writing about that same player numerous times over the course of his or her career. Arguably Indiana's most successful male touring pro was Todd Witsken, who was once ranked among the top five on the tour in doubles. Witsken died following a two-year battle with brain cancer in 1998. The following are the first few paragraphs of a story I wrote two months before his death.

FORMER TENNIS PRO OPTS TO SKIP "LONGSHOT"

March 24, 1998

Todd Witsken needs help to walk anywhere beyond his own bathroom. His speech is slurred. His eyes won't focus unless he wears a patch over one eye.

His heart? Still as big as it was the day he surprised the tennis world by beating Jimmy Connors in the U.S. Open in 1986.

The one-time touring pro and Indianapolis Tennis Center director has staged a tenacious battle with brain cancer but is losing the 20-month struggle.

"Physically I'm not good, but mentally I'm fine," he said in a recent interview at his Zionsville home. "The support from family and friends has been great."

He talked hopefully of reaching his 35th birthday in November and of being there for his wife and four young children, but he knows the odds are nearly insurmountable.

The relationship I built with the Witsken family allowed me access during a trying time. Building relationships with players, coaches, local tennis officials, and clubs will broaden the type of stories you can present to your readers.

9. Baseball

Howard Sinker

Howard Sinker is the State/General Assignment Editor at the Minneapolis *Star Tribune* and teaches news reporting at Macalester College in St. Paul, Minnesota. In addition to covering the Minnesota Twins, he has held an assortment of other writing and editing positions at the newspaper. He is a graduate of Macalester.

In all of sports journalism, there is perhaps no beat that's as taxing—emotionally, physically, and mentally—as baseball. I know this because I've been there and done that, and I'm too old or smart to do it again. The five seasons I spent covering the Minnesota Twins did more for me as a journalist—as a writer, as a reporter, and as a person—than just about anything else I've experienced. It's like construction work, in a way. You work your butt off from February to October, fighting tight deadlines, extreme conditions, and unforeseen circumstances, and then you spend a few months puttering around waiting to do it again. Of course, it doesn't always work like that, because the contemporary baseball writer is expected to know the business side of the game as well as the things that go bump on the field, and the off-the-field news turns your winters in a series of stops and starts.

Oh yes, and did I mention that nobody wants you around?

Maybe you've been a feature writer or maybe you wrote about your high school team for the school paper or maybe you've gone to places where the thrill of having a newspaper reporter around made you into a small-time celebrity for the time you spent with your subject. There are a lot of places where sportswriters are treated like royalty. The

Major League Baseball clubhouse is not one of them. And at the other end of the pipeline, everyone in the office knows so darn much about your beat that they all think they could do it better—if only someone would liberate them from the copy desk.

I remember that when I was made the Twins' beat writer at the Minneapolis *Star Tribune* in 1983, a wise old editor said to me: "Now we'll see how good you are writing about people who don't like you." At the time, I was making the leap from regional feature writing, which included a healthy dose of high school and small-college sports, to a professional team. It was more than a little bit like being called up from the minor leagues. Suddenly, the car trips to the middle of nowhere were replaced by air travel. The hotels had concierges instead of fly-swatters. Radio stations wanted my time, and some were willing to pay more than a penny for my thoughts. It was a heady time, the first time I stepped foot on a field, thinking about all of those things: It was September 1983, Labor Day evening in Arlington, Texas, the Twins versus the Rangers. It was also opening night for the Dallas Cowboys, so about 1,000 people actually witnessed the game.

To tell you everything about what it was like would be to take away some of the surprise if you ever get the chance to cover baseball. But the purpose of this chapter is to tell you a bit about what to expect if you decide that being a baseball-beat writer is one of your dreams. It's hard work. There's no way to sugarcoat it. The hours are long, the work is hard, the travel is a bear. Many of the things a journalist can do after covering the baseball beat seem like a paid vacation.

So you want to know what a typical day is like?

Well, there's no such thing. But here's a look at what my schedule might have been like on a typical weekday covering a night game at the Metrodome, the Twins' home stadium. The late Red Smith, the great New York columnist, used to talk about taking the reader by the hand and walking him through the dugout. What I'm going to do here is to drag you through the press box and the other places where I'd spend a few minutes or more during the day. The sum total of these experiences will tell you a lot about what you can expect if you ever decide that covering baseball is what you want to do.

10 A.M.—The phone rings, waking you up after the previous night's game. It's a writer from another city wanting to know about a possible trade involving her team and your team. You haven't heard anything about it and you add it to your list of things to do during the day. You pick up your newspaper and the other one in town, hoping the other

one doesn't have anything about that trade—or anything else that you don't have, for that matter.

Your editors may never want to admit this, but covering the baseball beat—and most other pro sports beats—is a lot about forging partnerships with peers at other newspapers. You need them to fill in the blanks of what's going on around the league. Is "their" team interested in "your" player? What's the loose talk? The front office of Team X is more likely to have loose lips about Team Y than about its own operation, so you need to build trust with beat reporters in other cities. You can't let their reporting replace your own, but those partnerships are absolutely essential.

1 P.M.—Stop in the office on the way to work. Sports-beat writers spend so much time away from the office—on the road or at the stadiums—that they often feel disconnected from their colleagues and supervisors. Copy editors are voices on the phone to be dealt with on deadlines, clerks hardly have an identity beyond the voices that answer when you call, news-side reporters barely exist regardless of their profile in the rest of the newspaper and community. It's a good idea to wander through the office and remind people that you're more than 10 blabberfingers on the other end of a modem. You check mail—electronic, voice, and "snail"—and make small talk with people who know more about your beat than you do (In their minds, anyway).

You really need to do the best you can to have good rapport with your editors—both the assignment editors who are thinking great thoughts during the day and the copy editors who will be working your copy on a quick turnaround at night. Feature writers have time to go back and forth with those folks; you don't. And if you don't take the first step in establishing a good relationship, your copy is going to suffer.

3 P.M.—Arrive at the stadium. The game doesn't begin for another four hours, but this is the time that a lot of the real work gets done. There are still a couple of hours until batting practice and all of the other pre-game rituals. The manager can be found in his office, and often he will be ready for some quality time that doesn't exist when the TV guys start showing up a couple of hours later. The players are lounging around in the clubhouse, maybe waiting for time with the trainer or in the weight room or getting in some early batting practice. The mood is relaxed. If you want to do something in depth about a player or an issue with the team, this is the best time to find someone willing to kick back and chat.

It's also a great thing to spring on your friends—that you arrive at the ballpark four hours before game time and don't leave until the cleanup-crew members are the only ones remaining.

One thing you'll notice on the beat: In the pecking order, the newspaper-beat writers and the radio announcers are at the top of any pyramid. The players might not like having you around, but most of them come to have a grudging respect for the members of the media they see at home and on the road. The hometown clubhouse is filled with TV guys and radio stringers who are basically faces without names to most ballplayers. That's why most big stories are broken by newspapers and most of the stories that turn out to be hot air come from the "instant" and not-as-well-sourced world of radio and TV.

Remember this: Basketball and football players have locker rooms. In baseball, it's called the clubhouse. Hockey players get ready in the dressing room, by the way.

4 P.M.—Wander through the main office. Not all of the action takes place on the field. If the general manager's door is closed, there's a good chance that something's happening that you should know about. Think about that 10 A.M. phone call that started your day, and find someone to spring it on. The front offices of baseball teams are filled with underpaid underlings, and in any organization there are one or two of them that think it's in their best interest to court the media. If you can find someone like that, work them well and use them discreetly. Needless to say, you wouldn't use their information directly because they're often three or four levels removed from the truly powerful.

But when you talk to the decision makers, it's the little people in the organization who can point you toward what to ask.

Once upon a time, the Minnesota Twins had a journeyman catcher named Mark Salas who worked his way into the starting lineup because the team didn't have anyone better. One night about an hour before game time, a friend from another newspaper called and told me to be on the lookout for a trade after the game. The Twins were going to trade Salas to the Yankees for Joe Niekro, a veteran pitcher who would help them in the pennant race.

A couple of minutes later, Salas's name was mysteriously removed from the Twins' lineup.

What was happening?

Well, the deal had been made, with the understanding that it wouldn't be announced until after both the Twins and Yankees were finished with their games that night—and that nobody got hurt. The

Twins weren't taking any chances with Salas. I wandered back down to the dugout and asked the manager was what happening. He assured me that nothing was up, he just wanted to make a change.

I knew better but didn't want to say.

When the game started, I tracked down someone in the organization who was a good enough source that I could use their information. I asked about the Salas-for-Niekro trade. I got one of those looks and a promise that the trade would be announced after the game. Then I went up the food chain to the general manager, being just as specific so he knew that I knew what was going down. I got confirmation and some quotes from the general manager.

Why did I need to do that during the game? Well, the game was at 7 P.M., and the deadline for my copy that night was at 10:40 P.M. I had my game story to write, I had the nightly team notebook of news that didn't fit into the game story—and now I had a significant trade. I was able to write the story during the game, and plug in a few details afterward, rather than scramble at the 11th hour, which is what the writer from the other newspaper in town had to do. The game even went into extra innings, testing deadlines and (more important) keeping the trade off the 10 o'clock news. One footnote: Salas entered the game as a pinch hitter in the late innings. His last act as a Minnesota Twin was to hit a home run.

5 P.M.—You're on the field. In baseball, the home team takes batting practice first, and a well-choreographed series of events is taking place on the field. Position players are taking their swings, pitchers are running in the outfield and shagging fly balls, a couple of pitchers may be throwing in the bullpen for one reason or another, some other players may be working on fundamentals with a coach. The mood is still pretty relaxed and there's time to grab a few minutes with a player or the manager, and there's also the chance to set up short interviews for after batting practice.

Players pretty much tend to their own business and often rely on the beat writers as a source of inside information. Because players are into a routine during batting practice—or "BP," as they call it—it's a time when someone can be talked to without the prying ears of teammates or coaches overhearing. Also, players from the visiting team are starting to show up on the field, and it's a good time to grab a few minutes with one of them if there's a need.

Because most players aren't going to use road trips for sightseeing, a chance to visit with a visiting-team player can frequently be had during the middle of the afternoon if the team's playing at night. The team bus usually leaves for the stadium 2½ or 3 hours before game time, but sometimes only a handful of players are on it because the others have opted to walk or take taxis.

Here's a reporter's tip I copped from a veteran sportswriter: When the team you're covering is taking batting practice, it's a good time to pay a quick visit to the clubhouse.

Why?

To make sure everybody has shown up.

Huh?

The only player who should be in the clubhouse during batting practice is that night's starting pitcher.

So how can you tell if anyone's missing?

Easy. Look for the street shoes. Make sure that each player has a pair of street shoes in their locker. It sounds a little bit like a children's math problem: If the Minnesota Twins have 25 players, how many street shoes should be in the lockers during BP?

Fifty, of course.

In 1986, the Twins signed a relief pitcher named Steve Howe, who was best known for his ongoing problems with chemical dependency and his suspensions from the game while playing for other teams. While the Twins were in Chicago, Howe was asked to appear on ABC-TV's *Nightline,* which was doing a program on drug abuse and athletes. Among the others appearing that night were Peter Gent, the former Dallas Cowboys football player who wrote the satiric novel *North Dallas Forty* that purported to describe a football player's life, and Dock Ellis, a one-time pitcher who said he'd pitched while on LSD.

Howe was supposed to take a private plane and meet the team in Cleveland, where it was scheduled to play a doubleheader the next night. Guess what? A pre-game check of street shoes showed that he never made it. The writer from the other newspaper covering the team knew what was up as well, and we started pestering the Twins' traveling secretary about Howe's disappearance.

The official line early in the evening was that he was simply delayed, for reasons that were never made clear to us. By later in the evening, midway through the second game of a boring September doubleheader, it became obvious that the Twins had no idea about the whereabouts of their troubled pitcher. The mystery continued throughout the weekend . . . and finally was solved at the beginning of the next week when, having blown off the series in Cleveland, Howe returned to the Twin Cities from Detroit, where he was whisked off a commercial flight by team officials and led away, never to wear the team's uniform again.

I was at the airport and watched him being led down the stairs in such a way that we couldn't talk to him. How did I know he was on that flight? Simple. I called the airline and told them "I" had a reservation from Detroit to Minneapolis, a popular route, and couldn't for the life of me remember which flight I'd been booked on.

Sometimes it works.

6 P.M.—The teams have retreated to their clubhouses, where they will change into game uniforms and take infield practice. That's when most teams serve meals to the media and team officials. One perk of working in a baseball front office, where the salaries tend to be surprisingly low, is the free food in return for working long days. Media members used to eat free but now, typically, are charged for their food—a good thing. That half-hour is a good time to catch up with your colleagues and check in with team officials, again in a more relaxed environment than you might find them otherwise. The Twins had an oversized round table in their dining room that was where team officials ate . . . and almost without fail it was possible to grab someone for a question or two that had popped up based on other things I'd learned during the day.

6:30 P.M.—It's half an hour before the game and it's time to get to the press box. The routine for most reporters includes a lot more than writing a story following the game. There are notebook items to be filed, most of which are written during the first few innings, and a running story (this happened, that happened—no quotes, just the facts) for the early edition of the newspaper. More often than not, that story gets scrapped entirely for the final edition, when stories tend to have a much more analytical tone. Some reporters have other items that need to be filed, depending on their newspaper's needs, and the good beat writers are always on the lookout for a news story to augment the game coverage of the day.

7 P.M.—Game time. You may not want to know this: Most reporters write, keep a scorecard, talk on the phone, and drink soda at the same time that they're covering the game. The task is made a little bit easier by press box TVs, but "multitasking" is a way of life on the beat, and the first-rate writers find a way to do three or four things at once without thinking that they're doing anything extraordinary. As a beat writer, you'll need to figure out what works for you while watching others for style tips.

Sometimes, especially at home, the beat writer isn't the only writer from the newspaper covering the game. A columnist might write his column off pre-game interviews or write a live column off something that happened during the game. A feature writer might be working on a story about a player or an issue on the team. News-side reporters might show up for one reason or another if there's a special promotion or if it's opening night or the post-season. A good beat reporter serves as captain of the team in the press box, knowing what everyone is doing and keeping conflicts nonexistent.

If you know that your columnist is writing about problems with the starting pitching, you'll gear your game story to something else. Beware of the columnist who says he's going to write about "a little of this, a little of that" because, darn it, that's your job covering the beat.

10 P.M.—The game is over. You have filed your forgettable running story for the first edition and you're going downstairs to collect wit and wisdom from those who have just played the game and coached it. Often, there is a 10-minute "cooling off" period following games, during which the clubhouse is closed to the media. Sometimes, when you're first let in, the clubhouse appears deserted.

Some players are in the trainer's room receiving treatment, others are in their dining area, a few others are in the weight rooms, and a handful of others have opted for a quick shower. None of those places are open to reporters. You must wait for players to be done with whatever they're doing and return to their lockers before chatting them up. Often the manager is available right after the game, and his office makes a good place to start the post-game circuit. If your deadline is 11:45 P.M., you know that you have about 30 to 45 minutes to do interviews before it's time to hustle back to the press box and write.

Interviews come in two flavors: individual and group. The best ones are individual interviews, one-on-one dialogue between you and the player you need to talk to. Sometimes a radio guy will stick his microphone in your player's face to get a quote that you wanted for tomorrow's story. That's an occupational hazard. Of course, it's also an occupational hazard for you to curse in the vicinity of the microphone while the player is talking or to keep repositioning yourself between the player and the mike. It's very aggravating when somebody co-opts your work in that way, and you need to decide how you're going to handle those situations, knowing full well that from time to time you're going to be late to a group interview with a player that you need for tomorrow's story.

Competing beat writers, on the other hand, tend to understand that everyone is trying to do the same job on a tight deadline. Sure, you'd like that quote for your own, but over the course of a 162-game season there are going to be times when competitors are going to bail each other out in deadline situations. It's one of those things that editors will never admit to, but you can't ride roughshod over your beat-writing competitors. Payback is a bear.

11:45 P.M.—You have filed your story and are packing up for the night. Are you finished? Not quite. Your work isn't completed until the desk lets you know that there are no questions about what you've done. Only then can you shut down the computer, file away your notes, and get ready to do it all again the next day. A postscript: Most beat writers will cover between 125 and 140 games per season, not including spring training and post-season games. In addition, there are all the other stories that aren't based on those games and the nuts and bolts that come with the turf of being a baseball writer. In other words, there's no such thing as a five-day workweek and an eight-hour workday. Then there's the off-season, which comes complete with trades, free-agent arrivals and departures, contract signings, and all sorts of rigors.

When you take the job, you need to discuss with your sports editor the kind of help that you'll receive. Can you miss a couple of road trips during the season to reacquaint yourself with the other people in your life? Who will get called when an off-season story needs to be done? How much time off will you get? The reason that few baseball writers cover a team for years and years is that the rigors of the beat have the potential to grind them down.

A good baseball writer can go on to just about anything else at her or his newspaper. Covering the beat is like riding the wildest roller-coaster at the amusement park, getting stuck a couple of times in incredible positions with amazing views—and then living to tell about it when you go on to do something else with your life.

BILLY BEANE

March 2, 1986

Some people figure that Billy Beane is a star waiting to happen, a young fellow who can't help but leave an impression. It's the type of advance notice that has gone to such Twins as Kent

Hrbek and Tom Brunansky. And such ex-Twins as Rick Sofield and Bryan Oelkers.

"In anything he would do, I couldn't picture Billy being mediocre," said Bill Latham, the left-handed pitcher the Twins got with Beane from the New York Mets for Tim Teufel. "He seems to have a quality that makes him destined to be a glamour type of player. I can see him as the star quarterback, the star outfielder, anything. You could invent a game and he would be good at it."

It would make so much sense. The name Billy Beane is cut out more for a baseball player than someone in a three-piece suit. The image, 6-feet-4 and 195 pounds with a ready smile and California tan, is the stuff of which marketing dreams are made.

William Lamar Beane III, age 23, doesn't mind being noticed.

"My dad was Bill so I was always Billy," Beane said. "Bill Beane sounds too much like Joe Smith. People say that Billy is kind of a stupid name for someone as old as I am, but in baseball you're always a big kid, anyway. So I'll probably always be Billy."

Unlike some of the other untested Twins talent, Beane has a chance at immediate success because manager Ray Miller wasn't overly impressed with any of his left fielders in 1985. If nothing else, Beane already is considered superior defensively to Mickey Hatcher and Randy Bush.

"I want to make a good first impression because that's going to be a lasting one," Beane said. "So I'm putting some pressure on myself. People are going to tell me not to, but it's natural. Everything I do here is going to be under the eye."

Beane has spent a total of 46 days in the major leagues since the Mets made him a first-round draft pick in June 1980. The Mets had three No. 1 picks that summer and used the first of the entire draft to take Darryl Strawberry. There had been some organizational debate, Strawberry vs. Beane, and since then it has been natural to compare the two. Beane hasn't come out well. Nineteen home runs at Class AAA Tidewater doesn't compare well with Strawberry's 29 for the Mets.

"I try not to compare myself to him," Beane said. "But with other people, especially the media, it was always there. We were both outfielders from Southern California, but Darryl was good enough to be in the big leagues at age 20. He's going to be in the Hall of Fame someday."

The Mets didn't exactly have a position waiting for Beane. George Foster was their left fielder and Strawberry was in right. Beane knew "that if I hit 10 home runs in a row at spring training it was no big deal" because their outfield appeared set.

His power has been accompanied by frustration. While batting .285 with 19 home runs last year for Tidewater, Beane also led all Triple-A players with 130 strikeouts. From 1981–83, he struck out in 31.4 percent of his 1,244 at-bats while hitting 25 homers.

The Mets, chafing for an immediate title, couldn't afford to keep grooming Beane. They needed proven bench help, which Miller said is probably why the Mets agreed to the deal.

Beane wasn't the Twins' first choice. "We shot high in the beginning, always knowing what would be acceptable," Twins vice president Andy MacPhail said. "Billy Beane always was part of what was acceptable." Shooting high reportedly meant the Twins' first suggestion was a one-for-one deal, Teufel for Sid Fernandez, a left-handed pitcher who was 9-9 but had a 2.80 ERA and 180 strikeouts in 170⅓ innings. Their next unrealized hope was for Len Dykstra, a left-handed-hitting outfielder and leadoff batter, and a lesser pitcher. Eventually, the Beane-Latham combination was agreed upon.

"There wouldn't have been a deal without Billy Beane," MacPhail said. "He has great talent and he does all five things in the game well. He can run, has arm strength, is a good defensive player, can hit for power and hit for average. We acquired him with the idea that he would become a very productive regular outfielder even though nobody has put a timetable on when that will come about."

That Beane was available for baseball executives to haggle over goes back to his senior year at Mount Carmel High School in San Diego, Calif. He was a three-sport star, good enough to be the city's basketball player of the year and be offered a scholarship by Stanford for both football and baseball.

Baseball or football? Pro or college? There were tugs in both directions.

"It was funny," Beane said. "When I was in high school and trying to decide, all I heard about was Tom Brunansky. He was in the same situation and even though I'd never met him, I knew so much about him that he was like my next-door neighbor."

In 1978, Brunansky had been a standout athlete in Los Angeles and was offered the same choice, a Stanford scholarship or baseball. He chose to sign with the California Angels.

"To play football in front of 80,000 people and go to a great school, that would have been nice," Beane said. "But I was looking at the amount of money that was being offered and I saw that I could get that as well as a baseball opportunity. I could sit here and tell you about how I wanted to play baseball, but when you're 18 and people are offering that kind of money, it's kind of your basic greed."

Beane laughed. The price wasn't cheap. In fact, after the Mets decided they would take Strawberry, he said, "the Mets didn't expect that I would still be around for their next pick. But other teams were calling and I was telling them that it would take a lot of money to sign me because I was planning on going to college."

So Beane was still available and the Mets made him the 23rd player taken in the first round. He signed for $125,000 and left home for Little Falls, N.Y.

Long bus rides and a .210 batting average that summer gave Beane plenty of time to ponder the benefits of a Stanford education.

"When you're 18 years old and in the New York-Penn League, there's going to be a lot of time to wonder, 'What am I doing here?'" Beane said. "There would have been the same thing at Stanford, staying up all night for finals three nights in a row and wondering why I'm not playing baseball."

The doubts finally ceased when Beane reached the International League last season. He batted clean-up for Tidewater, and despite all the strikeouts was among league leaders in several categories and made the postseason All-Star team. His reward was to spend the final weeks of the season with the Mets, witness to a hot pennant race his team lost to St. Louis.

"When I got called up we were playing the Cardinals and you'd come into the locker room and there would be 50 media people," Beane said. "Six or seven camera crews, ESPN, George Plimpton walking around. All I had to do was observe and enjoy it. It's amazing. I'd be watching Lenny Dykstra. One minute we were rooming together in Tidewater, Va., and then the next time I see him, he's got 500 letters in his locker and getting paid for public appearances. Now that I've seen people have things like that, I think I could handle it."

Whether he gets the opportunity depends on how well the weakest part of his game, making contact, comes around.

"He's your typical power hitter who has a chance to be more than that because he can hit for average and steal some bases," said Latham, who has been Beane's teammate for most of the past three years. "I've seen him come a long way. . . . I'm sure he's gotten frustrated at times because he wasn't getting good pitches to hit. I know that when a batter is frustrated, a pitcher can take advantage of that." Said Beane, "If you're looking at my walks, I don't get a lot of them. I'll do things like swing at the first pitch sometimes even when it's not good. If I could balance that out, I think I could hit .300 or .310.

"It's never been like I'm swinging and missing at pitches that are right down the middle. It's maturity, something that's going to come with time. Like sometimes I get so darn anxious when I'm hitting. I'll have two hits and I want that third one so badly that I'll swing no matter where the ball is thrown. A lack of knowledge of the strike zone, that's what it's always been."

Because he engineered the trade, MacPhail has a vested interest in that happening. Because he could fill a void, the rest of the organization must hope Beane is more than another outfield pretender.

"I couldn't ask for a better situation," Beane said. "After last year in Triple-A, I feel I deserve a chance to play every day. I'm here with the attitude that I can win the job. In New York, I knew where I stood no matter what I did in spring training. Here, I can grab as much as I can handle."

CRITIQUE

Spring training is the hopeful time of a baseball season. No matter how badly things went the previous year, things are supposed to happen over the winter that bode well for the season to come. In the case of the 1986 Minnesota Twins, the team was supposed to be significantly improved because a veteran second baseman was traded for two hot prospects, including an outfielder named Billy Beane, who was said to be the key to the trade.

Beane could have been a poster child for the phrase "hope springs eternal." He came to the Twins from the New York Mets amid stories of his potential and all-around athletic ability. The reason he'd spent too many years in the minors was that the Mets had an established outfield that was anchored by Darryl Strawberry, who had been drafted the same year as Beane and already was considered to be in the prime of his career.

The story was about the Twins' hopes for Beane. And it's an example of why it's a good thing that most newspapers are recycled and comparisons to hits and errors made by a beat writer are seldom invoked. Sure, the story never predicted that Beane would find stardom with the Twins. In fact, Beane's minor-league floundering was well documented, but to devote this many words to a prospect . . . well, that was done with the assumption Beane was going to make it after all.

The story's lead compared Beane to four players, all of them promising young players a few years previously. Two of them went on to stardom, two of them disappeared in a haze of mediocrity. The lines were drawn in the first 30 words, which was good.

Then the slobbering began. The player who came to the Twins with Beane was quoted heavily, as were Twins officials who had an interest in selling the trade to the fans. In retrospect, the negative statistics cited in the narrative all seemed to be explained away by words of wisdom from the front office and others, including Beane himself.

Yet the story did not hide the mediocre statistics that were Beane's hallmark. And there were articulate comments from Beane throughout the story—he was a literate interview subject, and not all athletes are. I think the best part was when he talked about choosing a baseball contract over accepting a football scholarship from Stanford. He admitted that he sometimes thought about the thrill of playing football in front of 80,000 people on a Saturday afternoon, and then noted that had he selected football, he most certainly would have had wistful thoughts about baseball while cramming for final exams. That kind of introspection makes a writer look good.

What should I have done to make this story stronger? The main thing, looking back, would have been to tell part of the story from the Mets' perspective. Why did they give up on Beane? His statistics would have been a good talking point to get someone in the Mets minor-league system, maybe one of his former managers, to chat about Beane's liabilities. He was no longer a part of the organization, so the right source may been freer with his words.

Whatever the case, the story does seem a little bit comical in that

Beane never was a regular player for the Twins. That season, slowed by injuries, he hit just .213 with three home runs in 80 games. He didn't last long with the Twins and his career ended a couple of years later.

One more thing: names can be deceiving. The third paragraph notes, "The name Billy Beane is cut out more for a baseball player than someone in a three-piece suit."

Well, when Beane's playing career ended, he started working his way up through the management side of baseball, eventually becoming the general manager of the Oakland A's.

10. Writing Columns

Pat Forde

Pat Forde writes sports columns for *The* (Louisville) *Courier-Journal.*

Welcome to the chapter on column writing, young journalists. Let me start by saying you're not ready to be a columnist. If that's a rude introduction, I apologize. But I will not issue a retraction. You no doubt disagree. You believe you are prepared to dazzle the world with your prose style, rapier wit, startling insight, and Solomonic opinions.

You're not. Trust me.

In a fit of optimism, my employer, *The Courier-Journal* in Louisville, Kentucky, promoted me to columnist at the absurd age of 27. After five years covering preps, then small colleges, and then the University of Kentucky, I was utterly convinced that I was ready for my dream job. The body of evidence from those early days shows that I was every bit as ready for that position as Ryan Leaf was ready for the NFL.

I was a grandstanding, shrill, shrieking, pound-your-shoe-on-the-table blowhard. If you could call my style anything at the time, it would have been rhetorical road rage. If an opinion was worth stating, it was worth overstating. I thought that was the way you were supposed to do it.

Ten years later, after baking the readership with scorching gusts of hot air, I believe (hope) that I have toned down without being tamed. I can still pound my shoe on the table—but no longer feel compelled to do it four times a week. I have, in short, developed that vaguely defined thing called voice—my own voice—and with it a better understanding of what writing a column is about.

It's about this: grit, wit, and bullshit. That's a gross—and crass—generalization, but it hits upon three key tenets: courage/conviction, cleverness, and creativity. We'll discuss all three as we go along.

Because most writers graduate to column writing from byline work, the early stages are intrinsically disastrous. The writer is catapulted into a great unknown:

- After years of living in mortal fear of the vertical pronoun, the "I Formation" is at your disposal to use as you see fit.
- Same with overt opinion, which is taboo for the beat hack.
- Interviews and reportorial skills, while still prized and used regularly by almost all the best columnists, are optional on some occasions.
- Style suddenly is as important as substance, which can lead to an outbreak of a disease I call, "Look, Ma, I'm writing!" (Nothing worse than forced lines that aren't funny.)
- The comfort of ready-made story topics focusing on a single team or sport—advances, gamers, follow-ups, features—is partially replaced by the challenge of manufacturing your own ideas.
- Readers actually notice you're alive and don't mind telling you if they think you stink. (I've been Bronx-cheered in bars, restaurants, supermarkets—and, once, cornered for what seemed like hours by a dogged critic at my sister-in-law's wedding.)

Trial and error—sometimes gross error—is the inevitable result.

So the best advice I can offer aspiring columnists is to stop aspiring. Learn the craft as best you can before charging off to inflict your opinion on the unsuspecting masses.

My firsthand experience tells me that column writing is way too often seen as a Holy Grail. Get your mug in the paper and you've made it. That attitude devalues the other jobs in the sports department and what can be learned by doing them.

My first job at *The Courier-Journal* was as a preps writer in southern Indiana. I had approximately 90 schools to keep tabs on—a cornucopia of potential stories. Basketball was truly a cultural bonding agent in that state. How lucky are you to cover something like that, where the games and life are so tightly woven together?

My last beat job was covering the University of Kentucky. The final game I covered was Duke 104, Kentucky 103, only considered the greatest game in college basketball history.

I get cranky when writers tell me they want to do columns so they can write great stories. There are plenty of great stories out there, on all levels. Pick up a copy of *The Best American Sports Writing of the Century*—a book no college sports department should be without—and you'll see that most of our genre's best work was not in column form.

Nevertheless, I admit that it is undeniably cool to write columns. I would not trade it for another job, now that I have some vague idea what I'm doing. Not that I can't do it better. Not that I don't occasionally expose myself as a complete knucklehead. Not that my story ideas couldn't use an upgrade. Not that dozens of my colleagues don't write rings around me on any given Sunday, Monday, Wednesday, or Friday.

But I do feel comfortable as a columnist. I believe I've grown into the one sportswriting job that requires the most time, experience, and perspective to master.

Here's what I've learned in the growing process:

1. It's hard.

We're talking about the physical act of writing here. If column writing comes to you easily and breezily, you're one of two things: a savant or not trying hard enough. If you find writing "fun," you probably need a reality check and a writing coach. You certainly don't know what you're missing—and what your readers are missing—if you're not agonizing over word choice, laboring over transitions, and relentlessly rewriting. (Very, very rarely these days is my first lede the one that gets in the paper. It's usually Plan B, C, or D.) The best writers don't settle for sloppy sentences, dull verbs, and trite phrases; they grind over their copy and make it better.

Ancient journalism proverb, which I just made up: He who writes fast from an afternoon game writes poorly. That's true of beat writers as well, but the personal ownership intrinsic to a column ups the ante even more. The late Red Smith, who is on the very short list of finest sports columnists in the history of the English language, described the job thusly in Jerome Holtzman's *No Cheering in the Press Box*:

> I don't enjoy the actual labor of writing. I love my job, but I found one of the disadvantages is the several hours at the typewriter each day. That's how I pay for this nice job. And I pay pretty dearly. I sweat. I bleed. I'm a slow writer. Once, through necessity, I was a fast rewrite man. I had no choice.

But when I began doing a column, which is a much more personal thing, I found it wasn't something that I could rip off the top of my head. I had to do it painstakingly. I'm always unhappy, very unhappy, at anything that takes less than two hours. I can do it in two hours, if I must. But my usual answer to the question, "How long does it take to write a column?" is "How much time do I have?" If I have six hours, I take it.

And remember this: At one point Red wrote *seven columns per week.* That's every day, for those who aren't mathematically inclined (and I know you're out there—this is journalism, remember?). That's an unimaginable amount of sweating and bleeding over the typewriter. In fact, that might make Red Smith the job's only certified martyr.

2. The methods are virtually limitless.

"The best sports columns inform and entertain in a distinctive voice," said Dave Kindred, who has written gracefully for a number of publications, currently *The Sporting News.* "From that starting point, possibilities are limited only by imagination. The column can be a piece of humor, a human interest story, a dissection of strategy—always colored by the writer's world view."

In other words, it's you out there on the high wire, talking to the reader in your own tone and style. So it's highly advisable to have a personality that transfers to that tone and style. Fakers and posers are easily exposed, and readers don't dig insincerity.

"Don't fake it. Ever," said Ray Ratto, who writes for the *San Francisco Chronicle* and *ESPN.com.* "Nobody's good enough to get away with that more than once, because people can read lack of conviction and going through the motions. Believe what you're saying, and say what you believe. Your readers are smart (if they're not, you might try getting different readers, or smarten up yourself). Treat them like they're smart, or you'll be stuck with moron letter-writers forever."

"Some columnists, following the lead of sports talk radio, write primarily to titillate or be provocative without a lot of honesty behind their writing," said Ann Killion of *The* (San Jose) *Mercury News.* "I think columnists—more than any other writers, have a pact with their readers: to be honest and straightforward and personal—revealing something about themselves (without boring the reader to death)."

"Whatever the style, you have to be yourself," said David Whitley of the *Orlando Sentinel.* "I can often tell who wrote what without even looking at the byline, simply because their words reflect the way they are sitting around the bar or dinner table."

There are about as many styles as there are columnists. You can write with the linear, no-nonsense sentence structure of Mark Bradley of *The Atlanta Journal-Constitution.* Or with the verbal curlicues of Chuck Culpepper of *The* (Portland) *Oregonian.*

You can write with the withering sarcasm of Bernie Lincicome of the *Rocky Mountain News.* Or the personable warmth of Joe Posnanski of *The Kansas City Star.*

You can write fat paragraphs like Michael Wilbon of *The Washington Post.* Or sentence fragments like Martin Fennelly of *The Tampa Tribune.*

You can jerk tears like Mitch Albom of the *Detroit Free Press* or Bill Plaschke of *The Los Angeles Times.* Or play for laughs like Rick Reilly and Steve Rushin of *Sports Illustrated.*

"It's very hard to define what makes a good column," said Mark Woods of *The Florida Times-Union.* "And it is clearly very subjective. Throw out a name of a columnist and you can easily get a wide range of views."

There's no how-to guide. Each of the writers above found a style and polished it to a high sheen.

3. Imitation is okay.

At least in general terms and reasonable doses.

Once again, Red Smith from *No Cheering in the Press Box*: "I've had many writing heroes, writers who have influenced me. . . . When I was a very young sportswriter I knowingly and unashamedly imitated others. I had a series of heroes who would delight me for a while and I'd imitate them—Damon Runyon, Westbrook Pegler, Joe Williams. . . .

"I think you pick up something from this guy and something from that. I know that I deliberately imitated those three guys, one by one, never together. I'd read one daily, faithfully, and be delighted by him and imitate him. Then someone else would catch my fancy. That's a shameful admission. But slowly, by what process I have no idea, your own writing tends to crystallize, to take shape. Yet you have learned some moves from all these guys and they are somehow incorporated into your own style. Pretty soon you're not imitating any longer."

When I was in college at the University of Missouri, Rick Reilly was My Guy. I was captivated by his jaunty, conversational style (Reilly himself was influenced by the legendary Jim Murray). I laughed out loud at his jokes. I was amazed by his creative story construction. I tried mightily to write like him—until I figured out I wasn't nearly as funny or inventive. Learning your limits and knowing your faults is important in developing your own style.

The sporting analogy would be Kobe Bryant. Down to the smallest detail—the form on his jumper, the way he walks, even his voice— Bryant grew up emulating Michael Jordan. But his hands are nowhere near Jordan's size, so he had to abandon some of MJ's midair ballet in favor of developing other areas—like a midrange jumper and post-up game that Jordan didn't rely upon until he was older.

4. Columnists tend to be the quarterbacks of the sports section: overly celebrated and overly vilified.

Get used to both, without letting either going to your head. Best piece of advice I've heard in this area: "What other people have to say about me is none of my business." Of course, now that most columns come with e-mail addresses and/or phone numbers at the bottom, minding your own business is harder to do. But developing a thick skin is vital to anyone who inflicts his opinion on the populace for a living.

If you're polarizing enough and lucky enough, you might one day have someone say something about you as hilarious as what Randall "Tex" Cobb said about Howard Cosell. Cosell, just about the last television man with an opinion of any kind, quit televising boxing after watching Larry Holmes bludgeon Tomato Can Tex for 15 rounds. When told that the fight had chased Cosell out of pugilism journalism, Cobb said, "I'd go another 15 rounds if it could get him off 'Monday Night Football.'"

Which is just too perfect.

Everybody wants to be liked, but your job is not a popularity contest. If you're overly concerned about hearing positive reviews, you might tend toward writing what you think everyone wants to hear— occasionally at the expense of the truth.

"You're not writing to preach to the choir," Ratto said. "You're writing to inform and entertain, and if you're only writing what people already believe, you can't inform them, because they likely hold their positions more dearly than you. Thus, fear nothing and nobody. When somebody actually has committed a laudable act, praise them for it. But make sure they've earned it. Nobody gets praise just for being somebody, except of course your own personal god and your parole officer."

When you decide it's time to rip, be accountable. Present yourself to the victim of the rip at your earliest convenience, so he/she can reply if he/she desires. One of the meanest things I've ever written was about famed thoroughbred racing trainer D. Wayne Lukas. He foisted a horrible nag named Deeds Not Words into the 1997 Kentucky Derby just to keep his 20-year streak of Derby appearances alive. I referred to him as D(elusional) Wayne throughout my column.

Then I reported to his barn promptly the next morning. Unfortunately, after an hour of waiting, Lukas did not materialize. It was after I left that he told other reporters that he wanted to meet me in the Churchill Downs parking lot at midnight for a fistfight. (Deeds Not Words finished 13th and last in the '97 Derby.)

5. Be timely, be entertaining and be where the action is.

My goal is to write about whatever the sports fans are talking about that day—at the office, the breakfast table, or the corner bar. For that reason, it's often necessary to jettison preliminary plans as events warrant. And to write it in a different or unique way. Readers come to the paper—especially to the columnist's spot—looking for entertainment. Try to give them some.

It also can be necessary to go where the story is playing out. These days especially, too many columnists want to cover the news from their recliner—especially if the news is evolving on deadline. (In this business, bigger can sometimes not be better. When the columnist decides he's too big to travel, too big to work on deadline, and too big to go to the ballpark, there's a problem.)

The best stories take you—and by extension, the reader—to places you never dreamed you'd visit. Like a tiny graveyard in Adairville, Kentucky. I wound up there recently in the company of a young man named Joseph Jefferson. He grew up in this community of a couple thousand less than a mile from the Tennessee state line working with his sharecropper father in the tobacco fields from age 5 on.

Joseph was a cornerback for Western Kentucky University. He was about two days away from being selected in the third round of the NFL draft by the Indianapolis Colts, and he was telling me about his life.

We were standing above his mother's grave. Joseph had wandered into her bedroom one morning when he was 8 and found her very cold and still. She had died in her sleep of heart failure. A flat headstone marked her grave. Joseph said that when he signed his first NFL contract, he would buy a more grand marker—an angel, spreading its wings as if to rise up from this obscure place. It symbolized his rise from tragedy and poverty to a new life.

It was a pretty good story. The kind that make this job one of the best jobs on earth.

FIELD OF DREAMS: WESTERN'S JEFFERSON ALREADY HAS COVERED A LOT OF GROUND

April 20, 2002

The party will be at the small brick house on Beauchamp Road. The site of Joseph Jefferson's saddest moment will be the site of his happiest.

As the National Football League draft commences at noon today, about 100 of the Western Kentucky University defensive back's family members and friends will gather at his boyhood home. Adults will sit on couches and lawn chairs in the front yard; kids will frolic in back. The big screen television will be brought out onto the concrete porch. Meat will sizzle on grills beneath an arching pine tree. And sometime this afternoon, during the first three rounds of the draft, Jefferson expects to hear his name called as one of the most unlikely new professional football players. Like Shoeless Joe Jackson emerging from the corn in "Field of Dreams," Jefferson will have walked out of a Logan County tobacco patch and into the NFL.

The joyous shouts will echo across the fields then. This remote farming town hard by the Tennessee line, with 920 residents and a single stop sign, will be on the map.

At that point Joseph Jefferson will take a quiet moment amid the tumult to thank God and think of his mother.

Anna Jean Spencer died in that house 13½ years ago. It was Joseph, her 8-year-old son, who found her.

He slept in the room next door but came into her bedroom on Labor Day morning, Sept. 5, 1988, as he was pulling on his clothes. He was going to meet his father, Joe Sr., in the tobacco field.

"Mom," he said, "I'm fixin' to go."

Joseph went to her bedside and kissed her on the forehead. He found it weirdly cold. He tried to shake her and found her body hard.

"Right then I knew," he said. "But I didn't want to believe it."

His mother and father were divorced, but Joe Sr. lived just a few hundred yards up the road. Joseph tore out of the house and sprinted that way, terrified. His dog, T.J., an accomplished car chaser, ran alongside.

"I believe I outran that dog that day," Joseph recalled.

His father saw him coming.

"He looked like he'd been crying," Joe Sr. said. "I said, 'What's wrong?'

"He said, 'Daddy, I can't wake Mama up.' I jumped in the truck and drove up there. Sure enough, she had passed."

A faulty heart finally had broken down. Anna Spencer was 39.

Joseph thinks of her constantly. But now, as the sharecropper's son who grew up in poverty and played football in obscurity approaches this life-altering weekend, she is especially present.

"He's doing this for her," Joe Sr. said.

Joe Jefferson said his youngest child and only son was the strong one at the funeral.

"He held up better than any of us did," he said.

At age 8, Joseph already had done considerable growing up.

At home, his mother made him dress and feed himself at an early age. When he complained, she told him, "One day I might not be here to help you do this."

He remembers her saying those kinds of things more and more in the months before she died. She'd had a heart attack two or three years earlier.

"I think she might have known something was going to happen," he said. "But she never let us know. She always had that same smile."

In the fields, Joseph had been helping strip tobacco since he was 3 or 4. He was driving a tractor by the time he was 5 or 6—standing on the pedals to make them work.

By the time he was 12, he had a job cutting and bundling wheat on a nearby farm. He worked in the fields—somebody's fields, any kind of crop—until he went off to college.

So did many of the kids he knew. Les May, the Logan County High School football coach when Joseph was there, remembers scheduling August practices for the mornings so the players could go home to work in the fields from noon until dark. If they weren't careful, the nicotine absorbed from wet plants would make them sick.

"I had several kids who wound up in the hospital with tobacco poisoning," May said.

Since sharecropping is hardly the path to enrichment, Joseph needed the money he earned for shoes and school clothes. Joe

Sr. was a Herculean worker who farmed and labored long hours at a nearby sausage plant, but there were many mouths to feed.

And the dirty, exhausting, endless job of stripping tobacco was the most natural way to earn money. Lives were tethered to cultivating the weed.

"Next time I set foot in a tobacco field, it's to say hello to somebody I know," Joseph said. "Not to work."

He is a true child of the Logan County soil. Five generations of his family have lived there. Three of those generations have worked the land at Robey Farms, a 7,000-acre operation.

Joe Sr. drives a tractor these days for the Robeys, who are sixth-generation farmers. The two families—one white, one black—have grown up in concert around the same patch of land. A Robey family patriarch even gave Joe Sr. his nickname: Rooster.

Lee Robey grew up on the landowning side of the relationship, but that didn't make him too good for discipline from the Jefferson side. He recalls Joseph's grandmother, Sarah, as a southpaw—"because she'd lay that leather strap to me when I was bad with her left hand."

Lee Robey and his family will be at the party today.

"We're really proud of Joseph," he said. "Besides his athletic ability, to hold everything together and get this opportunity is a testament to what kind of person he is."

To the folks outside of southern Kentucky, here's what kind of person Joseph Jefferson was until very recently: a nobody.

His high school football career was little more than mythology, because it was played out so far off radar. But May believed.

"I timed him in the 40 at 4.35 (seconds)," May said. "I went back to mark the 40 yards off again to make sure it was right. Then he ran it again. I said, 'Joseph, I'll mark it off one more time.' Then he ran it faster."

Joseph ran for 3,800 yards and scored 55 touchdowns at Logan County, but the University of Kentucky and the University of Louisville both yawned. He appeared headed for Division II Kentucky State until I-AA Western entered the picture very late.

Hilltoppers coach Jack Harbaugh still wasn't sure what he had until he watched Joseph play basketball in a regional tournament.

Diddle Arena. When Joseph soared from just inside the foul

line for a dunk, Harbaugh thought to himself, "I think we got a steal here."

He knew it for sure when Joseph intercepted a pass in the Kentucky-Tennessee All-Star Game and ran it back 78 yards for a touchdown.

Joseph played as a true freshman and was a four-year starter and stellar return man at Western, yet he wasn't even the biggest name in his team's secondary. He was overshadowed by Mel Mitchell and Bobby Sippio—both of whom also could be drafted this weekend—until the all-star circuit and draft combine.

Last December, for the first time in his 56-year life, Joe Jefferson Sr. spent Christmas outside of Logan County, joining 27 friends and family members to see his son play in the Blue-Gray Game in Montgomery, Ala. About two-thirds of that support group went to the Senior Bowl in Mobile, Ala., a couple of weeks later, where Joseph intercepted a pass.

Then at the NFL scouting combine in Indianapolis, Joseph tested spectacularly. He ran, jumped and lifted his way into the top 10 cornerbacks in the draft—as high as No. 6 according to one scouting service.

"His measurables were just out of sight," Harbaugh said.

A star, undetected for all those years in rural Kentucky, was born. Or at least uncovered. To the bigwigs in the NFL, Joseph Jefferson no longer was a nobody.

Since then his cell phone has been glued to his ear. If it isn't his agent on the line, it's someone from an NFL team.

Seattle and Washington called Thursday afternoon. The Jets called yesterday morning. Joseph gives them plenty of yes-sirs and no-sirs, but he isn't afraid to speak up.

"So," he said to the Redskins rep, "are you going to call my name Saturday? You've got some good corners to learn behind in Darrell (Green), Champ (Bailey) and (Fred) Smoot. I wouldn't mind that."

He wouldn't mind going anywhere, as long as it happens today. That's when the first three rounds will be held, with four more to follow tomorrow. He doesn't want to throw a premature party.

Curl around a bend in the road on the outskirts of Adairville, and Joseph casually points to a small field out the right window.

"That's where my mom is," he says.

Drive in. The tiny cemetery isn't marked in any way. The grass is long, and the dandelions are in full bloom. It is very quiet.

"What's up, baby," Joseph says, kissing his hand and rubbing it on Anna Jean Spencer's headstone. A wreath of plastic flowers sits behind it.

"We've been through a lot of adversity and heartaches," he says. "But that's life. We've been blessed."

Joseph has plans for what he'll do with the wealth expected to come his way after today. He'll pay off his father's debts, buy himself a nice car. Someday he'll build his dream house down here, too, "away from all that noise in the city."

And one more thing.

He'd like to replace the small, flat headstone with a grand statue of an angel with its wings extended—ready to take flight from this remote place, to a new life in a destination only dreamed of.

Until the statue comes, Joseph Jefferson will perform that role himself.

Western Kentucky cornerback Joseph Jefferson, a probably early-round pick in the NFL draft, and his dad, Joe Sr., are products of the fertile soil near Adairville.

Joseph Jefferson, dwarfed by a tractor, said: "Next time I set foot in a tobacco field, it's to say hello to somebody I know. Not to work."

Part II

The Rest of the Story

Introduction

Bill Buchalter

Barry D. "Bill" Buchalter has covered sports at the *St. Petersburg Times* and *Orlando Sentinel* for more than 40 years, reporting on everything from Little League baseball to a dozen NCCA tourneys and seven Olympics. He's lived in Florida most of his life and graduated from the University of Florida in 1962.

So you want to be a sportswriter? Hah!

Are you ready to prowl the sidelines at high school games, keeping your own statistics and chasing down players to interview? Or how about, around the five-minute mark of the fourth quarter of the college rivalry you are covering, you join the rush of other reporters going down the elevator to the field for post-game and during your trip to field level you miss the winning touchdown but you do hear the roar of the crowd?

Then there is the next level, professional sports or perhaps the Olympic Games. At Sydney, Australia, for example, you gather around the mixed zone with 500 of your closest colleagues hoping to get a glimpse of your athlete as he or she walks through the only area set aside for interviews of athletes who did not medal. And you quietly pray that your athlete, unhappy with his or her performance, recognizes you or respects you enough to stop and talk. Obviously, you won't get your feature takeout, but you can cover the top story of the day for your paper.

So you still want to become a sportswriter? Okay! I don't blame you.

You've read about covering specific beats such as baseball, football, and soccer in Part I of this book. Part II will cover themes that cut across those beats, such as ethics or covering women in sports. Read those chapters and take them to heart—what the contributors have to say in these and other chapters matters.

I want to add my 2 cents' worth, or rather tell you about the Four Rules that have guided me in my career.

Rule No. 1: Don't let anybody else do your work for you. Doing the little things yourself focuses your attention on trends, a key play, a critical error, all the intangible things that occur during a game that make your story better. Veteran high school reporter Buddy Collings tells about hearing when he was with *The Gainesville Sun* of a small-school phenom running back on the verge of establishing school and area rushing records. He decided to see for himself.

Collings keeps his own statistics and had compiled the numbers at halftime. He checked with the statistician, a student, who informed him the running back had twice the yardage Collings had compiled. Stunned, he asked the student to compare play-by-play and noted that a four-yard run was eight on the official statistics. The student explained that the back had received a pitchout four yards deep in the backfield and had run four yards past the line of scrimmage, a total of eight yards.

"It made perfect sense to her, but that's why you have to keep your own stats," he said.

Rule No. 2: Don't be afraid to ask.

I was covering my first Olympics, the 1972 Munich Games. The U.S. media were having a friendly argument over just how much English the Soviet Union athletes really knew or understood. The late great Sam Skinner, from San Francisco, put it all in perspective for all those who doubted the language capabilities of the Soviets. After the finish of the 100-meter dash, as gold-medal winner Valeriy Borzov was being escorted to the interview area, Skinner fired a question at him. Nobody expected an answer. "Valeriy," he asked. "How does it feel to be the first Russian to be called the World's Fastest Human?"

Borzov did a double take, turned toward Skinner, and replied, "Sam, I'm a Ukrainian."

Talk about your journalistic stunner, and so much for the Russians not knowing English.

And so much for solidifying the rule to ask all the questions necessary to get the answer you are seeking.

That doesn't mean that you don't want to do your pre-interview preparation. It's not a stupid question when you don't understand the answer and seek clarification.

It's only a stupid question when you ask something where you could have found the answer by looking it up before the interview. A high school coach may only shake his head at an unprepared question. A college coach like Bob Knight may terminate the press conference.

Rule No. 3, which is good in any department in the paper: Verify your facts. This dictum may seem as obvious as double-checking the spelling of someone's name, but consider the case of Houston McTear, who was timed in 9.0 seconds in the 100-yard dash at Showalter Field in Winter Park, Florida, at the 1975 Class 2A state high school track meet. That time, if true, would have equaled the world record.

McTear's performance, during a morning qualifying heat, shook the nation.

The Associated Press bureau in Miami reluctantly took the information and put it on the wire. Immediately, telephone calls came to the track press box from newspapers throughout the country, including *The Los Angeles Times*. The *Orlando Sentinel* was the paper of record covering the meet. We put the story out on the wire, so we took all the telephone calls and told the story that there were three watches on the race. Two timers had McTear clocked at 9.0 seconds, and the third in 8.9. An Accutrack, an automatic timing device, was hooked up for the race, but it was only for picture-taking purposes to separate runners in anticipated photo finishes. The Accutrack did record a 9.30 at the finish line, but since it was not official, and the humidity and heat made the device work for some races and not for others, it was disregarded.

The finals, which started at 7 P.M. the same evening, were obviously overshadowed by the qualifying heat and the record. Almost lost in the transmitting of information and stories from the track to the office was the fact that an editor thought the reporter had made a mistake in identifying McTear as being from Baker, a tiny dot on the map in northwest Florida. He changed the school name to Baker County, located in Maclenny, Florida, not too far from the University of Florida, which the editor had attended. The editor never verified the change with the reporter. Thus the paper of record was the only one to have the wrong hometown for the biggest high school story of the year. The reporter, who did not return to the office that evening, didn't see the error until the next day. Twenty-five years later, he still gets teased by his track-coaching buddies. All this helps to magnify the reminder of verification and its importance.

Oh, by the way: McTear didn't come close to a 9.0 in the finals.

Rule No. 4, which really applies to all reporting for all media (in fact, it's a good rule in the game of life, too): Keep your promises.

Several years ago, the football coach at Mount Dora High School called a local reporter to confirm a rumor. Yes, he was leaving his post as football coach, he admitted. The soon-to-leave coach then gave a heartfelt 20-minute interview about his successes and failures as a coach and what his plans were for the future. At the end of the interview, he asked for one favor from the reporter. "Just don't say I quit," he said. "That's a four-letter word and I sat here and told my players never to give up, and I don't want them to think I gave up on them. I was here all season, and I waited until after the season to leave. I have my reasons for leaving, but I'm not quitting."

The reporter agreed to the concession, writing a story about the coach "resigning" his job. Just one problem. The night copy editors made no distinction between "resigning" and "quitting." And the reporter never asked the headline writer to try not to use the word "quit."

So the next day's paper read: "Coach quits."

Although the headline wasn't his to write, the reporter felt the brunt of the coach's ire. The coach left for another nearby school—but he refused to talk to the reporter. And he still doesn't talk to him today.

Sure, the reporter could have said, with some justification, that he wasn't responsible for the headline. But you have to take responsibility; you have to be professional; you have to double-check all facts.

That's it. Of course, a willingness to work long shifts, an ability to write fast, and a penchant for the most unbelievable detail and trivia won't hurt either.

11. Covering High School Sports

Larry Ames

Larry Ames is Assistant Sports Editor of the *Ventura County Star* in Ventura, California. He is chair of the West Region of the Associated Press Sports Editors Association. A native of Boston, he was Assistant Sports Editor/ Schools for *The Boston Globe* for 16 years. At *The Globe,* Ames supervised the college cooperative program and helped train more than 300 student journalists.

Covering high school sports will be the toughest job you'll ever have. What makes it even tougher is the lack of experience that characterizes most people who handle the prep beat. The high school beat in any newspaper, or on-line, often goes to the first-year reporter just out of journalism school. It is the least desirable of all jobs in the sports department and the most difficult. That doesn't mean the assignment should be avoided . . . only that for you to succeed as a high school writer, you need to be totally organized and prepared.

Young writers aspire to the glamour beats, covering the pro or college teams or becoming a columnist. People in those jobs are often treated royally. When they show up for a game or a news conference, statistics, comfortable surroundings, sandwiches and hot meals, and cooperation are usually provided.

A high school writer gets none of these conveniences. There may be no press box or even any rosters when you show up for a game. You may freeze while sitting on a cold bench covering a four-hour baseball game in early April. The coach who has promised to be there for an interview may be swamped with emergencies and may be unable to talk with you. The athlete you are scheduled to interview may not be there because he/she has decided to take a recruiting trip at the last moment.

How, then, do you make your beat work? Organization and preparation are great starters.

Call ahead to make sure the coach and the athlete will be available. Show up an hour and a half early for the game to check the starting lineups and to make sure the rosters have first and last names and that the team records are included. Talk with the coach and a few athletes before the game and get an insight into what's expected. The pre-game talk often provides you with notebook and future feature material.

By showing up early, you also demonstrate that you care about your beat and the people with whom you are working.

Demonstrate enthusiasm by becoming an expert on the schools you will be covering. If you start your new high school beat during the summer, research the school's and your newspaper's archives and gain knowledge about the people, history, and traditions. Your readers will expect you to provide comprehensive information. They aren't interested in your inexperience.

Talk with coaches and athletes, past and present, to get a better understanding of the different schools and communities.

In conducting the interviews with the coaches and athletes, learn to be a good listener. Some interviewees need only one question to get them going. I remember covering a Muhammad Ali news conference in which only one question was asked. Ali provided the rest. Others need coaxing. You'll have to have more questions ready for those who provide short and boring answers.

By showing enthusiasm, you are more likely to win your subjects over. How much you win them over with your enthusiasm may well determine your success.

Each community and the schools in that community have a special pulse, something that makes them special. It's your job to know what that is.

No matter what you do, establishing credibility and a reputation for fairness and accuracy are among your most important responsibilities. Always deal with all people honestly, even if you fear that what you will be telling them will either hurt or anger them.

I once sent a reporter to a school to do an advance for a football playoff game. When the reporter returned from the school, he related a conversation he had had with the school's athletic director. The AD wanted to know if we had selected a football player of the year for our all-area team.

The reporter knew that we had made the choice but that it wasn't the player from the school he was covering that day. Fearing an angry response, the reporter told the athletic director that we had not made the selection.

When the reporter told me the story, I immediately called the athletic director and told him that we had made the choice and it wasn't his star player.

You don't ever want to tarnish your reputation or credibility. They are cherished commodities. People may not agree with you on everything, but they will respect you as a journalist and a person if you have proven that you are trustworthy.

I have worked with college journalism students most of my newspaper career and have developed a simple yet vital approach to writing.

It is: Never assume, figure, guess, or think you know.

Any time you use any one of those words, you need to stop yourself in midsentence and reexamine what you've just said. That's because you either know something or you don't. There's no gray area when it comes to facts. It either is or it isn't.

Therefore, when you assume, figure, guess, or think you know, there's a 50 percent chance you will be wrong. My experience has taught me that there's closer to a 100 percent chance you'll be wrong.

Always check your facts. If you have any doubt at all, make phone calls or check sources. Today, with all that's available on the Internet, there's no excuse for not checking a fact, a date, or a time.

Ethics, sensitivity, and fairness are important for any journalist, but they are even more important for high school writers.

How do you develop ethics when you may just be starting out on your career? All you have to follow is the same guidelines that you've followed in your personal development when it comes to right and wrong. When you are writing an article or column where you might pose an ethical question, ask yourself if you were in the shoes of the person or institution about whom you are writing, how would you feel?

It's important to remember that you are writing about 14- to 18-year-olds. They are neither professional athletes who may be earning millions nor are they college students who may be receiving scholarships. High school athletes do not receive compensation, and the number of high school students who go on to receive scholarships is small in comparison to the total number of participants. The coaches you are writing about aren't making millions a year. In many cases, given the time necessary to do their jobs, prep coaches make about 10 cents an hour.

I compare starting your career with the construction of a building. In preparing the foundation, if you use excellent concrete and proper mixing techniques, the edifice you build will last for a long time. However, if you cut corners and use inferior concrete or fall short in laying the foundation, even if you construct the most magnificent building, it won't take long before it crumbles.

Sensitivity is becoming more important because readers react to negative journalism.

Using a negative lead in a story can create controversy. Here are two examples of leads on a state championship game:

Smith High batters struck out 17 times as it lost the Division 1 state championship with a 2-0 defeat to Jones High yesterday at State U. field.

Smith High became the second best team in the state in Division 1 this year after its 2-0 loss to Jones High in the state final yesterday at State U. field.

In the first lead, the writer focuses on the negative and the failure of the team. In the second lead, the loss is reflected but put in perspective with the accomplishment of achieving the championship game rather than focusing on its defeat.

Sensitivity is also important when you write about officiating in game stories because coaches often rant and rave over an officiating call. It's not ethical reporting if:

a) There is, according to the reporter's observation, no merit in the coach's comments and the reporter still publishes the comment.

b) There is no attempt by the reporter to get the official's reaction. If the official refuses comment, then it is the writer's obligation to inform the reader that the official had no comment.

In many cases, a basketball game may have been lost because the team may have missed 15 free throws or had 21 turnovers. In a one-point game, the outcome was determined more by the team's errors than by one call at the end of the game. A football game may not necessarily be lost because of a call late in the game if the team turned the ball over four times and was penalized 12 times for 115 yards.

I cite two examples of game coverage I experienced and how sensitivity and lack of sensitivity were handled by a reporter and the copy desk:

One: A freshman girls' basketball player fouls the ball carrier at midcourt with the state championship game tied and a half-second left on the clock. The ball carrier makes both free throws as her team wins the state championship. I'm faced with this: a 14-year-old freshman has committed a foul at midcourt with a half-second left, and her team loses the state championship.

Here's how I handled it:

I stated the facts, then came in with a quote from the coach: "Without her, we wouldn't have made the state final."

Don't embellish on the error in judgment and get away from that aspect of the story as quickly as you can.

Two: In the quarterfinals of the hockey tournament, a team is leading midway through the game, 2-0, when the coach whose team is leading the game switches goalies. The other team scores three quick goals. The issue is handled sensitively in the story, and the coach takes pressure off the goalie by saying: "We've split the goaltending all year long and I have no regrets. This system got us here."

However, the copy desk person, writing a Sports Page 1 caption describing one of the three goals, targets the second goalie by writing that he surrendered three goals in a substitute role and the team lost, 3-2.

We were flooded with calls complaining about our insensitivity. The school's administration and the residents of the town were angry at the newspaper for a long time.

In dealing with stories involving high school, youth, and amateur sports, you have to consider how the words you use may affect a young person and his/her life.

A big part of ethics is fairness. And fairness can be subjective. Naturally, when you are working on a story, you need to get both sides of an issue. If you can't reach one side, you have to make sure you make it clear to the reader that you attempted to reach the other side. When the other side won't respond, you need to report the no comment.

But fairness goes well beyond that. You have to remove your own feelings from a news story. There is a tendency to favor one side of an issue. In writing a news story, you have to remove your feelings from any coverage.

If you have any doubts, check with an editor before you turn in a story. In fact, any time you are uneasy about any problem, it is best to ask a supervisor.

(In fact, I often tell young writers that they need to find a mentor early in their careers. It could be a supervisor or someone else in the business who has shown an interest in the development of young writers. A mentor is a person who can provide inspiration and guidance. It should be someone you trust to bring any and all of your problems.)

One of the earliest newspaper axioms I learned was this: When in doubt, throw it out. Always go with your gut feeling. If you question or doubt something, don't try to convince yourself that it's proper. Just as in any multiple-choice question, your first instinct is usually the best one.

The cornerstone of prep coverage is the statistic. Outside of fantasy fanatics, high school fans follow standings and statistics more than most other sports observers. In addition, because many high schools have decades of traditions, records are closely followed.

Until the 1970s, it was easier to compile statistics because most newspapers concentrated only on boys' sports such as football, basketball, and baseball. Over the last three decades, with Title IX and the proliferation of girls' sports and the increased popularity of such sports as soccer, track, volleyball, ice and field hockey, gymnastics, wrestling, and lacrosse, it's become a greater task to gather and print statistics and standings.

It doesn't have to be a daunting task, though. All you need is to determine your resources and the willingness of your school constituencies to cooperate. A traditional method of gathering statistics and standings is to have designated league representatives in each sport call in their information at a prescribed time each week. To assure the success of a call-in program, you must tease the procedure in the newspaper at least three weeks prior to the first week of publication. Provide telephone numbers and the time frame in which the calls should be made. A newspaper with limited resources could request the league representatives to either fax or e-mail the information.

While factoids and records are published more today than in the past, the people who have traditionally recorded prep history have dwindled to a precious few. If you can find an individual with a passion for a school or a league's history, meet with that person and find a way to publish his/her work. Always give the person credit and, if you can, pay for his/her work.

The most difficult part of covering high school sports is dealing with complaints and coping with criticisms. College and professional beat writers and columnists are somewhat immune from criticism because they are rarely in the office and they have either the sports editor or assistant sports editor to respond to readers' complaints. Even at an event, the beat writers and columnists are isolated from the reader because they operate in places off-limits to fans—the press box and clubhouse or locker room.

High school beat writers get no such protection. Fans unhappy with coverage can find the prep beat writer at the school, at a game, or in the office.

Readers who complain about high school coverage usually have a vested interest beyond love of the town team or the alma mater. Readers who aren't happy with your coverage usually have a friend, a relative, or some other close family member playing on the high school team.

Often the biggest complaint is about coverage. Readers are not interested in your resources or your space. They also complain about alleged bias against their favorite sport or their favorite player. They may also be upset about the way you wrote a feature or how you predicted the team would do in its weekly Friday-night game.

How do you cope with this onslaught? First, allow your supervisor to handle the complaints. This is what they are trained to do.

If you are confronted at a school or at a game, remember to be courteous. Listen to the complaint and try to explain your position. If you are wrong, apologize and explain how you will make a correction.

Your position may be correct, but you still need to remember that your are representing your newspaper and yourself. There are some who might not accept either your explanation or your apology. You can't please all the readers all the time.

Your journey covering prep sports will be difficult, but it will only enhance your experience as a journalist and will put you in good stead for future assignments.

12. Covering College Sports

Jim Rossow

Jim Rossow has been at *The* (Champaign) *News-Gazette* since 1994 and has been Sports Editor since 1996. University of Illinois head basketball coach Lou Henson made sure the transition from writer to editor was a quick one by unexpectedly announcing his retirement a week into Rossow's new job. Since then, *The News-Gazette* has been recognized as an Associated Press Sports Editors top-10 national section in all three categories—daily, Sunday, and special sections.

My first assignment as a professional journalist was to cover a drag race on sand in the middle of a desert in Arizona. It was hot, dusty, and not much fun.

My latest assignment was covering an Illinois basketball game against archrival Iowa in a sauna of a gym with Dick Vitale courtside. It was hot, rowdy, and a whole lot of fun.

I can't begin to describe the difference between the two events. But I realize that reaching what I always have considered a top spot in our profession—sports editor of a daily in a Big Ten town (*The* [Champaign] *News-Gazette*)—was made possible by starting somewhere near the bottom. In my case, it was writing about middle-aged men racing strange-looking cars on what looked like a beach.

Not many readers of the *Mohave Daily Miner* cared about the sport and, as a graduate of a midwestern college, I had never heard of it. But as I look back at my experience, I understand that what I learned then still is helpful today. I learned to interview. I learned to investigate. I learned to edit my own copy. Mostly, I learned to be patient.

I figured if I spent quality time covering middle school football, high school basketball, and park district softball as a one-person staff— I even took photos—someone at a bigger newspaper would take notice. That's what happened.

Not that spending years at a small daily is a requirement for landing a major college beat. When our men's basketball beat opened in 2000, several of the candidates I seriously considered were recent college graduates with apparent writing skills and boundless energy (we ended up hiring someone with three years' experience covering a high-profile Division I program).

Once you land a major college beat—and cover it successfully— more doors spring open. *The News-Gazette* (circulation 50,000) has seen a number of sportswriters move on to more prominent positions, including Bill Lyon (now at *The Philadelphia Inquirer*), Tom Reitmann and David Woods (*The Indianapolis Star*), Dave Van Dyke (Fox Sports), Dave Campbell (*The* [Cleveland] *Plain Dealer*), Dave Hackett (managing editor of *The* [Bloomington, Ind.] *Herald-Times*), Jeff Pearlman (*Sports Illustrated*) and, most recently, Jeff D'Alessio (*Florida Today*). Even Roger Ebert, the renowned film critic, covered high school games for the paper (he'll tell you it was a thumbs-up experience).

Keep in mind that not everyone leaves the beat. Our football writer, Bob Asmussen, has been at the paper since 1989 and still approaches his work with the enthusiasm of a rookie. Our lead columnist, Loren Tate, has been in town since 1966, turning down several offers throughout the years. He considers it a way of life, one that he thoroughly enjoys. When he doesn't have anything to do, he's unhappy. And he's 70 years old.

Tate will be the first to tell you that the beat has changed significantly since he typed his first story (on an Underwood typewriter). It is no longer just Saturday afternoons in the press box. It's Monday morning in traffic court, Tuesday night at a three-hour practice, Wednesday evening at a student council meeting, Thursday afternoon on a teleconference, and all day Friday chasing down wild Internet rumors: Is the coach looking to leave? Is the linebacker's ankle really broken? Is the all-state receiver wavering on his commitment? Is the beat writer in Bermuda?

There are times when getting out of town seems like your best option.

When Tate disclosed improprieties within the University of Illinois athletic department in the late 1980s, two things happened: the athletic director was forced to resign and Tate was badgered by those close to the AD for digging up the truth. For a while, Tate wasn't welcome at a popular Champaign restaurant, the owner of which was friends with the athletic director.

Still, Tate agrees that a college sports beat—with all its challenges, long hours, and last-second rewrites—is as rewarding as any you'll find in journalism.

That's because college athletics, despite the fact that pro-type problems are seeping in through every crack, still come equipped with a genuine feel. Most student-athletes still care about winning (and have manners, too). Most coaches still care about their players no matter how many years and millions their contracts guarantee. And most fans, who are as rabid and loyal as you'll find anywhere, will gladly plunk down 50 cents to read the next day's newspaper. Preferably your newspaper.

To ensure that they do read your paper, and your stories, you can't miss a beat. That means attending practices on your day off. It means keeping in constant touch with coaches, assistants, and players. It means developing relationships with people not directly tied to the program but who have insight to its inner workings, like janitors, ushers, ball boys, and even parents . It means working with and working around sports information department staffs that want only positive headlines. It means working with your newspaper's police and business reporters, who have access to information not readily available to you. It means working with your newspaper's photography department to make sure they're shooting the star of the game instead of the other team's sixth man. It means answering the phone at 2 A.M., responding to a page at 6 A.M., and answering e-mail at noon. It means keeping in touch with the high school ranks to assure access into the ever-popular world of recruiting.

It also means monitoring fan forums on the Internet which, despite an extra helping of hearsay, sometimes produce nuggets of truth. It means sifting through academic charts, filing Freedom of Information Act requests and finding the best deals on hotel rooms and rental cars so your boss doesn't go ballistic.

Most important, it means venturing outside the stadium to find the best story, stories your managing editor should and will demand.

Some sports bring in the big crowds and television cameras and should be covered extensively (for example, *The News-Gazette* staffs Illinois home football games with five writers and three photographers).

But the college beat offers a whole lot more than first downs and free throws.

The best story might be at a shoe store, where student-athletes are given a discount on shoes. That happened at the University of Wisconsin, which was penalized by the NCAA after a newspaper reported the misdoings of a Madison businessman.

It might be at the wrestling room, where a senior is working out frantically through the night—wearing what looks like a winter coat—in order to make weight. In the mid-1990s, a wrestler at the University of Michigan died while attempting to cut weight. As a result, changes were made in rules on making weight, and schools became more attuned to the dangers of the sport.

It might be at a neighborhood bar, where a basketball player is agreeing to shave points for a bookie. Northwestern in the 1990s was hit by gambling scandals that rocked both the basketball and football programs. Both were made public by newspaper accounts.

It might be at the natatorium, where men's scholarships are being eliminated and women's scholarships are being added in the name of gender equity, a federally mandated and controversial rule put in place to bring male and female participation rates into balance. In the early 1990s, Illinois eliminated men's swimming and diving and men's fencing. The cutbacks allowed the school to make progress toward gender equity—by offering fewer men's scholarships—and cut into a financial deficit the department faced.

A lawsuit was filed by members of the men's swim team, claiming their sport was unfairly singled out. The lawsuit was dismissed, but the ruckus put gender equity in the spotlight for the first time at Illinois. Today gender equity continues to be both a goal and a front-burner issue for the department. In the past five years, two women's sports have been added—soccer and softball—while the men's program has remained as is.

Coaching searches make for great copy, too. When Illinois replaced the coaches of its two revenue-producing programs—men's basketball and football—in 1996, reader interest peaked. Receiving no cooperation from the school's search committee—don't ever count on getting help on personnel matters—we came up with our own candidates and profiled our top 16 choices in each sport. Our work got us lambasted on national TV by Billy Packer—he thought we were putting the candidates in an unfair light because they had not announced their interest in the Illinois position—and lauded by our readers. Fortunately, we had the eventual new coaches (Lon Kruger and Ron Turner) on each of our published lists.

Remember, not every 72-point headline needs to deal with inflammatory issues. Tales of academic success, community service, and personal achievement are easy to find, especially in non-revenue sports such as volleyball and swimming and softball. A profile of a diver who aced metaphysics and won a conference title on the same day—and is happy to talk about it while using four-syllable words—can be as intriguing as a feature on the starting point guard on a nationally ranked team who is tired of the media spotlight.

Adam Tirapelle won an NCAA wrestling championship at Illinois. But the more compelling story—and better picture—was that he taught physical education at a Champaign high school and the kids loved him. Our writer went 20 inches before first mentioning "half-nelson."

Collinus Newsome was an All-American shot putter for the Illinois women's track and field team. But the better angle was Newsome as an accomplished singer who often delivered the national anthem before basketball games to rousing applause. The lead picture for our section was of her belting out "The Star-Spangled Banner" at halfcourt.

Travis Romagnoli was an NCAA gymnastics champion at Illinois. But he was better known around campus as a guitar player for a grunge band that performed at area clubs. The words "balance beam" didn't appear in the story.

Itch Jones is one of college baseball's all-time-winningest coaches. But the story we did on the Illinois coach fighting a rare form of cancer was a better read than any we did detailing his work on the field.

There are more story lines on campus than there are seats at the football stadium—it's up to you to smoke them out. Sometimes the sports information staff or a coach will tip you off. Other times it might be the guy serving roast beef at the deli. Good story ideas travel fast.

Finding the time to do them is another matter. There are 21 athletic programs at Illinois, all clamoring for attention from our staff of eight writers. We have beat writers for football, men's basketball, and women's basketball. The remaining 18 sports get sporadic coverage, which doesn't always go over well with team or reader. Volleyball, for instance, is a popular sport in town, often drawing more than 2,000 fans for a home match. The wrestling team is a perennial top-10 program. The men's tennis team is a threat to win a national title. And the baseball team is an NCAA tournament regular.

Yet we can't be there every time they're at home. We'd need a staff of 20 to pull it off. Instead, we have one writer assigned to the 18 minor sports. He spends 40 percent of his work week covering games, 40 percent previewing them with features and other non-game stories, and 10 percent helping out on the desk, editing copy and writing headlines.

Of course, he gets help. The writers who cover preps enjoy taking a break and staffing a college event now and then. We also hire stringers to cover important games on the road.

The rise in popularity of women's sports also forced our coverage hand. Before Hall of Fame coach Theresa Grentz arrived at Illinois, we often relied on the sports information department to fax us results of women's basketball games. On one of her first road trips, Grentz was handed a phone to talk to one of our part-timers. She threw a fit, appalled that an Olympic coach would have to supply quotes in order to get coverage from the hometown newspaper. Sports information never asked her to do it again and, because of the newfound success of the women's program under Grentz, we started staffing every game played in the Midwest. Sometimes even farther away.

The pull of women's basketball hit me when, a couple of days before Illinois was to play at Connecticut in the late 1990s, our managing editor pulled me aside and asked why we weren't staffing it. I told him it cost too much. He told me he didn't care. For men's NCAA tournament games, we send four writers and a photographer. For women's NCAA tournament games, we send two writers and a photographer. The gap is closing every day.

Delivering news from the mainstream sports—including women's basketball—requires clearing a number of hurdles. Like an angry coach, which is as much a part of campus life as fraternity parties. Deal with someone for four consecutive months and disagreements will happen. When I first started covering Illinois football, the head coach phoned me at home to unleash a four-letter diatribe concerning my assessment of the season opener. On a Sunday morning, no less. I listened to his opinion, stuck to mine, and went to church. By Monday, all was well.

When Kruger took over in basketball, he took exception to the way our newspaper graded each game (we attach letter grades to backcourt, frontcourt, bench, coaching, and overall). He thought we were being too picky, hinting at possible access problems if we didn't make some changes. I let him have his say, made some changes to our approach (no longer is it anonymous; we run a byline with the grades), and he kept practices open to our beat writer.

High-profile college coaches come with big salaries and bigger egos who rule with a heavy hand in the gym—they have scholarships as a trump card. But that doesn't mean they're always right. Don't be afraid to disagree with them; they'll get over it eventually. They want stories that benefit the program. You want stories that benefit the reader. The two approaches often clash. Consider the number of times the football coach at Illinois and our beat writer had disagreements about coverage during a recent four-month season. The coach was upset about:

- The way practice was described. He basically said, "Don't write what you see, write what I say."
- The way recruiting was reported. The coach did not like the fact that we ran a list of visiting prep players—obtained independently—in our paper. He thought it would leak to other coaches who would use the list against Illinois.
- The way games were reported. He thought our tone was much too negative even after wins, going as far as saying his wife cancelled their subscription to the paper (which in fact she did).
- The whereabouts of our beat writer during practice. The coach eventually established what he called "a penalty box," a 40-yard area far from some of the practice fields where media got its only glimpse of the action. In the past, our beat writer was free to roam sideline to sideline.

Again, letting the coach have his say face to face alleviated a lot of the tension. He made his point, we defended ours, and both parties moved on to more important things, like winning games and selling newspapers.

Not to single out football. Coaches of all college sports want control over what's written about their programs.

Okay, let's single out football again. Our writer, using a source close to the situation, correctly wrote that the head coach had fired two of his assistants after a sub-par season. The coach, who we tried unsuccessfully to reach before the story ran, disputed what appeared in print, saying the coaches weren't fired. Instead, he said, there was a mutual agreement that the assistants would look elsewhere for employment (in other words, they were fired).

He also said the reason he didn't want to talk about the situation was because he didn't want the coaches made out to look bad before landing other jobs.

Those types of dilemmas crop up every week, be it at the high school, college, or pro level. The key is maintaining a working relationship during the tense times. Talk off the record. Talk about another sport. Talk about the economy. Just keep talking to keep the lines of communication open.

It can't work any other way. The first writer I assigned to cover women's basketball full-time drew Grentz's wrath with a story she didn't particularly like. Instead of discussing their differences, the two grew farther apart. Eventually, the writer asked off the beat because of Grentz's lack of cooperation, forcing me to juggle assignments within the staff. Not that the head coach—whose on-the-record vocabulary often is riddled with clichés—is necessary for a story's well-being. There are plenty of sources nearby to provide candor: assistant coaches and players are refreshingly honest when given the opportunity.

If they're given an opportunity. Access is another obstacle for many reporters on major college beats. Professional leagues require their employees to be available to the media at certain times and places, using fines as incentive. On the prep level, the player-reporter relationship is so informal that guidelines don't need to be in place. But in college, access becomes a guessing game because—again—the coach rules with a heavy hand. He or she often dictates who is available even if his or her choice doesn't make much sense.

When Bob Knight was at Indiana, reporters covering his games would request the leading scorer or the leading rebounder for the post-game Q&A. Knight instead would bring with him a fifth-year senior who didn't play a second. Try getting a 12-inch sidebar out of that.

At Illinois, football and men's basketball practices are open to the media and the players generally are available after practice (just don't ask to talk to the starting quarterback after Monday). But the nationwide trend is to close practice, limit player availability, and make the media's life miserable.

Sometimes the folks in sports information—whom a beat writer has to deal with on a daily basis to line up interviews and retrieve statistical data—can help by hinting to a coach the benefits of exposure. Sometimes they can't. Before its annual football grudge match against Michigan State in 2001, Michigan did not allow one-on-one interviews with any players, thereby eliminating the chance of bulletin-board material slipping out (or the chance of stories with much meat seeing the light of day). It was the first time writers covering the school remembered such a policy being implemented, but they expect it to be the case from now on. Contrast that to Duke basketball, which has an open locker room, or the NCAA basketball tournaments, which require all players and coaches to be available after each game.

Sometimes access is excellent. Sometimes it's lousy. Rarely is it consistent, which makes planning a bit tricky. At one game, the columnist, beat writer, and sidebar writer might have the coach and five players to divvy up. The next game, they all might be stuck using the same single source. If the topic is considered a "positive" one by the coach or sports information staff—a feature on a sophomore with good grades and a better attitude—lining up interviews isn't a problem. But if you're seeking reaction to the star quarterback's arrest, you'll need a toolbox to pry out information. The quarterback isn't available (at Illinois and most other major schools, all interview requests must pass through the sports information office. Their guidelines discourage you from calling him at home. And even if he answers, he has been told when he first arrived on campus not to talk to reporters without prior consent.) The coach's comment consists of a vague statement probably written by someone else. That day's practice is closed. And your boss wants an A-1 story by 10 P.M.

So you try the quarterback's parents, whom you met after practice one day. You try his high school coach, whom you dealt with during the recruiting process. You try the kid who lugs the sack of footballs during practice, whom you got to know while watching endless hours of late-August drills. You try everyone and anyone you've bumped into on the beat. There are ways to work around the public-relations machine that is in place at most major colleges. You'd better hope that your Rolodex is a thick as this book.

Of course, your assigned seat, which is now on the 50-yard line, might be moved to the end zone for the next game. The coach might not answer your next question. The elevator operator might give you a dirty look. And the bartender who is a season-ticket holder might have this to say the next time he takes your order: "Why are trying to dig up all this dirt on us? Whose side are you on anyway?"

At Illinois, we discovered that an NCAA-qualifying pole vaulter was declared ineligible because he flunked a drug test. We called the student-athlete without consent from the school—against their regulations—and confirmed the story. However, no one from Illinois would comment on the matter other than to phone me and express their anger about how we went about getting the story and that we had the audacity to run it. They chose to get angry at the messenger—an associate athletic director requested a meeting with the newspaper's editor to complain—instead of the student-athlete.

Those are the prices to be paid for not becoming a fan which, on the college beat, is the most important requirement and, in a lot of cases, the most difficult to pull off. The temptation to root for the home team is very real, especially in college towns cozy enough that you can bump into the athletic director at the cleaner's and his assistant at the gas station on the same day (and have both ask you how the kids are). You're offered perks at every stop, from free pre-game meals (pay for your own hot dog and charge the company) to free sweatshirts at Big Ten tournaments (give 'em to Goodwill) to discounted rooms at the team hotel (stay across the street) to courtesy golf outings with the coaching staff (greens fees aren't that high). The CEO of your newspaper might even show up to work wearing an Illinois jacket. He is, after all, a member of the community, and most everyone in the community plan their weekends so as not to interfere with the big game. But you must be independent and impartial.

Retaining objectivity can be—like the beat itself—a struggle, every bit as much a hassle as the 60-hour weeks during peak season, the propeller-plane flights into tiny airports (try landing at State College, Pennsylvania, in January), and the deadline pressures created by late-night tip-offs and kickoffs (thanks, television). But when objectivity is achieved, it can be—like the beat itself—fulfilling, every bit as rewarding as breaking a story on deadline, interviewing a 20-year-old who has a fantastic tale and is both able and eager to tell it, or covering a game that 100,000 alumni will log on to read about and then send to a friend.

That's the pull of the beat: it's high maintenance, high interest, and highly competitive.

13. Memoir: Covering Sports in Small Communities

Larry Anderson

Larry Anderson teaches journalism at Georgia Southern University (home of the Eagles) in Statesboro, Georgia.

It's the first Friday night in September 1976, and I'm on the sidelines of the high school football stadium in Beckville, Texas, population 825, all of whom are sitting behind me in the stands, screaming their heads off as their beloved Wildcats sprint onto the field. Adrenaline rushes through my veins because I'm here to cover a live game for the first time in my life. I count the six pens in my pocket for the 27th time. I check my notepads again. One in my hip pocket, one in my shirt, and one in my hand. The camera has film (community journalists often have to shoot their own photos) and I have 10 more rolls stuffed into various pockets. I'm ready.

Earlier in the week, Beckville coach Gary Clark had given me an idea of what to expect. He knew he didn't have good athletes. "When you stand on the sidelines during this game, you will be able to see the difference between real speed and talent on one team and a bunch of good-hearted, hard-working kids without a lick of talent on the other team," he said. Clark was right. His kids suffered through a painful loss that night. They went on to lose most of their games that season, and I, as a reporter for the *Panola Watchman,* a semi-weekly newspaper in nearby Carthage, saw every loss. In the process I began to learn the craft of community sports journalism. I learned how to write accurate stories under severe deadline pressure and how to deal with coaches and players who were frustrated by losing week after week. And I learned that community sports journalists thrive on long hours.

In Carthage, however, we went beyond the call of duty by working 24-hour shifts on fall Fridays. Non-daily newspapers as a rule don't rely on next-day coverage of sports events, but we did because we had a competing newspaper in town. *Watchman* editor Jim Stevens, as competitive a person as I've ever known, wanted better and faster coverage than our competitors could deliver. In fact, he insisted on it. Some of our employees thought he was a harsh taskmaster, but I found that he was a pushover as long as you produced 10 to 12 well-written, accurate stories every week.

When the football season of '76 began, Stevens called for volunteers to produce a Saturday sports section with Friday-night results. That meant working a 10-hour day shift Friday because everyone had some nonsports duties that were essential and then working all night to "put the paper to bed," as they say in community journalism. Stevens and I were usually the only volunteers for the night shift, although occasionally a third person showed up. We wrote stories, typeset stories, wrote headlines, pasted up the pages, and sent them to press. Then we collapsed into a booth at The Coffee Shop next door for breakfast before going home for a few hours of sleep. It was a brutal routine, but we never missed a deadline or a story and our competitors never beat us on a story. The competitive attitude that I acquired in Carthage served me well throughout my career.

Those long Friday nights were a matter of personal and professional pride. We neither expected nor received a bonus for the extra work. I earned $125 per week whether I worked those extra hours or not. This was the era immediately after Woodward and Bernstein glamorized investigative reporting with their work on the Watergate burglary and its aftermath. It seemed that everyone wanted to be a reporter in those days, and publishers took advantage of us by lowering salaries. I survived because I lived in an $80-per-month, three-room upstairs apartment located so close to the local Sonic drive-in that on summer nights when I had the windows open I could hear customers place their orders. I had no air conditioning, no computer, no VCR, no electric alarm clock, and no radio. My stove was gas and I had a small black-and-white television (but I preferred to read). Consequently, my power bills ranged from $5 to $20 each month. The landlady's mother lived downstairs in what had been a garage before it was converted into an apartment. I couldn't afford noisy parties, so she and I got along very well. On Saturdays, when she cooked lunch for her daughter and grand-daughter, she always invited me. When you earn $125 per week, you don't refuse free meals. My social life consisted of an occasional movie and a weekly trip to Longview for beer and pizza with Stevens and his wife, Suzanne. I had no car payment because I drove a 10-year-old Volkswagen that sputtered and skipped and coughed but usually got me where I wanted to go.

Usually is the key word here, because there were noteworthy exceptions. I covered a basketball game one night in Karnack, as desolate a place as I have ever visited. After the game I interviewed a player and a coach before I went to my car for the trip back to the office. The night was so cold that the air hurt my lungs when I breathed, and I couldn't wait to get the car started and the heater warmed up. My fingers were numb and I dropped the keys a couple of times before I finally got the right key in the ignition and turned it. Silence. I tried again. Silence again. I had jumper cables, but the parking lot was empty by this time. A smart person would have returned to the gym and asked for a ride home on the team bus. I didn't do that. I would have missed a deadline. I tried to start the car by pushing it, jumping inside, and popping the clutch. After three attempts, I was about 100 yards closer to home, but the car still wouldn't start.

Meanwhile, everyone had left the gym and I was alone in a dark parking lot in a remote town where I knew no one, and our deadline was drawing closer. I had enough change to make a call from a pay phone (there were no cell phones in the '70s), so I walked to an intersection where I could see a phone booth under the street light. I called the office and relayed my information on the game. Then I asked if someone could rescue me. I explained that I was afraid I would freeze to death if I didn't get murdered first in that dark parking lot. About half an hour later, help arrived, and I was able to jump-start my car and head home.

Living cheaply was essential on $125 per week, and that meant staying healthy because even in the '70s a couple of medical bills would consume a week's pay. My health was fine until one unseasonably warm afternoon in late February when I went to the baseball field at Panola Junior College to interview the coach for an advance on the upcoming season. The team was taking advantage of the warm weather by practicing outside. The entire scene was a little surreal. The Texas sun was shining brightly, but some snow and ice remained in the shadows from one of only two snowfalls I saw in five years of living in northeast

Texas. Impatient as always, I didn't wait for the practice to end. I walked out to the first-base box where the coach was watching his players take batting practice. I was asking questions and scribbling away, so I didn't pay as much attention to what was going on between the lines as I should have.

I didn't see the line drive that broke my leg. I imagine it must have been a wicked shot because one moment I was jotting notes and the next I was flat on my back screaming in agony. I spent the next five weeks on crutches, which was not only expensive but was also a serious handicap for a sports reporter. Climbing into press boxes, for example, was no longer an option. Nor was chasing players and coaches for interviews after games. I covered the last month of the basketball season and most of the baseball season from the stands, and I learned to position myself to intercept players and coaches after games instead of chasing them. Except for the medical bills and the pain, however, the experience was not bad. You get a different perspective on games when you see them from the stands, primarily because the fans have a different point of view from the sportswriters and coaches. It's probably a good idea for all community sports journalists to occasionally cover a game from the stands. Talk to people and find out what they think about the coaches and the players and the strategy. They are usually less cynical than veteran sportswriters.

Team sports occupied most of my time, but my favorite sports story had nothing to do with team sports. It was a feature about Festus, an award-winning coon-hunting dog. Festus's owner came into the newsroom one day and offered to take a reporter on a hunting trip the following Saturday night. Suddenly everyone developed flu-like symptoms or had relatives visiting for the weekend, so I got the assignment.

On Saturday night I met Festus, his owner, and a couple of other guys at a café near town. We climbed into pickup trucks and drove into the woods, rattling along a narrow trail for what seemed like hours. Several times I wondered whether I would become a slimmed-down version of Ned Beatty's character in *Deliverance*. We finally reached a clearing and stopped. The night was crisp and clear and dark. You could almost feel the darkness brush against your skin. As I stood beside the pickup, I became aware of a constant rhythmic, metallic screech. I shuddered and felt the hair on the back of my neck bristle. I don't believe in ghosts or witches, but I was absolutely frightened for a moment. I fumbled for my flashlight and snapped it on. As the beam danced around in the dark, I saw that we were in the middle of a field of gas wells, each well looking like a giant heron bobbing its head up and down along a great black shoreline. Each time a well bobbed, it screeched, and each time it screeched, my skin crawled.

I calmed down a little as the hunters released Festus. As the dog went to work, the hunters built a fire, opened a bottle, and passed it around. They told crude jokes and stories as we listened to Festus barking in the distance. Then the barking changed timbre and the hunters jumped up, stomped out the fire, and began walking rapidly toward the dog. As we walked, one of them warned me not to use my flashlight again.

We came to a shallow ditch, which I didn't see in the darkness. I fell in and rolled to the bottom, but I sprained only my pride. The hunters chuckled at the greenhorn and kept going. We finally caught up with Festus, who was howling toward the branches of a large oak tree. The hunters shined lights into the tree, but there was no coon. "He follered a cold trail," one of the hunters said. "That coon was up there all right," the dog's owner replied. "He just jumped to another tree. Ain't no dog can track a coon through the trees."

That scenario repeated itself several times until finally, toward morning, the hunters played their lights into a tree and a pair of eyes flickered back. But it was a cat instead of a coon. When the cat saw the hunters, it came out of the tree like spitfire, raked Festus across the face and disappeared into the darkness.

On Monday I wrote the story, and it appeared in the next edition. The headline in 48-point type said, "Festus Barks Up Wrong Tree." That afternoon we received a visit from the irate owner of Festus. He disappeared into the editor's office. An hour later, he emerged and stalked out of the office. I never saw him again.

The conflict with the coon hunter was unusual. I seldom had confrontational relationships with the coaches and players I covered. On two occasions, however, I angered coaches simply by reporting what they did and said. In one case I was justified, but I still regret the other. In the first, the local junior college basketball team had played the junior varsity of Centenary University in Shreveport, Louisiana, in the final game before the Christmas break. When I returned to Carthage, I stopped at the gym to check on a statistic or a quote before going on to the office. As I walked into the gym, I was surprised to see the team on the floor in their uniforms. It was about 11 P.M. and the players had just finished a one-hour bus ride from Shreveport. I discovered that the coach was so angry at the lack of effort by his players that he forced them to ride home without a shower and then to work out. "They think they are already on Christmas break," he said. I reported the incident as part of the game coverage. The coach didn't like the reference to the workout because it got him into hot water with the administration. He said the workout was not relevant to the game, but I disagreed. It not only showed his attitude about the game but it also revealed a questionable motivational tactic.

The second incident occurred when I went to a high school stadium to interview a football coach for a story that would be a combination of preview on the upcoming game and commentary on the previous game. Although his team had lost Friday night's game, the coach was in a jolly mood. He jokingly said, "If they had played as well as I had coached, we would have won." I quoted him, and the coach had a lot of explaining to do to players, parents, and administrators. If I had it to do again, I would leave that quote out because I don't think it revealed the coach's real attitude toward his players.

When I left Carthage, I went to work for *The* (Henderson, Tex.) *Daily News,* where Buster Hale was editor. He insisted on good, accurate reporting and writing, but he was also a stickler for deadlines. A survivor of the Bataan Death March during World War II, he was acid-tongued and irascible. He was nearing the end of his career when I worked for him, but he had lost none of his grit. One day a young reporter made the mistake of agonizing too long over a lead for a high school baseball game. The clock clicked steadily toward deadline as the reporter sat and stared and sweated. Finally Buster walked over and stood behind him for a couple of seconds. "What the hell are you doing?" Buster asked. "I'm trying to think of a good lead," the reporter answered. "God damn it, boy, it's time to stop thinkin' and go to writin,'" Buster snarled. The reporter immediately went to writin' and had the story done before deadline.

As colorful as he was, Buster would have run a close second in a race for most flamboyant newsroom employee at *The Daily News.* Ted Leach, the sports editor, was famous in East Texas for his clear writing and accuracy, his antics, and his false teeth, which he once threw across a newsroom in a fit of anger. In fact, Ted's teeth spent more time out of his mouth than in. When Ted wrote, he usually took his teeth out and placed them on the desk—unless he had left them home.

Ted's teeth once played a part in a speech *The Daily News* publisher delivered to the Henderson Rotary Club. The publisher instructed me to take a photograph of several employees so that he could make slides for his speech. I dutifully photographed people in the mailroom, the pressroom, the composing room, and the newsroom. I shot an advertising salesman and I photographed Buster at his typewriter. Then I asked Ted if he would pose for a photo. "Okay," he said. "But first let me get my teeth out of the car." In a few minutes Ted returned without his teeth. "I left them in the other car," he said. "Go ahead and shoot me without them."

Leach, who is now editor of *The Panola Watchman* in Carthage, covered high school athletics for the same reasons I did. We enjoyed the games, we enjoyed interviewing players who were not jaded, and we enjoyed the communities we covered. Although the rewards of covering high school athletics are great, the job is just as demanding as covering the colleges or pros. High school fans expect the same kind of coverage of their teams as the fans of colleges and pros expect. A woman once called a newspaper I worked for a "hick-town rag with nothing better to put on the front page than a kid's game." She was upset because we had published a front-page story on a high school game that determined the league championship. I referred her to that Monday's edition of the *Houston Chronicle,* which had not one, but three photos of Billy "White Shoes" Johnson. The photos showed Johnson fielding a kickoff, avoiding a tackler, and dancing in the end zone. I don't know that she was convinced, but I argued that the high school team is as important to a small community as the Oilers were to Houston or the Cowboys are to Dallas.

High school athletics also provide reporters a chance to write about the best and worst of human nature. Among the best examples was a football player in East Texas whom the coaches described as "little but slow." He wasn't very strong either, compared to the guys he played against. He was the most obscure player on the team until his senior season, when he finally earned a starting position as an offensive guard. Week after week he tried to block bigger and faster players. I interviewed him after what I thought was a particularly brutal game for him. I thought a big and fast defensive lineman had overwhelmed him, but the young man had a different perspective. "He beat me most of the time, but when I blocked him, I can't tell you how good it felt. I know now I can do anything if I don't quit," he said.

Among the worst examples of human nature was a parent who became too involved in his son's high school athletic career. The player had a world of talent, but he crumbled under the pressure brought about by his father. He was at least 6'2" as a high school freshman and started for the football, basketball, and baseball teams. Football seemed to be his best sport, and that's where his problem arose. During his freshman season, his father frequently called him to the fence that separated the field from the bleachers. Although I could not hear what he said, Dad was clearly instructing his son. Naturally Dad and the coach clashed over this, and the son was caught in the middle. The player's performance declined toward the end of the season, and it got worse during his sophomore season. When the coaches moved him to defensive back during spring practice after his sophomore season, his father transferred him to another school for his junior year. By the time the young man was a senior, he was a reserve quarterback. He attended junior college on a basketball scholarship, but his athletic career ended there.

Although I always loved writing about high school sports, there were times I would get discouraged. Sometimes on a fall Friday night I would question my sanity as I began another 10 hectic hours of high school football. I would think about how I could, if I chose, cover a big game on Saturday instead of a high school game. I could enjoy a pre-game buffet in a fancy press box instead of a hot dog and a Coke at a tiny high school field. I could sit in a comfortable chair in an air-conditioned press box instead of squeezing a metal folding chair between the principal and the public address announcer at a crowded press table. I could interview players and coaches at a press conference instead of chasing them across the field as they ran to the locker room after a game. Most of the time, though, I thought, "What a great way to make a living; just watching kids play ball because they love it and then writing about it." I wouldn't have had it any other way.

14. Sports Reporting and Investigative Journalism

Danny Robbins

Danny Robbins is a member of the investigative projects team at the Fort Worth *Star-Telegram*. He previously worked as an enterprise/investigative reporter in the sports departments at several newspapers, including the *Houston Chronicle,* the *Los Angeles Times, Newsday,* and the *Dallas Times Herald.* He was named Investigative Reporter of the Year by the Headliners foundation of Texas in 1997 and received the Texas Associated Press Managing Editors Freedom of Information Award in 1996. He is a graduate of the University of Texas.

A college athletic program must explain its woeful graduation rate. A high school basketball star contemplates his future with advice from shoe-company representatives and would-be agents. An Olympic athlete is stripped of a medal for using a banned substance. A pro sports owner holds a community hostage in an attempt to gain public financing for a stadium.

Arriving almost daily, such headlines provide a constant reminder of how covering sports in this day and age can be a complex undertaking and how it cries out for one of journalism's most noble elements, investigative reporting. If only the cries were answered more frequently. Traditionally a tool for covering government, business, and other so-called hard news, investigative reporting is too often viewed by sports editors and reporters as something that belongs elsewhere in the newsroom. Out of sight. Out of mind. Out of touch.

Why should investigative reporting be an integral part of covering sports? And why is it often overlooked in that regard?

Let me start by dealing with a few myths. Investigative reporting is neither glamorous, as it is sometimes depicted by movies and television programs, nor does it require a particularly complex set of skills, such as those you might acquire in a class or workshop. More than anything, it takes persistence—the proverbial "shoe leather" factor.

It is true that covering sports as an investigative reporter means operating differently from your colleagues. While they do their jobs in press boxes and locker rooms, you knock on doors in small towns looking for long-forgotten former players from State U. or hunker down in courthouses and government offices to sift through records. But the basic ingredient for success—a strong work ethic—is the same. A baseball writer who isn't afraid to dig can easily be an investigative reporter by putting his or her mind to it.

Okay, so you think you can do it. How to begin. First, you need an idea. Simple as it sounds, that, to me, is the most important part of the process. Good idea, good story. Bad idea . . . usually doomed. Good ideas are those you know will make an impact on your readers and, most important, tell them something they didn't already know. If they pick up the paper and say, "Man, I didn't realize . . ." or, even better, "Holy. . . . ," then you have done your job. If they pick up the paper and say, "Didn't I just read this in *Sports Illustrated*?" or, worse, "So what?" you have wasted your time.

Where do good story ideas come from? As you might expect, some do arrive in the form of unsolicited letters, e-mails, and phone calls. Never ignore anyone or anything; even the most over-the-top caller can provide a nugget. But most story ideas don't land in your lap. They come from conversations with sources and others you encounter on a daily basis, small items in the newspaper, perhaps something on the Internet. Any snippet of information that raises a red flag.

My first experience with investigative reporting, which occurred when I was working as a sports feature writer at the *Dallas Times Herald,* might be instructive in this regard. Assistant football coaches in what was then the Southwest Conference floated the notion in conversations with me and some of my colleagues that boosters affiliated with Southern Methodist University were "buying" football players. Initially, there wasn't much to go on, just the coaches' vague (and off-the-record) suspicions and the names of some high school recruits who might have been involved. But the information was enough to take us places where much of what we were being told could be confirmed.

We found individuals who described how a highly regarded recruit in North Texas had signed with SMU after "committing" to numerous other schools and disappearing with his brother (and self-appointed "agent") on the night before the signing date. We found a district court judge in South Texas who had taken legal steps to show how another coveted recruit who signed with the Mustangs had visited Lake Tahoe with an SMU-connected family friend before signing. And ultimately we started finding recruits and others with firsthand knowledge of improper offers and payoffs, the birthing stage of a saga that would make SMU the first, and still only, school to receive the NCAA's so-called death penalty.

Another example: At the *Houston Chronicle,* I received a call from a friend who told me she knew the parents of a teenage girl in Houston who had been sexually harassed by an assistant football coach at her high school. The parents were particularly upset because the head coach at the school had helped the offending assistant land a job in another school district by providing him with a glowing recommendation. While looking into the situation, I met a state investigator who mentioned he had regularly seen such situations, particularly with coaches. He referred to the phenomenon as "passing the trash." After completing a story on the matter detailed in the initial tip, I was able to find numerous examples of "passing the trash" in the Texas high school coaching ranks and made them the centerpiece of a series on sexual misconduct by Texas high school coaches.

Working as an investigative reporter, in sports or elsewhere, does not necessarily mean you will be out of pocket for six months at a time while attempting to unlock the great secrets of life. Sometimes you *will* be in that mode, but often you won't. Many investigative stories are in essence a sequence of stories, one building on the other, not all that different from covering a beat.

How do you know when stories require months of research and when they don't? Basically, it's a matter of feel. Is there competitive pressure from other media? If you are alone in pursuing a story, you may have the luxury of pulling everything together and publishing on your own terms. But in a competitive environment, particularly one in which some of the facts are already public knowledge, it often makes sense to publish what you can and pursue other aspects of the story later.

When the *Dallas Times Herald* scrutinized the SMU football program, the "investigation" wasn't one or two big splashy stories. It was numerous relatively small stories, some published only days apart, a circumstance dictated by two factors: One, a Dallas television station, WFAA, had already reported that SMU was being investigated by the NCAA. Two, our competition, *The Dallas Morning News,* also was following the story. To hold information and produce stories with greater context would have been nice, but it also could have meant being scooped.

An investigation of the University of Washington football program by myself and a colleague at *The Los Angeles Times,* Elliott Almond, shows you the other side. It began when Almond encountered a former University of Washington football player who mentioned that he had been paid for a summer job at a booster's construction site and had done virtually no work, an obvious story. Our preliminary reporting indicated the ex-player's claim had merit, but we didn't rush to get something in print, mainly because there was simply no reason to do so, competitive or otherwise. We fleshed out the situation, found other former Washington players who had worked at the site, and ultimately produced a long comprehensive story on the "jobs" program as a whole. In that instance, the long-range approach fit the circumstances.

In some ways, an investigative reporter in sports is not much different from one who deals in more traditional coverage. The investigative reporter must develop and nurture contacts in a variety of areas (law enforcement, the NCAA, high school athletic associations, etc.) just as the traditional sportswriter must develop contacts within teams and leagues. The investigative reporter must strive to get all sides of a story in the same way the football writer who deals with a dispute between a coach and a quarterback must duly note the views of both. The difference, as I see it, is that investigative reporting requires a sense of patience that typically isn't associated with the daily journalism grind, a factor that, from my point of view, causes a lot of sports reporters and editors to bail.

In many instances, covering sports is based on the "quickie" interview. A few minutes with a player in front of a locker or in an interview room. A call to a hotel or dormitory. Get some quotes and pound out a story. While such thinking may be okay in some cases, it typically doesn't work when stories raise questions about the behavior of individuals or how institutions conduct their business. In those situations, you must be willing to take the time to learn as much as you can about your sources. It's important to put people at ease, to make them feel comfortable enough to trust you. It's also critical to know as much as possible about the people you are dealing with so you can better judge their character and veracity and seek corroboration for what they say. If someone tells you, "Well, my aunt was there, too," you want to be able to locate the aunt and speak to her. Was she really there? What does *she* remember? You simply can't make that kind of connection in 30 minutes.

Sometimes the issue comes down to simple logistics. How far are you willing to go to make meaningful contact with someone you think can help you with a story? Talking on the phone can get the job done in some circumstances, but not often. Face-to-face meetings are usually better. If someone can't be contacted by phone or doesn't appear receptive to setting up a meeting, there's nothing wrong with showing up unannounced at his or her home or workplace as long as you are civil about it. And if someone won't talk to you at first, don't be afraid to go back and try again. On many occasions, the second or third try is the charm.

Realize, too, that a lot of the people you'll want to talk to generally won't be well-known or readily available. Some will be hard to find. Some won't want to be found. In that regard, learning how to find addresses and other personal data through Internet databases, state driver's-license records, or court files is extremely important. My dealings with two former Texas Tech athletes who were key sources in *Houston Chronicle* stories on academic irregularities at the university, Nate Jackson and Stephen Gaines, illustrate some of the points I am trying to make.

I started looking for Jackson when I got a tip indicating he had received credit for an unconventional correspondence course while attempting to become eligible to play basketball at Tech. After looking through some old media guides and making calls to friends and family members, I found him living with an uncle in Atlanta. He was willing to talk about the situation on the phone but was vague about what had happened—so vague, in fact, that he wasn't sure of the name of the junior college from which he had received the credit. By meeting him in Atlanta and drawing him out on the subject, I was able to fill in the gaps, resulting in a story that showed how he had received credit for a Spanish course from a West Texas junior college without leaving his home state of California and with the assistance of a Tech-connected coach.

I subsequently learned that Gaines, a former Tech football player, had been involved in a similar situation and sought him out in his home town of Electra, Texas. When numerous phone messages went unanswered, I drove to Electra, where I finally spoke to Gaines and learned the reason for his reluctance to talk: He had already been interviewed by NCAA investigators and feared that making his involvement public would bring reprisals. Over the next several weeks, I made more visits to Electra. Each time, Gaines politely refused to discuss the matter, leading me to believe he knew something important. What do you do in that situation? Be honest. Of course, it is your job to get information in the paper, but you are not out to set people up as vindictive whistle-blowers if they don't fit that description. You just want the facts. Maybe bringing the situation to light will correct the situation. With Gaines, I got lucky. He eventually became comfortable enough to explain how he had completed a correspondence course with the help of a member of the Tech coaching staff and had provided that information to the NCAA.

Should all interviews be on the record? Absolutely. Also taped. But if someone wants to talk off the record, there's nothing wrong with going along and later asking that the information be placed on the record. Just because something is off the record on Tuesday doesn't mean it has to be that way on Friday. For example, say one of Mr. Smith's former employees tells you that Mr. Smith helped high school athletes find stand-ins to take their SATs. There is a catch, however—the former employee doesn't want to be quoted. Obviously, you can't put the information about Mr. Smith in the paper, at least not on the basis of the former employee's say-so, nor would you want to. But maybe the former employee knows others familiar with the test-taking scheme, including some of the athletes themselves, and maybe some of them *will* talk on the record. And once you get those individuals to talk, who can say that the former employee won't change his mind and speak on the record as well? Just because someone says, "You can't quote me," it doesn't mean you have to give up on a story.

As for unnamed sources, I don't consider them taboo, but I use them sparingly and only in certain instances—a source who might have a legitimate fear of retribution as a result of speaking out on some issue or a source who has knowledge of a particular fact that is contained in a confidential report or document. Again, the better you know your source, the better you can deal with his or her reason for not being identified. I have used unnamed sources to help corroborate information from named sources or documents but rarely as the primary sources in stories.

Another major element of the reporting process is seeking information from public records or other documents, the so-called paper trail. Again, I believe this is an area that often is neglected by sports reporters and editors, much to the detriment of their sections. How you use records will obviously depend on your story, but you should always consider using them in some manner. Maybe somebody steers you to a particular court case, which becomes your starting point. Or maybe you simply want to verify one aspect of something mentioned by someone in an interview. Either way, coming up with records is an integral part of the job. The best stories, I have found, often involve both the recollections of individuals and information contained in records, with one element serving to corroborate the other.

The first thing to be aware of is the wealth of information in the public domain and how useful it can be in your reporting. In addition to the obvious—court records, property records, articles of incorporation, and so forth—consider the less obvious as well, such as traffic tickets (a way to link college athletes to vehicles) and the personnel files of public school teachers and coaches (which often detail unpublicized disciplinary matters). Some public records are available through Internet Web sites. Some require contacting or visiting courthouses or state agencies. Still others can be obtained through state or federal open-records requests. Considering how much coverage is devoted to the ills of college and high school sports, much of which deals with public institutions, clearly one of the most critical aspects of investigative reporting in sports is having a thorough knowledge of your state's public-records law and how to use it. Usually a simple letter to the appropriate entity can provide you with the information you need.

Many records, of course, are not meant to be public—college and high school transcripts, for example. How can you get them? Well, someone has to provide them to you. Can you use them in your reporting? Sure. There is nothing that says you can't use a "leaked" document as long as you can determine its legitimacy and you came by it honestly. It is also possible in some circumstances to obtain such records by getting approval from the individuals involved. For instance, both former Texas Tech athletes cited earlier agreed to sign releases allowing the *Houston Chronicle* to obtain copies of their college transcripts and other academic records. What prompted the players to sign the releases? They were asked. Simple as that. In Gaines's case, obtaining records from the school from which he received his correspondence-course credit, Southeastern College of the Assemblies of God in Lakeland, Florida, proved particularly significant. The records showed that the course material had been sent to the home of the Texas Tech assistant coach identified by Gaines as having helped him complete the course. In addition, the handwriting on the enrollment documents matched the handwriting on the coach's expense accounts, which were provided to the *Chronicle* by the university in response to a request under the Texas Public Information Act. In short, the records meshed with what Gaines had said.

Most stories follow a pattern. You collect a certain amount of information and then seek answers from those individuals whose conduct could be called into question. These so-called confrontational interviews certainly can be tense, but bear in mind that you usually will get more information by being nonconfrontational and showing you have an open mind. A prosecutorial approach is often counterproductive. Be tough, sure, but also fair and respectful. Take everything in and compare it to what you already know.

Are you being lied to? Or have you gotten the wrong impression from a source or document? Remember, nothing is black and white.

Do you have to wait until the very end of the process before conducting interviews of that nature? Not necessarily. If you think the time is right to talk to someone, go ahead and do it. Frankly, sometimes that approach works better, creating the sort of relaxed environment that helps you get answers to your questions. Besides, there's nothing that says you can't go ahead and collect more information, then go back and ask more questions. If you hear, for example, that a certain high school looks the other way when its athletes take performance-enhancing drugs, obviously you don't go straight to the coach or principal and ask, "Hey, is it true . . . ?" You work around the edges, contacting former athletes, disgruntled parents, ex–assistant coaches, and so forth. You typically want your inquiries to remain as subtle as possible so those who might stifle your sources will not seek to do so. Eventually, of course, you go to the coach or principal and lay out what you have found. On the other hand, if it plays out that you wind up talking to those individuals earlier than you expected, don't consider yourself in a bind. Get their side and go on with your reporting. People often reveal more about themselves and their actions, questionable or otherwise, than you imagine they will.

How do you know when it's time to write? If you're doing a good job of reporting, you may never think it's time. Don't worry. It's the nature of the job to believe there's always one more person to contact, one more thing to check. Still, a great reporting effort is meaningless if it goes no farther than your computer. Developing a sense for when you have compiled enough information to publish something, if only a piece of a story, is difficult but necessary. The situation is infinitely better if you have a good editor, someone who understands what you're doing (and the difficulty you face in doing it) but is removed enough from the process to provide fresh perspective at crunch time. If you can work with such a person, consider yourself fortunate. Also, don't be afraid to seek the opinions of your colleagues. One of the difficulties of investigative reporting is that you can become so involved in what you're working on that you lose sight of your goal: letting the readers in on the secret.

You may be wondering at this point why nothing has been said about writing. The reason is simple: Writing is probably the least of your worries. There are basically two keys to writing an investigative story or stories: clarity and organization. If you want to be cute or clever, stand in line with all the other columnists-in-waiting.

Clarity means pretty much what you think. Nothing fancy. Just the facts. Some stories can be written in the basic style of who, what, when, where, why, and how. Some may require a "soft" lead, perhaps an anecdote. But all should be clear and lean. Let your information carry the story. The hardest thing, as I see it, is taking complex sets of facts or circumstances and making them understandable for readers who, by and large, are not readily familiar with them. You may know everything there is to know about how the NCAA punishes schools that ignore academic cheating or how NASCAR regulates safety belts, but the average reader does not. Lay out the facts for that reader as clearly as possible and without embellishment. Make sure you give the story a sense of context. Why is this something the reader should care about? If your story involves multiple individuals or topics, be sure to keep them all straight. Nothing can mess up two months of solid reporting quicker than a confusing or overwritten story.

Organization basically comes down to deciding how your work can best be presented. As with writing itself, the decision should be based on what can make the material most understandable to the reader. Some projects can best be presented as a single story tying together a number of elements. Some make more sense as several smaller stories or a series of stories. Many of the SMU stories I mentioned earlier were no more than 20 inches in length. They went in the paper basically when they were completed. On the opposite end of the spectrum, the project I cited regarding sexual misconduct by high school coaches in Texas was published as four stories and three charts in a single Sunday paper. It filled five open pages. Different circumstances; different approaches.

Another important thing to consider is how you can use photos and charts. The story I mentioned regarding the academic records of Stephen Gaines, the former Texas Tech football player, was illustrated with a chart that included elements of the records themselves and showed in step-by-step fashion how possible wrongdoing had occurred. Headlined "How to Earn Three Credits in Two Weeks," the chart probably gave readers a better feel for the situation than the 1,500 words that went with it.

Also, avoid thinking that the publication of a story means your job is done. It isn't. In fact, it may just be starting. One story usually leads to another—and often others after that. If what you have written results in an investigation of some sort, perhaps by law enforcement or the NCAA, stay on top of it. The university says no wrongdoing? What led to that conclusion? Remember, too, that something you may have put aside the first time out of the gate can be a story the next time. The worst thing you can do is write a story and fail to follow up.

As a final word: Try not to get discouraged. Just about every story will present some roadblocks. Somebody doesn't want to talk. A document you thought would be a matter of public record isn't public after all. Don't let it get to you. Maybe the story leads elsewhere. Maybe there's no story at all. Fight through it, keep digging, and know that your efforts will pay off eventually.

15. Sports Profiles

Nelson Price

Nelson Price is an Indianapolis-based author of three books and an award-winning journalist who specializes in profiles of newsmakers and historic figures. He's also done many in-depth profiles of athletes, including Olympic diver Greg Louganis and gymnast Kurt Thomas. He wrote for *The Indianapolis News* and *The Indianapolis Star* for 20 years.

Many people consider profiles—the "up close and personal" stories—to be soft news, whether the focus is on a sports figure, a movie star, an auto mechanic, or even a controversial politician.

But watch your step. Don't fall victim to a certain soft-news trap even if your profile subject is a beloved Olympic gold medalist who has overcome cancer or a pro football cheerleader who made the squad after toiling for years as a janitor.

What do I mean by soft-news trap? Well, I'm certainly not disparaging profiles that portray the subject in a sympathetic or positive light when justified. In fact, I would wonder about the agenda of a journalist who uses a profile about, say, figure skater Scott Hamilton's inspirational comeback from testicular cancer as a vehicle to tear down the 1984 Olympic gold medalist.

The term "soft-news trap" has to do with the writing style, not the approach to the profile subject. Today's newspaper and magazine readers are rushed for time. Surveys show that the average subscriber spends about 18 minutes reading the daily newspaper. An in-depth, magazine-style profile eats up a huge chunk of that total time allotment.

So profile writers need to state right away—in a fresh, clear, and artful way—why a profile subject's personal story is important. What's his or her connection to the news? Or what's the drama, conflict, tension, or revelation about human nature that's going to emerge in this profile?

If your profile subject is well-known to your readers—whether a nationally famous person such as basketball superstar Reggie Miller or the quarterback of a college football team familiar to fellow students—what new dimensions about him or her will the reader glimpse?

"Soft-focus" profile ledes—indulgent descriptions of the falling snow on the night of The Big Game or leisurely-paced looks at how a race car driver got his childhood "jump start" in the sport—lose readers lickety-split.

Book readers might be willing to settle in for a meandering, literary opening in a biography. Newspaper and magazine profile readers, though, want to know, pronto, why this athlete, coach, ball boy, or other sports subject is worth their precious minutes. Hit the significance swiftly and emphatically, not softly.

Remember the reference to a custodian who became a cheerleader? That wasn't hypothetical. I wrote just such a duckling-into-swan story for *The Indianapolis Star* in 1998 when I profiled a member of an NFL cheerleading squad. Here was my lede:

> It's easy to understand why Dorene Lewis says she was "a nervous wreck" when she debuted as an Indianapolis Colts Cheerleader in 1991.
>
> "As far as I know," she says, "I'm the first and only janitor to become an NFL cheerleader."
>
> Lewis, 32, was hired on the housekeeping staff of the Hoosier Dome (now RCA Dome) in 1986. That was two years after the stadium became the Colts' home when the NFL team moved here from Baltimore.
>
> Her custodial duties included scrubbing the cheerleaders' locker rooms.
>
> Talk about flips: She's now the veteran member of the 34-woman squad.

In the lede, I didn't take readers on a stroll around the catacombs or restroom stalls of the stadium, pausing to describe a hardworking woman pushing a mop and harboring a dream. Instead, the profile jumps right to the point: This woman apparently is the first and only janitor/cheerleader in the NFL.

Not that I'm against descriptions, details, and all of the sensory stuff. Far from it. I love nuance. I savor details. But details should be weaved into a profile seamlessly, not dumped in a lede or in an off-putting block of copy that slows the pace of a profile to a crawl. In fact, detail and description should *advance* the story.

I'll share one of my misjudgments. Several times over the years, I've profiled Olympic gold medalist Greg Louganis, generally considered the greatest diver in history. Greg has coped with almost every possible personal problem, from issues related to race, adoption, and dyslexia as a child to his battle with AIDS as an adult. Here's how I began a profile of Greg in 1987:

> Brandishing cocktail napkins for autographs and Kodaks for memories, they elbow their way to the adopted son of an immigrant Greek fisherman, ignoring six other top-caliber divers.
>
> Exclusive focus is on the Olympic athlete considered as close to perfection as possible in his endeavor. The stunning 27-year-old described by sports publications as the Adonis of American amateur athletics. The competitor so darkly handsome and perfectly shaped (chest 44 inches, waist 28 inches) he is said to pull down 7s just for showing up in his Speedo. Once, classmates tormented him. . . .

That lede was followed by heaping helpings of description of Louganis in practice:

> Again and again, he mounts the platform at the Indiana University Natatorium, two rungs per step, then peers down from 33 feet up. Again and again, he forgets fear and flings himself off, somersaulting, twisting, flipping and reversing his body as he executes just one more dive. . . .

How many readers, particularly those who are not diving fans, are going to wade through all of that? At the time, I was proud of the piece, which won some state journalism awards.

Yet thanks to the clarity and detachment that come with the passage of several years, I see now that my lede was far too "soft" and indulgent. Many readers surely didn't stay with me. To hook and hold them, I needed to tell them much sooner about Greg's dramatic struggles.

Speaking of dramatic struggles: I've been accused of fixating on them in profiles, a charge to which I plead guilty. My favorite sports profiles accomplish a couple of things, chief among them:

- They capture the power or artistry of an athlete, coach or other sports figure.
- They tell a compelling human story, a tale that often involves pain, conflict, struggle, irony, humor, comebacks, and at least one major crisis.

Quick examples from my clips include profiles of a brother-sister team of pairs figure skaters who grew up in a trailer park and were beset with "hard-luck" injuries before every moment of triumph and of a grizzled football coach whose grandchildren were dying of a rare mysterious disorder.

Why do I focus on the personal dramas and conflicts? Several reasons. For one thing, they humanize profile subjects, particularly people easily dismissed as (or whom readers only may know as) single-dimensional "winners" such as jocks, cheerleaders, and coaches.

My experience is that attaining success is never a breeze. Plenty of heartache—a trail of tears, if you will—is part of almost every person's life. People who have chosen to focus single-mindedly on achieving glory in sports (and in other ultracompetitive fields) often are driven by unusual or agonizing factors in their backgrounds.

Why did they spend hours in practice, waking up in the pre-dawn darkness day after day, sacrificing "normal" teenage lives and postponing typical pleasures, to chase some dream? The answers often reveal a lot about their personalities.

Sometimes an athlete's introduction to sports even came as a potential "cure" for a problem. As a preschooler, Reggie Miller suffered from a severe hip and leg bone disorder. Doctors told his parents that Reggie might never walk unassisted. He wore steel braces at night until he was four; his mother used to wake him once an hour to turn him so his leg bones would rotate.

To strengthen his spindly legs, young Reggie threw himself into basketball. He was fortunate enough to have talented older siblings—including his sister Cheryl, often considered the greatest women's basketball player ever—to teach him the game.

That kind of raw material makes a profile compelling. It also contrasts with all of the hoopla and victories that typically prevail in the life of a current newsmaker in sports. (Sometimes the triumphs and hardship coexist. I once profiled a 290-pound pro football center who suffers from diabetes and has to inject himself with insulin in the locker room. He almost lost his chance to play in the pros when recruiters learned of his disease.)

If, on the other hand, the profile subject is newsworthy *because* of his or her downfall—say, a former Olympic medalist who sank into a depression and even was rejected for a job as a pizza-delivery boy (I once profiled such an athlete)—then the crucial "contrast" material isn't the hardship stuff. The contrast is the spectacular success that's now a distant memory.

Of course, maintaining perspective and balance is crucial. A profile writer should guard against the temptation to pump up an episode or personal problem that may be colorful but has never been truly significant in the subject's life.

Was, say, that snub at the high school prom really such a big deal that it merits excavation and a description of four paragraphs? Does it deserve to be the lede—with all of the fanfare that goes along with being at the top of the story—or does restraint (and a supporting role in the profile) better reflect the profile subject's character?

Good profiles, you see, are word versions of portrait paintings. The "painting" is distorted if you focus on one feature and minimize others; it's like painting a person with a flawed nose as nothing but the schnozz.

A profile writer needs to be an accurate judge of character, probably even a bit of an analyst.

Back to the lede—and to that dreaded affliction called writer's block. My experience as a profile writer has been that when I find myself stumped or blocked, the reason has very little to do with frustrations about finding a catchy word or phrase. In other words, a thesaurus doesn't help remove a major "block." Why not? Well, invariably I'm blocked because of a basic reason: I don't know my profile subject thoroughly. Translation: I need to do more legwork, more reporting. I need to hunt up a coach, parent, teammate, rival, sibling, neighbor, or other secondary sources. (Surely it goes without saying that an in-depth profile should be multisourced. Single-source profiles lack credibility.)

I'm "blocked" because I haven't discovered the key to the profile subject's personality—and, as a result, find myself at a loss for a lede. I don't have the anecdote, paraphrased quote, or snippet of behavior that reveals character. Or that sums up—or at least hints at—the profile subject's "essence."

Maybe I need a second interview with the subject. Maybe I just need to observe him or her in action again. Potential solutions—courses of action for the block—are many. Paging through a thesaurus or dictionary is seldom among 'em.

When I turn to the printed page, it's to do "homework." That is, to read, digest, and take notes on articles written about profile subjects at the infancy of their careers and other coverage that supplies perspective and depth about them.

Once in a while, I make the previous coverage part of the lede. Such was the case with a profile I wrote of Kurt Thomas, generally considered the first truly great American male gymnast.

At the point of the profile—September of 1990—Kurt was attempting to make a comeback in his sport at the ancient (for gymnastics) age of 34. He'd also been struggling with a slew of personal problems since his glory days. I used the praise lavished on Kurt in early coverage of his career as a way to contrast with—and throw into sharp relief—his life since then.

Here's the profile, which won several Indiana journalism awards, as it appeared in *The Indianapolis News:*

KURT THOMAS BOUNDS BACK

©1990 The Indianapolis Star. Reprinted with permission.

September 14, 1990

Back when Kurt Thomas was an Indiana State University student turning the gymnastics world upside down, The *New York Times* dubbed the teen heartthrob "the Shaun Cassidy of sport."

Us magazine lauded the 5-feet-5, 126-pound sensation as "the Baryshnikov of the pommel horse."

Sports Illustrated came up with different celebrity comparisons, calling Thomas the "Bert Parks, Billy Graham and Bob Barker" of his sport. Those were salutes to his "showoff"-style enthusiasm, fervor and salesmanship.

All that was in the late 1970s and in 1980, when Thomas was winning the Sullivan Award in Indianapolis; becoming the first American male gymnast in 46 years to snatch a world gold medal, and being trumpeted as the red, white and blue's best bet to knock the Moscow Olympics for a loop.

Now—two divorces, a son, a bankruptcy, a decade, a weight loss, a motion picture, stints as a network commentator, a book, a TV pilot, a line of active wear and five appearances on *The Tonight Show* with Johnny Carson later—the 34-year-old with the modified spike haircut is attempting to bounce back in amateur athletics.

Observers say yet another celebrity comparison applies.

"Kurt is a John McEnroe," says Mike Jacki, executive director of U.S. Gymnastics, the sport's Indianapolis-based governing body.

"He is feisty. He is a bit cocky. But just like McEnroe in his heyday, Kurt makes good on his boasts."

But is the former "wonder boy"—who now quips he is the "grandfather" of his sport—in HIS heyday?

The question is relevant because, like Mark Spitz, another star amateur athlete who trained in the Hoosier state, Thomas has kicked off a comeback attempt he hopes will culminate in glory at the 1992 Olympics.

There are stark differences between the dark-haired swimmer and the blond gymnast, among them the fact that Spitz owns seven Olympic gold medals. Thomas, denied his chance to perform before his largest audience when then-President Jimmy Carter ordered a boycott of the Moscow games, has none.

He had to settle for being a torch-bearing symbol at the 1984 Olympics, sprinting with the flame on the last leg of its cross-country journey and handing it to Ronald Reagan.

"Until gymnastics, I hated being a short kid," Thomas commented, explaining his dedication to sports during a recent interview in Indianapolis.

The Florida native, who became a Sagamore of the Wabash in 1979, took a break from training to promote the 1991 World Gymnastics Championships. The event next September is expected to bring 500 athletes from about 55 countries to the Hoosier Dome. Thomas hopes to be among them, battling competitors barely more than tots when he created the Thomas Flair.

He unveiled the explosive trademark—in which he flairs his legs in a series of whirling, alternating, mid-air scissors kicks while shuttling down and back on the pommel horse—during a meet in Barcelona. The city will be the site of the 1992 Olympics.

"When you are short," Thomas explained, "there is a motivation to feel big. If you can't do it in size and bulk, you do it with sheer force."

With sheer force. That's probably as apt a phrase as any to describe the style—whether entering a party or executing a vault—of Thomas, who shared the national spotlight at ISU with a basketball player named Larry Bird. ("Pure Gold in the Corn Belt," *Time* magazine once proclaimed in dual profiles.)

And it is gold Thomas craves. At the worlds in Indianapolis. At the Olympics in Barcelona. At every competition.

"I'll take any medal, just make it gold," said Thomas, punching out the words as his intense brown eyes stared—as is his habit—straight at his questioner.

Aware of the force of his demeanor and words, he quickly softened both by grinning and adding, "If I get a bronze or silver . . . I'll paint 'em gold."

Nobody but Thomas would say such a thing, acquaintances note. But they also warn against underestimating the compact, V-shaped athlete whose long arms and short legs make him perfectly proportioned for gymnastics.

"If there is any 34-year-old human being on the planet who can do this, it's Kurt," said Olympic gold medalist Peter Vidmar, 29, a member of the 1984 team. "It's not going to be easy, though, even for Kurt. The older gymnasts get, the more we have to deal with our chronic injuries."

Thomas, who underwent shoulder surgery in May, insists his form, physique, stamina and abilities are as impressive as they were even a dozen years ago. Better even.

"I used to wake up with aches and pains," he reported. "I still ache every morning. I am stiffer going into workouts. But I used to roll out of bed and pound down aspirin. I don't do that now. For one thing, I am smarter about training. For another, I don't hurt as much as I used to. The other day a 19-year-old kid, a top gymnast, asked to train with me. At the end of the day this kid was hurting more than I was."

Coached by former ISU teammate Lee Battaglia, Thomas trains in suburban Chicago. Supported by a manufacturer of plastic food packages, he lives with his mother, Ellie.

"And with my girlfriend," Thomas added. She is Janine Creek, a gymnast who toured in some of his arena shows.

His father died when Kurt was 7. Thomas' son, 6-year-old Kurt Jr., was born during his second marriage to former gymnast Leanne Hartsgrove. (His first wife, Beth, is a native of Rushville, Ind.) Kurt Jr. lives with his mother in Sacramento.

The second divorce—which Thomas describes as "rough," although he is friendly now with Leanne—was a factor in his bankruptcy four years ago. He listed assets of $127,500 and debts of $864,827.

"I also had some problems with one of my managers, although nobody took me to the cleaners, legally or otherwise," Thomas commented. "I just got involved with high-risk investments that didn't pan out."

What with a financial crisis on the heels of a divorce—and scathing reviews for the movie in which he made his film debut (*Gymkata* in 1985)—was this a dark period?

"No way," Thomas replied, his gaze never flickering. "My head was cool the whole time. I never stressed out. I always remained positive."

Personal turbulence is a flip from the image projected by Thomas' arch-rival during the 1970s, 1984 Olympic gold medalist Bart Conner. Known for his sunny disposition and success as a motivational speaker, Conner is 32, single and a TV commentator.

But contrasting the two in "good boy/bad boy" terms—a frequent tendency—is inaccurate and unfair, some say.

"Sure, Bart is more serene. It's all been easier for him than for Kurt," Jacki said. "Bart is calculated. Kurt is raw and spontaneous. In 1978 and '79, it wasn't unusual for Kurt to compete in 13 top events. Bart would show up for maybe five.

"Bart is more polished, a great PR man who smiles, dresses impeccably, knows the buzz words, knows all the right people and says the right things. If you mentioned a name to Bart, he would exclaim, 'Oh, sure! I know him!' Kurt would tell you, 'That guy is an a———.' "

"And he may BE an a, which both of these guys know deep down. The difference is Kurt will tell you. Bart won't."

Similarly, Thomas is willing—even eager—to discuss the reaction of Conner and others to his comeback attempt.

"Bart said this was a marketing maneuver, that he wasn't sure I was doing it for the right reasons," Thomas said. "Sure, I miss the limelight. That's part of it. I am trying to market myself more, but isn't everyone in this world? Bart didn't even wish me luck . . .

"People say, 'Why don't these guys like Mark Spitz and Kurt Thomas get on with their lives?' I say, 'You don't know what makes a winner.' Look at Sugar Ray Leonard. He doesn't come back for the money. He does it because he is a champion.

"I want people to say, 'This guy Kurt Thomas proved himself. It wasn't a fluke in the '70s. He deserved Olympic medals. He is the best.'"

His comeback attempt startled many, including several top names in gymnastics.

"I was shocked because of his age," conceded Mary Lou Retton, the 1984 gold medalist. "But that misses the point. Kurt has the ideal body for a male gymnast and has an incredible fighting spirit.

"I am pulling for him. He has a strong personality. I have a strong personality." She smiled. "We understand each other."

Savvy as ever, with a showman's knack for building excitement, Thomas refers to his comeback struggle as a "miracle" attempt.

In doing so, he uses a word denied him in 1980.

Calling him the "unluckiest" athlete of all, a Boston sportswriter predicted a Thomas triumph against Soviet gymnasts in Moscow "would have become as enshrined as the entire 'Miracle on Ice' U.S. hockey team, the gallant underdog . . . that rose up and slew the Russians."

In the decade since, Thomas said he has grown an inch and is 5 feet 6. "I also have chest hairs now," he added, laughing. "Two or three at least."

It isn't the first time he matured at his own pace. When Kurt was 9, his mother, concerned her youngest son was a midget, took him to a genetics specialist. Medical problems that affected his growth eventually went away.

He was all of 77 pounds when, as a high school freshman in a tough section of central Miami, Thomas asked a coach to stick him on the gymnastics team. Assuming a squad of hulking jocks spelled success, the coach smirked and turned him away. Until, that is, he saw Thomas, clad in a pair of oversized gym shorts, pull off a rapid series of handstands and flips.

Even though he has been somersaulting over barriers ever since, Thomas concedes that mounting a comeback in his 30s is the toughest thing he has ever done.

He is told of the McEnroe comparison. Thomas takes a breath, then plunges ahead with—what else?—blunt remarks.

"Male gymnasts usually are a boring bunch. There is no spirit. I'm a rebel. No, I don't argue with judges. I don't fling down equipment. But do I have the fire of a McEnroe? You bet. Have I mellowed with age? Nope. I am crazier than ever."

Thomas is talking as he walks near the Hoosier Dome to pose for a photograph. He has been asked to execute a handstand a block away from the facility, so the dome could be captured in the background.

The former world champ complies, but offers a suggestion. He volunteers to perform the handstand on the stadium steps. Better yet, he will teeter on the railing near the top flight of stairs. High above the sidewalk and pedestrians.

His way, Thomas explains as he leaps into position, will be more eye-catching.

CRITIQUE

Although I continue to be proud of the profile—I think it captured a complex person in a colorful, balanced way—I would do some tinkering with the benefit of hindsight. Notice how often Kurt or the other quoted sources are "reporting," "commenting," "confiding," "whispering," or "explaining."

Why did I have such an aversion to "said?" In his introduction to this book, Bob Hammel is exactly right. Forcing a substitute just for the sake of variety is usually unnecessary. And often counterproductive. It pulls focus from the impact of the quoted material.

Bob's also correct when he implies that shorter usually is sweeter. Early in my career, I tended to "information pack"—that is, stuff a single sentence with as much material as possible. This was partially a maneuver in self-protection: If details, descriptions, and other material were woven into a sentence (for example, "Prodded by his teammates, the brown-eyed, muscular athlete . . ."), editors couldn't cut them. It would be too much of a hassle.

Then a fellow journalist pointed out to me the impact of short short sentences. One of the most unforgettable passages in the Bible consists of just two words: "Jesus wept."

Let's leave the tears, shift gears, and return to an aspect of profile writing that I mentioned earlier. The legwork. Specifically, interviewing. In no other form of journalism, in my opinion, is the success of the interview as crucial as in profile-writing.

Your challenge as a profile writer is to get interview subjects to open up. For that reason, it's almost never effective strategy to lead off with killer questions: "Why did you file for bankruptcy?" "How did your brother's death from AIDS affect you?" "What was the most difficult part of playing for Coach Knight?"

Unless you are super-pressed for time with your profile subjects—

and if they can't give you more than a minimum of 20 minutes, one-on-one, maybe you should rethink whether now is the best time to profile them—save the sensitive subjects for later in the interview.

The first several minutes of an interview—of any interaction between two people, really—are spent sizing each other up. What does she look like? What does he sound like? Is she sincere? Do I like them? Does it seem that they like me?

This internal dialogue is going on in the minds of both participants in the conversation. So what you are doing in the first few minutes is establishing—or trying to establish—rapport. By the way, that doesn't mean trying to become his/her best friend. Attempts to do that are transparent and come across as manipulative, opportunistic, and fake. Establishing rapport means creating a conversational climate that's frank, genuine, and as relaxed as possible. Because the first several minutes of an interview are loaded with all of the internal "sizing up," I try to keep questions as basic as possible. For instance, now is the time to verify factual information such as hometown, parents' occupation, and so forth.

For years, my favorite interview question has been, "What's the biggest misconception (or myth) about you?"

It offers a platform to interviewees. I may not use their replies in my story—as you can imagine, the answers often are self-serving—but the question lets the interviewees have their say.

And you never know. In their responses, the interviewees may bring up a painful matter—say, their shoplifting conviction or their image as a spoiled brat—thereby sparing you from having to be the one to introduce the topic in conversation. Now that the painful matter has been thrown into the water, you can just flow with it by asking further questions and seeking elaborations on their answers.

I used to assume the "biggest myth" question was primarily—maybe only—of use with newsmakers, people in the public eye. But then I realized that just about all of us—whether we're a jock, cheerleader, coach, umpire, housewife, politician, or journalist—walk around feeling that the world has gotten us wrong in some ways. This "misconception" question gives us the chance to voice our beefs.

My final question in any profile interview is invariably: "Is there anything you want to add that I haven't asked about?" I've learned that despite all of my homework—again, I can't stress its importance enough—there sometimes is a heretofore private matter that my interviewees are yearning to get off their chests. Plus, just as with the "misconception/myth" question, it's a way of making interviewees feel they've had a fair opportunity to explain themselves.

Which leads me to the conclusion of a profile—and the end of this chapter. I'm a believer in saving a "nugget" for a story's conclusion. The most important and compelling stuff, of course, should be at or near the lede. But don't neglect the ending of a profile. It establishes the tone that will linger in readers' minds. Try to conclude with an anecdote, insight, quote, or description that reinforces the profile's theme—the grit of the janitor-turned-cheerleader or the nonstop showmanship of Kurt Thomas, for example.

Profiles that don't conclude with a sense of tone or mood don't really end. They just stop.

16. Dramatic Narrative in Sportswriting

Elliott Almond

Elliott Almond is a staff writer at the *The* (San Jose) *Mercury News,* where he covers the Olympics and does enterprise and investigative pieces. He also has worked at *The Los Angeles Times* and *The Seattle Times* and has taught at Orange Coast College and California State University, Fullerton. The Associated Press Sports Editors has recognized his work 10 times.

It begins with an idea. An idea that is alive and passionate and filled with inspiration—one which, cultivated over time, will blossom into an in-depth chronicle that supersedes the tired formulas we're used to reading in newspapers. Some of the most distinguished work in sportswriting integrates fictional elements usually associated with literature. These stories often start tense, rhythmically building to a dramatic crescendo that enchants readers every step of the way. They underscore the power of storytelling.

In a February 2000 *Los Angeles Times* retrospective on the 10th anniversary of the death of basketball star Hank Gathers, Maryann Hudson Harvey illustrated the effectiveness of what is known as literary journalism:

> It is freezing, and the light is fading from the harsh Philadelphia sky. In a cemetery on the outskirts of the city, a car creeps past the field of unkempt graves, then jerks to a stop.
>
> "There it is, Hank Gathers," the photographer yells.

In the back seat, Aaron Crump awakens and shakes his head. The search for his father's grave had taken so long he had fallen asleep. "Hurry, Aaron, we're losing the light," the photographer calls.

Aaron looks quizzically at the photographer, who realizes what he has just said and apologizes profusely.

Aaron finds the irony amusing. He has never visited his father's grave, as far as he remembers, and here this guy is worried about the light.

Now compare her take with this more traditional, albeit acceptable, one from the *Los Angeles Daily News:*

First comes the shock of time.

So much of it has passed, yet there is the sad realization how ineffective it's been at blurring the images.

The death of Hank Gathers remains a memory sharply in focus.

Nearly 10 years have passed since Gathers, the charismatic forward who had led the nation in scoring and rebounding the previous season, collapsed on the floor at Loyola Marymount in a West Coast Conference tournament semifinal and was pronounced dead an hour and 41 minutes later.

The torch has been handed from Grantland Rice to Red Smith to Gary Smith and, well, so many other sportswriters who have borrowed from fiction to tell spellbinding stories. As newspaper space shrinks in the age of the time-stressed reader, as attention spans wither like overripe grapes, as editors become wedded to corporate jargon such as "directness," the tradition of storytelling in American daily journalism has eroded. But as long as the torch continues to pass down, the practitioners will breathe life into print.

The essence of this chapter is to examine how the elements of narrative and literary writing differ from standard newspaper fare and how components of such writing can enliven a small but good story— even one written under the strain of deadline. Entire books have been dedicated to the subject matter. One chapter, at best, can only introduce young writers to the idea and perhaps launch them on their own exploration. Consider this a rudimentary roadmap for a lifelong journey.

What Is Creative Nonfiction?

Think about a favorite piece of fiction. On the surface, it resonates because of the story. Great fiction has universal messages that massage the senses. But on the most basic level, it's the story, stupid. By borrowing from fiction, sportswriters can bring their subjects to life. They can bring their readers joy, sadness, pleasure, or tears. They can bring them love. One of the most fundamental ways to effectively tell a story is the narrative. This is the purest form of storytelling. Listen to children. When they tell stories they start at the beginning, perhaps commencing with, "You'll never believe what happened." They'll carry it through chronologically, innately knowing their audience will attentively wait for the kicker.

Instead of stringing together a set of facts and quotes, a story is told as a sequence of actions, according to Ira Glass, the radio host of *This American Life.*

Glass's groundbreaking show on WBEZ-FM in Chicago, which is syndicated across public-radio land, is a great place to study the power of the narrative. "Whenever there's a sequence of events—this happened then that happened then this happened—we inevitably want to find out what happened next," Glass wrote in his pamphlet, "How to Make Radio That's Good." Academicians have attached names to the narrative forms, but no matter what nomenclature you choose, it starts with identification of what makes a good story. Glass offered an excellent suggestion. "The story needs one character, a character that you identify with, who interacts with other characters in a very specific way, and there's conflict, change, and resolution (and not necessarily the resolution part) inherent to the story." Isn't this what Gary Smith does in his lyrical stories for *Sports Illustrated*? He finds characters—well known or unknown—and uses the elements of conflict, change, and sometimes resolution, sometimes not, to drive us through a profile.

Here's how Smith starts his March 5, 2001, piece in *Sports Illustrated* on an African American high school basketball coach's effect on a secular white Ohio community:

> This is a story about a man, and a place where magic happened. It was magic so powerful that the people there can't stop going back over it, trying to figure out who the man was and what happened right in front of their eyes, and how it'll change the time left to them on earth.
>
> See them coming into town to work, or for their cup of coffee at Boyd & Wurthmann, or to make a deposit at Killbuck Savings? One mention of his name is all it takes for everything else to stop, for it all to begin tumbling out . . .
>
> "I'm afraid we can't explain what he meant to us. I'm afraid it's so deep we can't bring it to words."

"It was almost like he was an angel."

"He was looked on as God."

There's Willie Mast. He's the one to start with. It's funny, he'll tell you, his eyes misting, he was so sure they'd all been hoodwinked that he almost did what's unthinkable now—run that man out of town before the magic had a chance.

The character is yet unnamed, but this clearly is about one person. The conflict is only hinted at but it is simmering just below the surface. And change? Well, Smith uses this ingredient as the story's plough. As for resolution, it comes with a collective transformation coursing through the townsfolk in a dramatic ending.

Smith's best work almost always employs the elements of great fiction. He rarely writes a profile about someone in the news whose athletic prowess alone has made him or her exceptional. For a long-term narrative to work it has to crackle with fictional elements that can be delivered in exceptional ways. Put simply, the local high school basketball star might make a nice feel-good profile, but she or he will not be a great story until the writer unearths something in her or his life that warrants exhaustive exploration. It doesn't take much. It could be a family tragedy that has been discussed by the newspaper but never told in story form. A daily sportswriter will rarely get the blanket canvas of a magazine writer, but a scaled-back narrative can effectively inspire readership. It's a matter of degrees.

Focusing on one person and a cast of supporting characters allows writers to humanize their stories. It takes patience and practice, but a good story, no matter what its length, needs crisp sentences. Listen for meter and rhythm. William Nack, who wrote elegantly in *Sports Illustrated* for 23 years, counts the beats of his sentences. He often wrote in iambic pentameter, a line of verse containing five metrical measures. Covering the Mike Tyson rape trial in Indianapolis in 1992, Nack considered his options minutes before deadline when the verdict was announced. He wanted to infuse his story with the tension of the moment but dismissed the clichés such as "The time had come." Then he thought of William Butler Yeats's "The Second Coming":

"And what rough beast, its hour come round at last,

Slouches towards Bethlehem to be born?"

Nack borrowed "The hour had come round at last." An editor didn't listen to the language closely and deleted round. Here's how it appeared, a lovely and atmospheric opening to be sure. But listen to what it lost by the extraction of one word:

> The hour had come at last, and with it the final silence that so many had been awaiting since the proceedings had begun two weeks before. It was 10:52 on Monday night, and the scene in Courtroom 4 of Marion County Superior Court was frozen into an eerie diorama. The lawyers sat staring fixedly into space. The jurors gazed blankly across the white light of the room. And Don King, carrying a Bible, sat as still as a statue in the front row of the spectator section. At the very center of it all, with the corners of his mouth turned down and his eyebrows furrowed, Mike Tyson sat motionless at the defense table. It had been here, in this courtroom, that the central drama of Tyson's life had been played out.

If we can ignore, for a moment, the lost melody of the first half of the first sentence, we can celebrate the rest of this example for achieving a theatrical quality with lucidity.

"Young writers should be attempting to wed euphony with clarity," Nack said. "If you can achieve both in a single sentence or story, you are on your way to being an artist."

Real Voices

One of the easiest ways to improve copy is the use of dialogue. Sometimes a dialect or an oddball speech pattern offers a sense of place without having to drench description in vivid hues of greens, yellows, or reds. Many authors have used dialogue as a centerpiece of their fiction. Readers of John Kennedy Toole's *Confederacy of Dunces* often come away with a deep attachment for the back alleys of New Orleans because the author effectively captured the patois. We can borrow from the great writers by incorporating dialogue in daily journalism. Good editors preach against overquoting because they know too well the nasty habit of this tired structure: paraphrase, quote, paraphrase, quote—paragraph after painful paragraph. The best editors suggest saving quotes for powerful moments to provide drama, not to use them as a crutch. That means carefully selecting colorful phrasing that the subject said better than the writer can paraphrase. It's good advice. It's also important in literary writing. An even more effective way to insert voices into the story is quoting dialogue.

Nack has many examples of effective use of dialogue. Here's a passage from a January 2000 story about a wheelchair athlete and his life of crime:

> "Do you have any guns?" [Larry] Streeter asked.
> "No, sir," [Ted] Ernst said.
> "Do you understand you are trespassing on private property?"
> "Yes, sir."
> "What are you guys doing back here?" Streeter asked. He had seen Ernst talking on the radio.
> "Just fooling around."
> "Where's the other guy?"
> "He's out by the gate."

Nack has put the reader into the scene, as if he or she is overhearing this conversation. Then he shifts back into the narrative:

> It was almost 11:50 p.m. Believing he had caught a burglar at work, Streeter demanded the ignition key to Ernst's car. Glancing into the back of the Tempo, he saw one of the .357 Magnums on the floor. He opened the door and picked up the gun, giving Ernst the moment he needed to ready his .22. "Give me your license," Streeter said.

That last use of dialogue is brilliant. It stitches this scene together, something Nack does so well. The dialogue mixed with real-time sequences keeps the action tense and moving forward. This kind of writing can be introduced into a breaking story or profile. It's not the sole province of magazine writers. Traditionally, a daily journalist might take the dialogue above apart and offer something such as this:

> "Streeter asked him if he had any guns," Ernst wrote in a detailed description of the murder.
> "I told him I didn't," he wrote.
> Ernst said he told the victim that he was just fooling around by the house.

This offers the reader the essential detail but lacks the raw voice and intensity of the situation. It lacks the tension and suspense of that chilling exchange before wheelchair-bound Ted Ernst fired four bullets into Larry Streeter's body Christmas night in 1997. The second version is more accepted because editors are under pressure to condense copy. So pick your spots carefully, but remember that taut dialogue can be pulled out of the cabinet like a seasoning, giving readers a vivid description of what is taking place. Sometimes it can offer the most revealing moments of a personality. The direct quotes to reporters are wooden because the subject is not using his or her real voice. Listen for voice and use it for effect.

Now Nack obviously didn't overhear the above dialogue. He reconstructed it from interviews with the murderer. Many narratives are reconstructions of a story. They have been labeled retrospective narratives. Another type is prospective, which follows the action as it is taking place. A great story often blends the two forms, especially in the narrow focus of dialogue. Here are two easy ways: 1) Use conversations between the main character and those he or she interacts with instead of standard interviews; and, 2) Re-create dialogue that emerges from intensive interviews to recount an important scene.

By forgoing traditional quotes, the writer can keep the story's tempo nicely paced. In other words, it will help prevent flat spots. If it seems that I am overemphasizing the use of voice, it is because learning to use quotes correctly is one of the easiest ways to improve writing. The old saw says people cannot learn to write, that it is an innate talent. It might be true. But anyone can learn to improve their writing by avoiding clichés, keeping it simple, and carefully choosing quotes.

Finding Middle Ground

Depending on the topic, writers often need an exposition of their material. This is the part of a narrative that feels more like traditional newspaper reportage, even when quoting sources. How do they marry the two forms to make a cohesive piece? They can effectively do this in blocks of text carefully interwoven into the narrative to expand the context and make the story more universal. In other words, it flows from the specific to the general. If handled attentively, the narrative's drama is not interrupted. Dave Davis of the *LA Weekly* didn't sacrifice the dramatic scenes of boxer Jerry Quarry's life in a 1995 profile when he introduced the scientific explanation of Quarry's medical condition. He found a perfect break in the narrative to introduce this:

> The connection between Jerry's condition and boxing echoed the findings that had begun to appear in the 1980s in the Journal of the American Medical Association (JAMA). Advances in technology and testing—including magnetic resonance imaging (MRI), computer-

ized axial tomography (CAT) scans, and neuropsychiatric testing—
were allowing researchers to confirm medically what had for years
been anecdotal material about "punch drunk" fighters. According to
one study done in the New York area, over 60 percent of professional
boxers who'd fought a large number of bouts would end up with
chronic brain damage. Unlike the harm caused by a knockout, when
a boxer renders another unconscious almost instantly, chronic brain
damage—more subtle and hard to measure—is the result of an ac-
cumulation of blows. Other factors that contribute to the severity of
the condition include the number of fights and at what age the boxer
began and ended his career. The more fights, the more likely he will
end up with cerebral atrophy: aging exacerbates the condition.

The exposition continues because it is essential to telling this story.
But even though Davis is introducing broad context, he cleverly re-
minds the reader this is all about Jerry Quarry a few paragraphs into
this segment:

> Ironically, just before his '83 comeback, Jerry took part in a
> *Sports Illustrated* study about brain damage among boxers. Neurol-
> ogists hired by *SI* administered a CAT scan and a neuropsych exam.
> They concluded then that Quarry, though still functional, had "prob-
> lems with certain cognitive functions—short-term memory and per-
> ceptual motor ability."

Creating Scenes

Atmospheric writing is another entrée into literary journalism. It perhaps is the most common and comfortable and shares so many values
with fiction. In fact, this is the intersection between the two, an often
confusing and complicated crisscrossing. Handled nonchalantly, it can
fail miserably in daily deadline journalism. It can become prescribed,
particularly in travel writing. What you want to do is construct realism
through a lucid scene, something Robert Caro, the Pulitzer Prize–winning biographer, calls creating atmosphere. Talking about history writing on NPR's *Talk of the Nation,* Caro said, "Then you have to give
the reader a sense of the place, the atmosphere that he would have seen
if he was there at the time. . . . You know, you have to write it so that
the people who are reading you will feel the same emotions as people
felt when they were actually seeing it." You also have to be careful of
wandering over the line into fiction. Above all, it has to be factual. The
best scenario is experiencing a scene and, through great observation

and insight, recounting it to the reader. The suspense can unfold without embellishment. You'll hook your readers.

Many times, if not most of the time, though, the journalist must recreate the images from interviews of witnesses or those who were involved. Nack's July 23, 2001, profile on Bob Kalsu, who died in Vietnam while still a member of the Buffalo Bills, reaches back to put the reader in the middle of hell:

> There were always lulls between the salvos of incoming mortars, moments of perishable relief. The last salvo had just ended, and the dust was still settling over Firebase Ripcord. In one command bunker, down where the reek of combat hung like whorehouse curtains, Lieut. Bob Kalsu and Pfc. Nick Fotias sat basting in the jungle heat. In that last salvo the North Vietnamese Army (NVA), as usual, had thrown in a round of tear gas, and the stinging gas and the smoke of burning cordite curled into the bunkers, making them all but unbearable to breathe in. It was so sweltering inside that many soldiers suffered the gas rather than gasp in their hot, stinking rubber masks. So, seeking relief, Kalsu and Fotias swam for the light, heading out the door of the bunker, the threat of mortars be damned. "Call us foolish or brave, we'd come out to get a breath of fresh air," Fotias recalls.

Even if you have never been in a bunker being heavily bombarded, Nack has painted the picture. He had reservations about recreating the scene but had the good sense to go with his instincts. Nack had served in Vietnam. He had participated in the Tet Offensive. He had hunkered down in bunkers like the one at Firebase Ripcord, flinching at each new salvo fired by the enemy. He said his editor liked the scene but asked about the phrase "whorehouse curtains." He was able to say he had written with authority. Sometimes the simple choice of words brings everything to life. In this scene, "basting" does it. He could have written "sweating," but the idea of cooking on a rotisserie gets under the surface about what the protagonist would do next—emerge from safety and become another casualty of war.

Report Before You Write

We're not dealing in fiction. We cannot make it up or imagine it. As much as we want our work to resonate with the reader, we are compelled by strict boundaries of accuracy and fairness. Whenever the journalist fails to honor this doctrine, he or she surrenders the art of non-fiction writing. Above all, the reporting must be impeccable or credibility is lost, not only for the individual but for all of us.

Other chapters in this book concentrate on reporting. They should be studied, particularly the one on investigative techniques. I cannot overemphasize the importance of good reporting as the stepping-stone to good writing. I've discussed dialogue and quotes, but they are worth noting again. Some of the best investigative reporters, such as Pulitzer Prize–winner Eric Nalder of *The* (San Jose) *Mercury News* or Danny Robbins of the Fort Worth *Star-Telegram,* have created interview techniques for all occasions. They can be hardnosed, sympathetic, engaging, or quiet. But whatever they choose, they primarily are good listeners for detail. For the nonfiction writer it is important to extract the essential facts, to draw out true emotions from the characters. It also is important to know how to work the court system, to read court transcripts, interrogatories, police reports, and so forth. Fascinating details of a character or subject often can be found in public records. These are indispensable sources of documentation that can transform the mundane to the extraordinary.

Writing coach Fran Smith tells her subjects to fill their notepads with every detail. Smith wants reporters to exercise their sense of observation—sights, smells, sounds. She advises leaving much of the detail in the notebook when writing. But the perfect colorful feature will be waiting when you need it if you have taken the time to jot it down. Personally, I like to step back and create scenes. It forces my antenna to connect with my surroundings. I've been able to lift passages from my notebook and turn them into beginnings, middles, and endings, with some refinement for meter and rhythm. Perhaps the most important point about reporting is that it will show in a good story. It stays in the background, but the reader intuitively knows the author is writing with authority. The only way to have command of a subject, to elevate it, is to have fully, passionately, and meticulously reported it first.

A Means to the End

Embarking on a narrative or long-form story takes courage and confidence. Courage in that the writer, like a salmon, must race upstream to reach the destination of publication. Confidence that the story is so riveting the reader must finish it. As a result, the ending becomes as important, if not more so, than the beginning. The ending, in fact, should be plotted in advance of writing unless you are following an ongoing story for which the final chapter is in doubt. Stories are not necessarily circular. Endings do not have to return to the beginning like so many Hollywood movie scripts. The conclusion can and should stand on its own power. Think theater or drama for a finish. Too many stories end with quotes. It has become a hackneyed formula.

In a March 6, 1995, *Sports Illustrated* profile on figure skater Surya Bonaly, Johnette Howard has a big windup for her finish. The power is not only in the words, but the pacing. It increases the drama.

> "And so?
> "So we must adapt," Suzanne [Bonaly] says.
> "In the mind you stay the same," says Surya. "But you change the appearance. The outside."
> And then?
> Then, though you might prefer the forest, you and your mother attend the French federation's reception following the European championships, smiling self-consciously when the champagne corks stop popping and the waiters carrying hors d'oeuvres trays pause, and the crowd—recognizing that you've arrived—begins to clap and backpedal until a horseshoe of empty space is left for you, the champion, to glide into and fill.
> Smiles hang on everyone's face. All the knives are sheathed. And it is no surprise—no surprise at all, really—that Didier Gailhaguet is among the first to step forward and take Surya Bonaly's hand and kiss her once on the cheek.

Howard took even more time than the example above shows to come to a close, slowly drawing the curtains on her character for lasting effect. This is how you want to leave your readers. Gripping their seats, wondering until the last syllable just how it will turn out.

Will It Be Okay?

Maybe. Maybe not. The hints are there for the possibility of redemption, retribution, or revival. Or nothing at all. It is part of chronicling the pathos and pleasures of our humanity. And all of it, good, bad, or indifferent, provides fertile soil to cultivate and grow into a tale, one as tall as Paul Bunyan and as wide as Babe the Blue Ox. A tale told from the heart.

17. Freelance Sportswriting

Steve Salerno

Steve Salerno writes on sports, business, and other themes for some of America's best-known publications, including *Esquire, Playboy, Good Housekeeping, The Wall Street Journal, Worth, The New York Times Magazine,* and the *Los Angeles Times Magazine.*

I began my career in freelance writing the same way almost all successful freelancers begin: as a custom-mirror salesman in Harlem.

I jest, of course. But only in part. The fact is, my decade selling $1,500 wall mirrors in one of New York's most famously distressed neighborhoods—to customers who, sometimes, didn't even have front doors—laid the groundwork for my first freelance sale, a memoir of those experiences to *Harper's.* I've gone back to that well many times since, for publications ranging from *Esquire* to *The New York Times Magazine* to *The Wall Street Journal.*

There's a pretty important point buried in my seemingly wacky entrée to freelancing, and it's this: The way "in" is to write about what you know about. Which also helps explain how I came to my career-long specialty, freelance sportswriting. You see, it wasn't long after I got the itch to write that my wife gave birth to my son, and it wasn't long after the blessed event that my son and I began arguing on a nonstop basis. As luck would have it, most of these arguments took place on, or en route to, various ballfields and other sporting venues. Thus, over the years, and to the eternal chagrin of TAFKAMS—The Anecdote Formerly Known As My Son—I was able to transform our dysfunctional on-field relationship into an authentic cottage industry.

I've sold literally dozens of pieces about Graig and me and our various misadventures in football, baseball, basketball, and other athletic pursuits. I'm not talking about quaint little pieces for those give-away weeklies you see lying in wet clumps outside your local grocery store. These sagas of our foibles, mishaps, and rare triumphs—and the lessons thereof—have appeared, among other places, in *The American Legion, Los Angeles Times Magazine, Sports Illustrated* and *The Washington Post.* Not quite A to Z, but close enough. They've earned me, on average, about $1,700 apiece. Not quite enough for a new Lexus, but a decent start toward the drive-off payment on the lease. They've also led to a slew of bigger, more ambitious assignments for many of these same publications.

What I'd like to do now is break down the umbrella rule mentioned above—"write about what you know about"—into three components that go very much against the grain of today's rah-rah, be-all-you-can-be motivational movement. To wit:

AIM LOW.

THINK SMALL.

WRITE ABOUT WHAT THE EDITORS DON'T CARE ABOUT.

This time I'm not jesting at all. *Aim low* means you probably need to content yourself with flying under the radar of the big glossies in Gotham until you have some decent clips to show. *Think small* means don't expect to be writing 5,000-word works of bellwether journalism that a publication is apt to put on its cover, at least not your first few times out of the chute. *Write about what editors don't care about* is a sly way of saying that if your story is already *the* de rigueur topic of conversation at those trendy watering holes where New York City editors buy their $9 martinis, well—put bluntly—what the hell do they need *you* for? There are dozens of proven writers in the average editor's Palm Pilot who've already shown that they can get the job done. *Your* job is to find subjects the editors don't quite care about because they haven't been made to care—yet. Then you have to make them care.

If you notice, the foregoing contrarian insights are just different ways of saying the same essential thing—that freelancers have to train themselves to think in the margins of the megastories, the footnotes of the flash and fuss. They have to learn to see the local or personal story that ties up to the big national buzz. If over the years I've come to realize any one thing that's enabled me to enjoy the success I've had in freelance sportswriting (and freelancing in general), it's that you must pick your spots. You must learn to distinguish between the assignments you have a decent shot at landing and the assignments where you might as well put the pitch letter right in the return envelope and mail it back to yourself, because that's where it's headed anyway.

In hopes of making this clearer, I'm about to introduce you to the 10 types of assignments a young freelancer should never, under any circumstances, expect to receive. Which implies that you shouldn't waste valuable time and energy pursuing them. I should preface this by saying that when I use the word "freelancer" in this context, I'm talking about the *true* freelancer, the guy or gal on the outside looking in, *not* the contract writer or contributing editor, whom editors tend to regard almost as members of staff.

Without further ado, then, here's the list of assignments to file under *fuggetaboutit:*

"I want to interview Michael Jordan."

Sure you do. You and everybody else, including world-class authors like Gore Vidal and Tom Wolfe and Joyce Carol Oates—celebrities in their own right. Top sports figures are in such ubiquitous demand that it can take many months, if not years, for even the glossiest publications to line up a one-on-one. And when they finally get the go-ahead from Jordan's agent or publicist, they're not going to dispatch an unknown freelancer to do the job; they're going to send one of those infernal staff writers, contract writers, or contributing editors. And don't think you're going to do an end run around the editors by locking up the interview with Jordan *first.* Ain't gonna happen. No major sports figures, or their handlers or gatekeepers, will green-light an interview with a freelancer unless they know for sure it's taking place with the publication's blessing. They don't want to waste their time on a speculative venture with some journalistic greenhorn.

Speaking of which: If you're going to take aim at this level, you damn well better know your stuff. There is *nothing* more humiliating and potentially disastrous than having to admit to your interview subject that he just referred to something that's common knowledge to everyone in sports but you. I invite you to try it in front of a Bobby Knight or a Bill Parcells sometime and see what happens.

"I want to write about that new football league they're starting up in Barcelona."

Don't bother, unless you happen to live in Barcelona to begin with. A veteran editor won't pony up millions of pesos in T&E* for a piece that may not be publishable (or so he fears). With that level of lucre at stake, he wants a reliable writer on the case. Yes, we know you're as reliable as the next guy, but the next guy's no more likely than you are to get that assignment from an editor who's unfamiliar with his work. Today's editors are exquisitely sensitive to journalistic boondoggles— that is, proposals that seem like they might just be some writer's opportunistic way of wangling a paid vacation in some exotic haunt. There used to be a running gag called "articles I'd love to write for *Esquire,*" number one on the list being "the world's 10 best topless bars." Enough said. And no, you won't be getting that assignment, either.

"I want to cover the Super Bowl."

Uh-huh. And I bet you wouldn't even demand to sit on the 50-yard line, right? Again, this is a plum assignment doled out to a favored, super-dependable writer—often a writer with a name that's expected to serve as a draw in its own right on the publication's cover or Web site. Other events in this same category: the World Series and any other professional sports playoff or championship, the Final Four (as well as the regional tournaments leading to it), any major collegiate football game, Olympic events, top-drawer boxing matches, and so forth. Common sense should tell you which events to save your breath and postage on.

"I want to write about that unbelievable game last night."

With the advent of on-line journalism, many delusional young writers thought they could just catch an especially dramatic contest on TV, pound out a few hundred well-chosen words, fire the results off to *ESPN.com* or another well-paying virtual market, and sit back and wait for the check to arrive. And that's exactly what they end up doing, most of them: waiting, and waiting, for the check to arrive. Because it doesn't work that way. This kind of spot journalism is exactly what publications (on-line and off) have staff writers and contributing editors for.

If at 10 P.M. something takes place at Madison Square Garden that's

---

*T&E? Shorthand for travel and entertainment expenses. If you didn't know that, invest some time in learning the lingo before you start chatting up editors. Much as we saw when we discussed celebrity interviews above, these things come up in casual conversation with editors. If you sound new to the jargon, you sound like a bad risk for a meaty story.

considered a milestone in sports history, you can bet that editors at *Salon* or *Sports Illustrated* or *ESPN: The Magazine* already have a trusted writer at work on the story by 10:30. Once again, you lose.

"I want to cover that big point-shaving scandal out in the Pac-10."

If you've got the investigative bona fides of a David Halberstam or Bob Woodward, and maybe a couple of awards for top-notch reporting under your belt, you *might* give this one a shot. Otherwise, leave the sticky, tricky, legally sensitive jobs to the real pros. Editors fret constantly about minor things like libel and malice and reckless disregard for truth, which is why they tap seasoned journalists for these assignments. They want writers who aren't going to get the publication embroiled in an embarrassing and expensive courtroom fiasco. Consider that if push comes to shove, the very fact that an editor knowingly dispatched an inexperienced writer to cover the story might work against the publication in court. I learned this the hard way when, very early in my career, I botched a sensitive story for *Rolling Stone.* My then editor, David Rosenthal, vowed that he would "never again send a freelancer to do this kind of piece." So if you can't land these types of assignments, feel free to blame yours truly.

"I want to write a piece that ranks the top 10 sports colleges in America!"

Look, I applaud your chutzpah, but these are buzz-generating potential cover pieces that involve a ton of detail work and methodical, coordinated reporting. When a magazine like *Sports Illustrated* or the sports section of *USAToday* undertakes such complex, detailed "roundup" stories, it may well commit more than half its staff to the effort, an effort that ultimately will include assorted sidebars, short Q&As, and relevant subordinate features. You can't handle this project solo, and you shouldn't try. If nothing else, to an editor, such brashness screams "I'm a novice!" Experienced writers know better.

Overall, the odds of failure and embarrassment are w-a-a-a-y too high here.

"I want to write about the various teams' prospects for the coming season in baseball/football/basketball/hockey/[fill in your own desired sport]."

There are several crippling problems with this notion. First, it's a very ambitious undertaking, along the lines of the roundup pieces described earlier; it's seldom a one-person job. (Even when you see stories in this category that carry a single byline, that doesn't mean there weren't a number of researchers and/or other apprentices involved behind the scencs.) Second, it presupposes an expertise that, fairly or not, few editors think freelancers possess. Third, it has a little bit of that boon-doggle scent, as it tends to entail travel to the far-flung locales where pro sports teams hold their pre-season workouts. Fourth, if you do get to write it and your predictions are horribly wrong, you've lost all credibility for the next go-round. In general, staff writers can afford to be way off base in their predictions; it's even considered comical when it happens. When freelancers are way off base, editors do not usually consider it comical. They may even accuse you of making their publications look foolish. Then they may stop offering assignments.

"I want to write about the history of [fill in the blank]."

Part of the trouble here is endemic to the nature of the article. A well-known editor at one magazine for which I often wrote liked to joke that "*history* is a seven-letter word spelled *b-o-r-r-i-n-g*." But let's assume that your idea has some inherent excitement or appeal—like, say, the history of a venerable baseball stadium that's about to be gutted and replaced by a new one. Be aware that you're bucking a recent trend wherein editors desirous of such pieces tend to avoid "regular writers" and go instead to established historians such as Alvin Josephy or Doris Kearns-Goodwin. It's hard to pin down when this started or why, but there's no mistaking its impact throughout feature journalism, in magazines in particular.

"I want to follow the Lakers through their season and write about it afterward."

You probably know without being told that this so-called diary approach to sports journalism—immortalized by John Feinstein in his marvelous best-selling work, *A Season on the Brink*—is not for amateurs. Of course, not all freelancers are amateurs. I've been a freelancer since 1981, and I stopped considering myself an amateur in, oh, 1981. (Hey, if *I* don't have confidence in my abilities, who will?) So why is this a bad idea even for established freelancers? Here are several reasons: 1) It's such a taxing, time-consuming project that an editor is going to want to assign a star writer to it, or at least a favored writer from his stable. 2) You're putting too many of your journalistic eggs in one basket. Feinstein can afford to do that because he gets colossal advances. You can't because you won't. If something goes terribly awry, you've blown months of productivity. 3) Nowadays, the teams themselves are ultrapicky about who gets unfettered access. If you're not a regular on the beat, or at least a known commodity, you're unlikely to get the level of organizational cooperation that makes for a convincing read in the end.

Pass on this one, for now. Once you become a household word, have your agent pitch the idea to a big New York publisher. Then lie back and wait for ESPN to call, offering you that job as a color commentator next to Howie and Terry and the gang.

"I want to write THE definitive essay on baseball's singular place in the American consciousness."

First a tiny sliver of good news: There is, and will always be, a place in American journalism for an unsolicited essay that just *nails* the spirit of this or that aspect of our national obsession with sports. I've been lucky enough to sell a few of 'em myself. So I don't want to discourage anyone with a truly original vision from trying that vision out on an editor. The operative phrase here is "truly original." You have no idea—really, you don't—how many maudlin, warmed-over riffs on "what baseball means to me" the average national magazine receives each spring (and of course, if you're first mailing them in the spring, you're already way too late, even if your stuff is awesome). This applies also to "what football means to me" and "what basketball means to me." I'm not sure about lacrosse.

As a rule, when a publication is looking for a thoughtful piece in this vein, it goes to somebody with a rep: a Roger Angell, a George Will, a Thomas Boswell, or our old friends Feinstein and Kearns-Goodwin. The editors aren't just sitting there four months before Opening Day thinking, *Gee, I hope something good drifts in soon because otherwise we're gonna have this huge hole in our April issue.* . . . If they want an essay about baseball's unique role in American life, they've already assigned it long before you think of it. But like I said at the top—there's always that slim chance. Just keep this caveat in mind if you're not ordinarily an essayist: There are an awful lot of writers out there who've got that special "essay voice" down pat. I like to think I'm one of them. We're in line ahead of you—and even we aren't selling as often as we'd like. Alas, there just aren't a lot of top-paying markets for good essays these days.

If you're still with me this far, no doubt there's a certain question buzzing around your brain—something along the lines of *Well, geez, what does that leave for me to write???*

Plenty.

Commit this to memory: *As a freelancer trying to break in, you want to write about small things that serve as symbols for, or help explain, big things.* So no, they're not going to let you write about Bobby Knight per se—but maybe there's a Little League or high school coach in your neighborhood who's a lot like Bobby Knight and who can give readers an additional lens into the Bobby Knight experience. Or maybe you know or played for a coach who couldn't be more *un*like Bobby Knight. Tell readers about it and show them how things worked out and what it all signifies.

No, you won't be asked to chronicle some NFL team's undefeated march to the Super Bowl. And sadly, if your neighborhood high school team is undefeated the past four years, you probably won't be asked to write about them, either. (We live in a world that's growing steadily smaller; today's high school teams get the kind of coverage major college teams got back when I was selling mirrors.) But maybe you know a team somewhere that's *unvictorious*—they just *never win.* Don't you think readers and—more to the point—editors are interested in the flip side of the American sports dream?

Want to write about how money is corrupting the sports world? Don't do it by asking for an assignment to interview baseball commissioner Bud Selig or D-Backs owner Jerry Colangelo (who says he lost money in 2001 despite sell-out crowds and a team that won the World Series). You're not going to get those assignments, and anyway, pretty much everybody who follows sports already knows what those guys have to say. So consider starting from the opposite end: Find some local 14-year-old high school stud who's already being hounded by scouts and agents. Skillfully weave the points you want to make into this kid's story.

Which brings me to something else you need to commit to memory if you really want to go places in this profession (or at least go hungry less often): Don't think *news.* Think *context.* Sure, you need to tell people what happened. But anybody with half a brain, some basic grammar skills, and an AP stylebook can do that. What's going to put you over the top in the freelancing game is your ability to tell readers what it *means.* This is all the more true if magazines are your intended quarry.

A few years ago a wonderful writer named Gary Smith did a mesmerizing, award-winning cover story for *Sports Illustrated* about a star high school basketball player for whom coaches, school administrators, and others continued to cut corners and open doors even after the young man apparently committed a rape. Smith's tale wasn't an award-winning piece of journalism just because it told a riveting yarn. It was an award-winning piece of journalism because it revealed the hypocrisy behind the high-minded rhetoric of scholastic sports. *That's* context. The story introduced readers to a cast of characters who talked about integrity and honor while they were also bending rules and making excuses for a player whom they thought, bottom line, could *help them win.* Which, by the way, also means that you should be thinking *people.* When possible, try to give your readers a sense of characterization. Who are the major players in the story and what are they like? What makes them memorable or at least worth hearing from and about?

Or think *service.* So-called service journalism—the signature ethic at my former employer, *Men's Health*—means you use your experiences or those of other successful athletes you know to show others the right way to approach the net, the wrong way to make the 7-10 split, the best way to throw a curve that actually curves. Just remember that what readers learn doesn't necessarily have to fall under the heading of technique. They can also learn a new way of thinking about the sport, a new way of dealing with crises and situations that may arise during athletic competition, and so forth.

Depending on where you hope to publish, the service angle may be more or less overt. If you're writing for *Men's Health*—and if you are, I'm impressed—your story may consist of a breezy lead that makes a quick, unceremonious segue to the hard-core info. ("As you can see from the foregoing vignette, I was not exactly the world's most successful Little League coach. How can you avoid similar catastrophe? Here are the top 10 things to keep in mind . . .") If you're writing for *Esquire*'s "Man at His Best" section, there's *a little* more room to stretch out. The service element can be implied or more creatively phrased.

Amid all this, you might find it helpful to know something about your target publication. I'm being ironic, of course. You need to know a *ton* about the publication, which is why, during my professorial days at Indiana University, I devoted many a lesson to drilling students in the various ways of recognizing and assimilating the "ethos," if you will, of each different publication. While we don't have space for that here, suffice it to say *Sports Illustrated* is not going to cover a story the same way *The New York Times Magazine* would cover it. (By the way,

I'm using these august magazines as familiar examples. You're not go-ing aim quite that high just yet.) And *The New York Times Magazine* is not going to cover it the same way that, say, *Worth* would. When assessing any given publication, ask yourself, among other things: Who is my audience? What do they want from me? How much knowledge do I take as a given? For example, *SI* makes more assumptions about its readership's familiarity with sports than would *The Times*. And *Worth* assumes its readers want to know far more about the financial underpinnings of sports than would *Maxim*'s audience.

A book called *Writer's Market,* updated annually, can be quite help-ful in making sense of the marketplace and figuring out where you fit. Still, there's no substitute for taking an afternoon or two and sitting down with the magazines themselves. *Inside tip:* Take a look at who the advertisers are. The ads, sometimes more than the articles them-selves, will tell you who the *magazine* thinks its audience is. A mag-azine chock-full of ads for Cadillacs and Range Rovers is aiming at a wholly different demographic than a magazine featuring Hondas and Outbacks.

Now we come to the part that brings us full circle, back to my experience with my son. The one thing common to all of us who like to write about sports is that we also like to play sports—or at least we used to, before our knees started making noises like a 12-year-old Fiat on a bumpy road in subfreezing weather. So we've all experienced things, for better or worse, that other readers might identify with, want to read about, and, above all, *profit from* in some way. And the truly great thing about this is, *Nobody can tell your story but you.* You can't get scooped!

Take a look at a book called *Chicken Soup for the Baseball Fan's Soul* (and not just because they reprinted, on page 315, something I wrote originally for *Sports Illustrated*). I'll admit up front that I'm less than crazy about the smarmy, pop-psychology overtones of that whole series. I also wonder how far they plan to take it: *Chicken Soup for the Ax-Murderer's Soul*? Still, from the freelance writer's perspective, the baseball book is a case study in the exact types of writing editors want, and need, from "outsiders." It includes dozens of short pieces of the sort I'm describing, personal pieces that bring a new perspective—which is to say, the writer's—to the sporting experience. (And when I say short, let me expand here on what I said at the outset about thinking "small." Editors won't give you the 10,000 words *SI* gave Gary Smith to make his point about scholastic athletics. In most cases, I'd think

1,000–1,500 words would just about do it. Cut that in half for newspapers.)

Right about now you're probably thinking, *Hold on a sec here, Stevie baby—didn't you just get finished telling us that we should forget about writing essays?* Thing is, there's a big difference between the flat-out essay and the type of writing I'm talking about here, which we might call the personal experience piece with an instructive or illuminating message. First of all, an essay, generally, tells readers what you think. It makes its points in terms of logical, point-by-point argumentation. It's mostly theory and supposition, and it has an overt agenda to sell. In contrast, the personal-experience pieces that fill the *Chicken Soup* book *show* readers something. They're mostly *action,* or at least they're focused around action. They unfold as stories that (a) are interesting and/or entertaining in their own right, and (b) have a larger, implied meaning. They have a moral, if you will.

As you sit down to map out your article, ask yourself these two questions: 1) Is this a story that would hold the reader's interest? and 2) In the end, of what use to readers is the piece I propose to write? Do they learn anything they can actually apply? If the answer to either question is no, go back to the drawing board. If the answer to both questions is yes, congratulations, you may already be a winner. . . .

Now for just a few final things that should apply to all human beings who aspire to call themselves writers, yet are especially critical in the case of freelancers. Remember that to an editor who's unfamiliar with your work, your correspondence doesn't just represent you. It *is* you. So:

- In general, you're going to be *querying* editors, not just writing the full manuscript and hoping for the best. A query is a succinct (usually, one- to one-and-a-half-page) description of the piece you want to write, why you're qualified to write it, and how it serves the publication's needs. This last point, by the way, must be made in terms of *specifics,* not just some generalized blather about how "this is the most important piece you'll ever run!" Show the editor how your idea matches up to his audience's tastes or, better still, its needs. That's the quickest route to a sale. Also—and by this juncture I really shouldn't have to say this—there's a world of difference between a topic and a story idea. If your notion of the latter is "I want to write, um, something about baseball for you," you need to go back to the beginning of this chapter and start over, preferably when you're sober.

- Despite the pervasiveness of today's computer culture, e-mail is still considered bad form for an initial contact with an editor, unless the publication makes clear in its writer's guidelines (which you should *always* ask to see) that it's open to e-mails from new writers. Many a top editor uses specialized screening software that automatically filters out e-mails from people he doesn't know or dumps them into a secondary mail folder that's routed to some gatekeeper anyway. Besides, writing just looks better on the printed page. And until an editor knows who you are, you need every advantage you can get. *Inside tip:* Speaking of the words on the page, use a font that complements the one they use for the body text in their publication. Nothing too fancy or flaky here. Just a nice serif font (like Times New Roman) for the more traditional publications, or a sans-serif (like Arial) for the ones that opt for a more modern look.
- Spell-check everything you send. You already knew that, right? Well, did you also know you can't *just* rely on spell-check to save you from grievous errors? A lot of young writers don't realize that many types of mistakes will just sail right through spell-check *and* grammar-check, too. For instance, neither program will save you from saying "I tried to right it before my parents got home." (For all the software knows, you could be talking about a lamp you'd knocked over.) During one of my several stints as an editor, I opened a query whose first line read, "Needles to say, early detection of cancer is paramount." Needles to say, I was underwhelmed with that writer's attention to detail. There's simply no substitute for printing out your letter and giving it a once-over, even a twice-over, before dropping it in the mail.
- Avoid at all costs the temptation to use that clever Internet shorthand that's become a staple in instant messaging (and, regrettably, has gained a foothold in other forms of "discourse" as well). Don't write things like, "btw, c u l8r b/c IMHO plz. r u ROFL?" The editors I know, most of whom were indeed born since the last Roosevelt administration, *hate* Web-speak in more formal correspondence and with a passion most of us reserve for Al-Qaeda members. Certainly you should refrain from falling into such hip-speak at least until you're given an opening to do so by the editor.

Now go get 'em! K?

18. Reporting on the Business of Sports

Jay Weiner

Jay Weiner, of the Minneapolis *Star Tribune,* has covered the Minnesota Twins and issues in college sports, reported on every Winter and Summer Olympics since 1984, and written a wide variety of sports features. He is the author of *Stadium Games: Fifty Years of Big League Greed and Bush League Boondoggles* (2000). He is a frequent contributor to *Business Week* magazine and a sports commentator for Minnesota Public Radio.

It was a cool, clear day in October 1993 when Paul Thatcher, a member of the Metropolitan Sports Facilities Commission, drove his spotless black Mercedes to the Minneapolis Metrodome. He was about to make Minnesota sports business history. He was about to provide an unsuspecting reporter with a page-one story.

For months, owners of the Minnesota Timberwolves of the National Basketball Association had threatened to move the team to another city. The owners were asserting that the finances of their privately built arena, the Target Center, were in freefall. To save their shaky empire, owners Marvin Wolfenson and Harvey Ratner declared that the taxpayers of Minnesota would have to bail them out and buy the three-year-old arena.

Opposition was rampant. Thatcher, a wealthy venture capitalist, was one of the noisiest of the opponents. But on this sparkling Minnesota autumn day, he decided to make a move that would change the face of sports business in a state that once embraced its teams but was now angered by the unpredictable economics of major league sports. Just six months earlier, the Minnesota North Stars hockey team had up and left for Dallas. This was a scorned community. It was fed up.

That day, Thatcher invited Bill Lester, the executive director of the Dome, which is owned and operated by the Sports Facilities Commission, for a walk around the concourses of the stadium, home to the baseball Twins and football Vikings. There, Thatcher, in his deep voice and authoritarian tone, surprised Lester by declaring: "It's time to get off the dime." Within minutes, at a subcommittee meeting of this tiny public agency, seven citizens, paid $50 a day when on duty, decided that the state of Minnesota or the city of Minneapolis should help subsidize two millionaire owners of a seemingly flourishing NBA franchise. The commission voted to hire investment bankers to begin a Target Center takeover.

History? Yes.

But news?

Well, it might not have been. It might have been just another public meeting among hundreds in Minnesota in any given month. A subcommittee meeting at that, announced, as required by law, three days earlier via U.S. mail. But I was there in the conference room of the commission for the 8 A.M. meeting. There because public meetings are the easiest forums at which to gather sports business news. There because public officials who see reporters at meetings appreciate the time it takes to sit through them. There because less dramatic but often fascinating tidbits emerge at public meetings and the brief meet-and-greet interviews afterward. There because it was my job to attend every meeting, just as it's a baseball-beat reporter's job to attend every game.

There, and a front-page story was born out of a presumed-routine early morning meeting. There to report a major shift in the Target Center process and to help a state begin to debate the merits of public financing of an arena. There to write a story for a broad swath of readers; not just sports fans, but taxpayers and those with knowledge of business.

The story, published in the October 28, 1993, *Star Tribune* of Minneapolis, read in part:

> The Metropolitan Sports Facilities Commission, long maligned for bystanding, turned aggressive Wednesday by laying the first bricks on a path that could lead to the public takeover of Target Center in Minneapolis.
>
> The commission voted 4-3 to invite Twin Cities investment bank-

ers to advise it on how it might structure a public acquisition of the arena.

"We want to be part of the solution," said commissioner Paul Thatcher, who proposed the commission's action. "We'd like to accommodate. We don't want to be the goat that we aren't and never have been." The commission, criticized for its inaction while the North Stars moved, owns and operates the Metrodome and Met Center. By state law, the commission is charged with overseeing "the betterment of sports facilities" in the state.

But the law applies only to those facilities that play host to college and professional baseball, football and soccer and to NHL hockey, specifically at Met Center. Thus, any final act by the commission to take over Target Center—primarily built for basketball and hockey—would require a change of its charter by the Legislature. . . .

What's my major point in relating this anecdote and inserting this selection from the original story?

It's this: The venues for most sports business reporting are rarely games played in stadiums or arenas and are rarely telecast into a sports fan's living room. Rather, sports business news develops in board rooms, league meetings, court rooms, and the public meetings that take place in every governmental agency and legislature from Albany to Sacramento.

The other point? In most reporting—but especially in sports business reporting—the story *does* belong to those who show up. I was not merely the sole reporter sitting in on that fateful meeting. I was the only member of the public. I was the audience, the public. Would I have been "wasting my time" if nothing had happened? Perhaps, but the Sports Facilities Commissioners would have at least seen me one more time, appreciated my diligence, and, perhaps, privately tipped me off to something else. Besides, I was good at multitasking and often brought my mail from the newspaper office to read.

In my opinion, sports business reporting is the most socially responsible category of sportswriting. For sure, sports business reporting is not what most aspiring sportswriters view as "pure" sportswriting. There's no tumult, no glamour, no hobnobbing with muscular jocks. Sure—athletes, coaches, and general managers can be sources. But during my years as a sports business reporter, I've dealt more with governors than third basemen, more with mayors than quarterbacks and more with Senate research assistants than the public-relations directors of major league franchises. Sports business reporting is business reporting about the sports industry. Sports business reporting is about placing the games fans watch into a context that turns spectators into taxpayers, that turns ticket-buyers into consumers, that turns athletes into workers and owners into captains of industry. Sports business reporting takes the façade off of sports; it helps to crack the myths that somehow sports is only about bats and balls and not about dollar signs. At its core it serves to demythologize the cocooned "world of sports" and places sports in the real capitalist world of banks, Wall Street, and balance sheets.

That's why I believe that sports business reporting is the most important beat—and sports business stories are the most significant stories—on a sports page. Like other stories that place sports in a social context, sports business stories place the games that we watch into their economic context.

At almost every level these days, sports is about money, from the funding of public-school sports to the facilities "arms race" in college sports to the issues of Title IX and gender equity on campuses to professional players' salaries to the public funding of stadiums and arenas to the sale of teams for a half-billion dollars.

Let's examine sports in your community and identify sports business story possibilities. Let's see how you can get at those stories. The best way is to examine sports business issues on a national level and then to localize those stories to your smaller community, your campus, your metropolitan daily and weekly or monthly magazine. (I focus on the newspaper and magazine—or their on-line partners—rather than the electronic media here, because sports business stories on radio and television are few and far between. Concepts are tough to disseminate in those media. Charts and graphs, which help so much in a sports business story, are difficult to examine on a TV screen. In many ways, the written format is the only way to fully communicate a sports business story, which is why newspapers and magazines have a monopoly on these kinds of stories. Realistically, it's tough to have a highlight on ESPN's *SportsCenter* after a dramatic meeting on stadium financing!)

We can begin with youth sports. Most communities have parks and recreation boards that sponsor youth sports. Funding information from city or county budgets should be readily available. Youth-sports organizations, which generally operate as nonprofits, must register with their respective state. Their budgets, in many states, are also available via open-meeting, data-practices, or sunshine laws. Or, if a reporter simply asks a member of a youth-sports board, it's generally easy to get a hold of such budgets.

School sports are a pressing issue of the day. Inner-city schools are funded at a significantly lower rate than suburban schools. All of these financial figures in most states are available, along with coaches' salaries. Plus, the various state high school leagues in each state are often worthy of examination. Each state has its own high school sports fiefdom doing business as state leagues and associations. They are a gold mine of good stories. Corporate sponsorships of high school sports tournaments are intriguing stories and raise issues about the over-commercialization of school sports.

A good example was an investigative story that I wrote along with a veteran reporter named Joe Rigert about the Minnesota State High School League, the umbrella organization of all high school sports in the state. Long considered a monolithic bureaucracy that was unresponsive to students and parents, the league was an agency that was never fully examined. Rigert and I began looking at the league's rules and regulations, which some parents and schools said were abusive; rules that restricted transfers from one school to another, rules that seemed to cost school districts too much money in dues, rules that allowed the league to pocket large rights fees for selling the popular Minnesota state high school hockey championship to a local television station.

Using the state's Data Practices Act, which is the analog to the federal Freedom of Information Act, we requested just about every piece of paper in the league's filing cabinets. It took us weeks to go through the data. And here's what we found, as revealed in a front-page story that caused quite a stir and eventually led to the resignation of the league's executive director:

> The Minnesota State High School League—the quasi-public agency that runs profitable state tournaments—spends money liberally and sometimes improperly to feed, lodge and transport board members, staff executives and, occasionally, their spouses.
>
> As part of this pattern, during the past fiscal year the league's officials treated themselves to a $4,600 Christmas dinner and meeting, a $21,600 trip to a national convention, and a $7,100 meeting at Madden's resort at Brainerd, Minn. Board members and executives who live in the Twin Cities area frequently stayed in Twin Cities hotels for board meetings at league expense. Liquor was served at league expense. Spouses dined at league expense.
>
> League records for the financial year that ended in July show that

the league spent more than $132,000 for 16 board members; five staff executives and others to eat, meet, sleep and travel. . . .

Public colleges and universities in most states must reveal the details of their budgets, too. Whether it's stories on the monstrous growth of college football or the laughable size of men's gymnastics budgets, whether it's stories on how women's sports are underfunded or how much money an assistant linebackers coach is being paid, there's data to be had. And issues to be raised: Why are football coaches paid more than university presidents?

Locally, the salaries and working perks of college coaches often raise the eyebrows and ire of the public. An unusual story emerged a few years back when a colleague of mine at the *Star Tribune,* Jon Roe, requested the details of a contract extension granted to University of Minnesota football coach Jim Wacker.

Inadvertently, a university staff person also sent along a side letter or "memorandum" that spelled out more than the dollars Wacker was to make; it detailed how many games he had to win to keep his job. Roe's story read in part:

> Gophers football coach Jim Wacker will be required to offer his resignation if his team doesn't win five games this season, according to documents obtained from the University of Minnesota. If Wacker's resignation is accepted by men's athletic director Mark Dienhart, Wacker will not be paid for any of the remaining two years on his contract. Dienhart, however, can take into consideration what he deems to be extenuating circumstances if the Gophers' record is not 5-6, and he does not have to accept Wacker's resignation.
>
> Wacker, who will start his fifth season as the Gophers coach on Saturday night at Northeast Louisiana, was given a two-year extension in November on his original five-year contract. His contract now runs through the 1998 season. But Wacker signed a two-page memorandum from Dienhart on Dec. 8 that defines the coach's on-field job expectations. . . .

What we learned from that experience was this: as a matter of policy, seek and keep the contracts of all the coaches at your area's public colleges; as a matter of policy, get the details of any contract extensions; more important, when making your request, ask not only for the contract of a coach, but for any and all side letters, letters of memoranda, extra agreements and all documents related to the coach's working conditions, job performance, salary or expectations.

Be as specific and as all-encompassing as you can be in seeking any public documents. You never know what you'll wind up with.

Even most private colleges are required to submit to the U.S. Department of Education some data as it pertains to gender equity. And in 2002, the Department of Education began posting on the Internet the so-called EADA (Equity in Athletics Disclosure Act) reports, data that every institution that receives federal funds is required to submit (Available on-line at http://ope.ed.gov/athletics). In those reports are budget numbers that go beyond men's and women's sports and often detail coaches' salaries, a very hot topic.

Of course, at the professional level, there is a wide swath of stories. Among the pros, some of the data is harder to get. But in some cities and states, as in Minnesota, public agencies are landlords to teams. Those public landlords often must disclose rental agreements and other financial transactions. Within this data, there are ways to extrapolate just how well a team is performing at the gate, via hot dog and popcorn sales, via the selling of advertising signage in their stadium, and so on.

Most professional-athlete salary data is made available to key national news media outlets by owners or players' unions. Unless you work for *The New York Times* or *USA Today* or *Fortune* magazine, there's really no reason to be chasing down the salary lists of players in the major sports. At the start of every season, those national outlets will gather such information—leaked to them by executives of the leagues or unions—and those figures become the standard for all reporters.

From youth sports to Yankee Stadium, from the Friday-night high school football game to the Saturday-night pay-per-view boxing match, an entire industry of sports business consultants, analysts, and academicians has sprung up. When pursuing stories at every level of sports on any matter about economics and sports, there are experts everywhere to use as sounding boards and as sources with authority.

Universities are good places to look for such experts. There is a terrific umbrella service called Profnet.com (http://www2.profnet.com), which is available to professional journalists but not to student journalists. This is a network of experts at institutions of higher education or in industry on specific topics. Queries can be sent via e-mail, and Profnet staffers find the right experts for reporters.

Colleges or universities in your town, state, or region can also assist you in searching for experts, be they in schools of business or law, departments of sociology and anthropology, or even physical education departments. Be careful to make sure that these "experts" are, indeed, experts.

The fact is, the longer you cover sports business issues—as in covering any topic area—the more likely it is that you will become as much of an expert on the subject as those you are interviewing. That is sometimes frustrating and maddening. But it's true.

(One more idea en route to becoming an expert: If you never took an accounting course in college, consider it as you begin diving into sports business news. Local community colleges or universities offer introductory accounting classes, and they will be invaluable in understanding annual reports and financial data of teams, stadium authorities, or the companies that owners control.)

As for sports business industry consultants, they can speak to issues such as stadium and arena construction. They consult on hiring athletic directors at universities. They consult on whether a college's football program should move from Division II small-college play to Division I big-time competition. There are architects. There are marketing experts. There are TV and radio consultants. Most were once team or league employees or staff members of accounting or investment-banking firms that once had teams or leagues as clients.

Most of these consultants are a reporter's lifeline: quote machines. Most love to talk with reporters. Just like the expert academicians you will chase down for input, all of them have biases and agendas. Be careful with that, but not so careful that you shy away from experts with opinions. For instance, there are economics professors at major universities who believe that public funding of stadiums and arenas is a waste of taxpayer dollars, and they never saw a stadium plan that was socially responsible. On the other hand, there are financial consultants who profit from stadium construction and thus who have never seen a stadium deal they didn't love. Know the biases of your experts even before you call them. This will make your questions and your skepticism most pressing and potent.

Obviously, officials of school districts, colleges and universities, and professional teams in your towns must be key sources. And not just the biggest fish, either. For instance, the general manager of a Minor League Baseball team might not want to reveal the salaries of his players. But the assistant GM in charge of operations might want to show how well he's minding the purse strings and could help you to piece together how much the team members are being paid. The stadium manager of a local facility might be loath to discuss the expenses of running a ballpark, but the chief groundskeeper—who needs more sod or new seats or a new sprinkling system—might be glad to tell you how underfunded his or her stadium is.

Like all reporting, sports business reporting blossoms the most in between the cracks. By that I mean that you must cultivate sources and see them and talk with them at times when news isn't happening. An off-the-record lunch with the chief financial officer of a football team in June will likely pay off when a frantic last-minute fact check in November is required. Do not expect to be a good sports business reporter by simply picking up the phone and asking some complex questions to a person you've never met. All reporting is stronger after face-to-face personal relationships are established, but in sports business reporting I believe that's even truer. Mostly that's because, unlike other sports reporting, very little sports business reporting is done among a pack of journalists. That is, state legislators and high school league directors don't go into a locker room after a meeting, change their clothes, and wait for the reporters to approach them about the vote on cutting back funding for girls' field hockey. Generally, it's you and the state representative. If he or she has seen you at earlier meetings or has met you before, your ability to get at the news will be that much easier.

The more sources you have, the more information you gather from experts, the more data you store from public documents, the more reading you do of sports-industry newsletters and insider publications—such as *Street and Smith's SportsBusiness Journal* or *Sports Business Daily* or *Sports Business News*—the more you will be armed to become the sports business expert on your campus or in your community, city, or state.

In some ways, the spectrum of sports business reporting is broader than other sports topic areas. The status of a company on the New York Stock Exchange could affect the wealth of the owner of your town's pro sports team. Know how your owner got rich and how he stays rich. Monitor those companies. The news of a world crisis could impact your sports business beat. Will the war on terrorism mean prohibitive insurance costs for the team or arena in your town? Is the arena or stadium on campus named after a once-high-flying company that has now hit on hard times? Could it be that the Arthur Andersen Pavilion will lose its name as fast as the accounting firm lost its reputation during the Enron scandal? (Need we mention that the Houston Astros' stadium, Enron Field, lost its name when that energy giant's fortunes tumbled? It was the ultimate sports business story.)

Sports business reporting has limitless boundaries. After all, President George W. Bush was once an owner of the Texas Rangers baseball team and profited handsomely from the construction of a publicly-funded stadium in Arlington, Texas.

So keep your eyes open along with your mind for good story ideas and for enterprise stories that reveal your growing expertise. Because that's when the fun begins. That's when you can begin to challenge financial assumptions made by teams that want stadiums or college athletic directors who say ticket prices must be raised. That's when you can begin to build charts and graphs that show readers how your team's salaries, ticket revenues, stadium concessions revenues, and parking fees compare to others.

As with all reporting in the twenty-first century, adept use of the Internet is critical. It's truly amazing how much information—including some that's accurate!!—resides on the 'Net. Meanwhile, cultivate professional sports business reporters in other markets. They could help you too, and you will share information with them.

In 1997, when the Minnesota Twins were threatening to leave the Metrodome for the Winston-Salem–Greensboro–High Point region of North Carolina, I established a terrific working relationship with Justin Catanoso of *The* (Greensboro) *News & Record.* It was born out of competition. I was working for the Minneapolis *Star Tribune.* My major competitor in Minnesota was the St. Paul *Pioneer Press.* The *Pioneer Press* is owned by the Knight Ridder chain of newspapers. Knight Ridder also owns *The Charlotte Observer.* My competitors at the *Pioneer Press* had a ready-made staff of on-site helpers in North Carolina at *The Observer.* Similarly, *Observer* reporters could rely on the St. Paul reporters to tip them off to doings in Minnesota. Catanoso and I, working at two independent papers, began consulting with each other on a daily basis. I was his eyes and ears in Minnesota, trying to ascertain if the Twins move was for real. (It wasn't.) He was my eyes and ears in North Carolina, monitoring what business and political leaders were saying and doing on the ground there. Together, we covered the story responsibly for our newspapers. Journalism is often a lonely independent job, but don't be afraid to collaborate with a trusted reporter elsewhere.

Still, showing up where sports business news is happening before your eyes . . . I can't emphasize that enough. The "games" of sports business aren't so regularly scheduled as those of a baseball or basketball team. But your city hall reporter, your state capitol reporter, your courts reporter, or your university-beat person will know when key boards or committees are meeting on sports matters or when a lawsuit is filed with sports implications. And you, as a sports business reporter, should sniff out these meetings too or keep your ears to the ground about any litigation that's been launched.

Then, at the most unsuspecting moment, you might see history happen, as I did that autumn day in 1993. And you'll have a page-one story and more. Indeed, I mark that event, when the Sports Facilities Commission decided to vote to take over Target Center, as a defining moment in Minnesota sports history. In a state where public financing for sports has been the subject of a decade-long debate, October 26, 1993, was the moment of liftoff. As the lone reporter there, I saw some well-meaning citizens make a decision about the buying of an arena that, in the end, meant—after two more years of debate in various public forums—the retention of a sports team in my town. Soon after, the baseball and football teams in Minnesota began seeking their own new stadiums. For years, they called me "the sports business reporter." Sounds boring, right? But I had one of the highest-profile positions in newsgathering in my community.

19. So You Want to Be a Sports Editor

Garry Howard

Garry Howard is Assistant Managing Editor/Sports at the *Milwaukee Journal Sentinel.* He is a past chairman of the National Association of Black Journalists Sports Task Force and a former chairman of the Associated Press Sports Editors Diversity Committee.

Everyone knows it.

The sports agate clerk who sits in the still of the night with a telephone stuck to his ear, taking endless high school scores and results. . . .

The copy editor, whose job it is to play better than any goalie in the National Hockey League. . . .

The slot, the twin of an air traffic controller. . . .

The reporters, who may find themselves challenged each and every day of their sometimes-brilliant careers. . . .

And, finally, the sports columnist who wants to cover the Super Bowl, the Final Four, the World Series, the NBA Finals, *and* the Masters, and all in the same day. . . .

Everybody connected to the sports department—big or small— knows that the sports editor is the real authority, the Chief Justice and *Il Duce* and Mother Teresa all rolled into one.

Yes, the sports editor does rule in his or her department at any newspaper. No question. And it has been that way since the inception of daily journalism, maybe before, and will continue, in my opinion, to operate in that manner because of this one fact: A last word is truly necessary in this complex fire drill of sports newsgathering and display that takes place each and every day of the calendar year.

Being a sports editor is a tough regimen, replete with pitfalls and lava, paradises and waterfalls, highs I promise you you've never experienced, and lows that make you wonder just how much further (not farther; we're speaking hypothetically) down can you go.

We will start at the very beginning and the first thing is . . .

Read, read, read and, well, read.

Anything you can get your hands on is a good enough start. Children's books, comics, short stories, *Reader's Digest,* and *Vogue.* Even the flyer at the corner store trumpeting the rummage sale of all sales. It will start training your eyes for what you're about to see. And believe me, you want to see everything.

It's never too early to start reading. When I was a boy growing up in the South Bronx, the New York *Daily News,* the *New York Post, Newsday,* and *The New York Times,* along with anything else that contained a score, was my fix. Had to have it daily—sometimes more often.

I absolutely loved the New York Knicks, beginning in the 1970–1971 season when Walt Frazier was the Man To Be and the team had a stranglehold on the biggest city in the world. As a sixth-grade student at P.S. 154, right smack in the heart of the Mitchell Houses, where I was raised along with my five brothers and sisters by my mother, Ann B. Howard, schoolwork was way too boring.

That year, the greatest teacher in my life, Mrs. Sessa, hollered at me daily for lack of attention, but it was really hard to concentrate on reading stuff like "Look at Spot" (obviously I'm exaggerating, Mrs. Sessa).

It seemed as if I knew the answer to anything we were studying that year. Every stinking answer, I'm not kidding. I couldn't explain it. Momma said it was something special. Mrs. Sessa called me a mess. An hour-long test would take about five minutes, if that. And after the first time I raised my hand for her to collect my test, Mrs. Sessa kindly took me outside the classroom. She began to tell me that some students (in this top class in the best elementary school in the South Bronx) needed more time to finish their tests and that my speed discouraged some.

I didn't have the temerity to tell her that I was just trying to get done so I could concentrate—some would call it daydream—on who Red Holtzman, the Knicks' future Hall of Fame coach, would use in the bench rotation that evening at Madison Square Garden. I was nuts in a very good way. That, my friends, is what a good a sports editor has to be: Nuts, but in a good way.

Yeah, that's it.

Now sit back and relax, because if this is indeed your calling, you will not stop reading. If it is not your calling, go sell insurance.

EDUCATION

This is your foundation. Build it strong and acknowledge your weaknesses. Then work on your weaknesses.

For me, it began when I graduated from Mrs. Sessa's class as her prized valedictorian, along with some other awards. I gave a speech, was not nervous at all, but couldn't stand when they called my name to go on stage to receive an award. Toward the end of the ceremony, after the song and the speeches and the Bronx dignitaries (there are some, you know), they finally called out an award and didn't call my name. I knew I had won that one too, but actually prayed they would just go on to the end.

At the last minute, however, the teacher blurted into the microphone: "Wait. We forgot somebody."

The whole auditorium then replied, in unison, "Gar . . . ry How . . . ard!"

I could have dropped through the floor. I couldn't get up because I had a gift watch and a dozen or so other awards in my lap. I just sat there for a few seconds until my classmates reached over and helped me unload my booty just so I could get more. It was humiliating, yet it made me cry tears of pride. After pictures and smiles, it finally hit me. This is education. This is what makes parents all gushy. This will get you all the pizza you can eat. This, my friends, is good.

Next up was Clark J.H.S. 149, where I was in a two-year special-progress class that went from seventh grade to ninth, skipping the eighth. Graduation was great. No speeches. No stage-walking. Just one—I had to stand up near my seat—for receiving a four-year scholarship to The Lawrenceville School, a prestigious boarding school that today costs over $25,000 per year, through the A Better Chance, a spectacular organization that has changed the landscape of this country with its success.

Finally, the cap and gown were off and I was headed to New Jersey the following fall. It was at Lawrenceville where I began to actually see the world. The academic scholarship that I received had to be renewed each year, so there was tremendous pressure to achieve. It was my first taste of deadlines.

And Lawrenceville is about as white and about as preppy as you can get. For a 13-year-old African American (we were still Black back then), it was terrifying. My high school was also the most beautiful place on earth that I had ever laid my eyes on. Breathtaking. It was to be my paradise for learning, but it came with just a little bit of, well, challenge.

You see, there were, like, tons of white people, more white people than I had ever seen assembled in one place. The campus was spread out over more than 100 acres of landscaped luxury, but like deer standing in the field, there were those white people. I was nervous. Once again. And I would find out that is a good thing. This is the absolute crux of education: learning about people.

By the end of my four years at Lawrenceville, I had come to respect, deeply, people of all colors, races, and creeds. It was the most important part of my high school years.

After graduation from Lawrenceville in 1977, I made my way to Lehigh University in Bethlehem, Pennsylvania, and it was, to some degree, just a bigger Lawrenceville . . . with coeds. Four years of boarding school with all boys was rough and was the main reason I almost flunked out of Lehigh my first semester.

The coeds at Lehigh were shaped much differently than the boys at Lawrenceville, and that would almost prove to be my downfall. I met Lynette that fall, another freshman from Newark, New Jersey, and, well, I tried to make up for four years in one semester, if you know what I'm talking about.

Bad decision.

Luckily, I was able to bounce back, save my scholarship, and keep my life in order by putting a more-than-solid spring semester together. I knew how to study; I just didn't that fall.

Don't let that happen to you.

You can fall in love, get a new hobby, anything, but don't forget the reason you came to that college or university. You want a degree. And if you want to be a sports editor, make sure you finish or your career will be finished before it ever begins.

At Lehigh, I took my first journalism course and caught the bug. If that happens to you, half the battle has been won. A solid journalism undergraduate degree is pretty much all you need to get started. It will give you the necessary core materials, like news-writing, editing, and the basic tenets of journalism.

If at all possible, stay involved in your school newspaper. I worked as a reporter and then was elected sports editor of *The Brown & White* at Lehigh. It was through the school paper, along with my courses, that I learned how to put together a news story, how to lay out pages, how to write a story. I knew sports. I just didn't know how to report.

The next part of your undergraduate education is the most important, aside from getting your degree. You must apply for every internship that you read about, hear about, think about. Don't worry whether you are qualified. They will let you know quickly. The more experience you accumulate during those years, the better you will be when you actually get a job at a newspaper.

While at Lehigh, I applied and won the Williams Undergraduate Prize for Feature Writing as well as an internship at Pennsylvania Power & Light, where I worked in the communications office for one semester. Then I won a biggie: a Dow Jones Newspaper Fund Copy-Editing Internship in 1981. I also played on the Division I basketball team under Brian Hill, who would later go on to become a head coach in the NBA for the Orlando Magic and the Vancouver Grizzlies.

That summer, however, when I worked on Wall Street in New York City on the copy desk of Dow Jones News Service, I learned more than I did in any classroom at college, and you learn a lot in college.

It was the cornerstone of my journalism education to that point and helped build a solid foundation for my future success.

The same can happen to you if, first, you prepare yourself by working hard in the classroom and, second, apply for the position. As I stated earlier, apply for everything. It will serve you greatly. Trust me.

After receiving my B.A. in journalism from Lehigh, I was prepared to launch a career that I hoped would lead me to the head of a sports department at a major daily newspaper. One thing got in the way, however: I didn't know how to start.

That is why you have to continue reading through the final parts of this chapter to understand your next move.

Follow along, now.

ROAD TO THE OFFICE

The road to the sports editor's office does not follow a straight path. You must be prepared to move to any city at the drop of a hat and you must realize that what you are doing at any one point—whether it be agate or obituaries—is but a means to a definite end.

For me, it began at the *Trenton Times* in Trenton, New Jersey. I did what the professors at Lehigh told me to do and applied for every newspaper entry-level job I could find—even the Associated Press in Japan (they actually sent a letter back!).

It just wasn't happening. I had a solid education, had won a few scholarships, and was full of vigor. I just needed a job. Any job. Remember, that is all you need. Your first job will set you on the right path. You just have to find one, and that can prove to be difficult. But persistence is one of the hallmarks of a good reporter, and I believe the right preparation for the sports editor's office begins with a stint as a reporter. And it doesn't even have to be in sports.

I was hired in Trenton by a former Dow Jones Newspaper Fund Copy-Editing Internship recipient, who just happened to be the managing editor of the paper. Good breaks—you will get some, but many you just have to make yourself.

At the *Trenton Times,* I covered high schools and was happier than a pig in a sty. I was doing what I went to college to do and I knew bigger things were ahead.

Four months after I began, I was fired.

Welcome to the big leagues, baby! About 25–30 newsroom employees were laid off when the paper was sold, and I was the last one hired and one of the first to go. Talk about lows. I was stunned, angry, sad, and confused about how to get up off the canvas from this obvious knockdown.

As luck would have it, I did. *The Home News* in New Brunswick, New Jersey, had two openings. One was a 24-hour-a-week obituary writer, and the other was a full-time clerk. I was offered, and accepted, the obituary job because it meant I was a reporter again. I made the right decision for the right reason. Yes, the clerk job was full-time, but I would not be able to write for the paper, even if I only wrote about dead people for the obituary job.

When you get knocked down, as I was, brush yourself off by making phone calls to professionals that you know. You must try to find the next available opening because you don't want big gaps in your resume. And that is what you are doing: building a resume that you hope will land you a job at a big paper.

After almost 15 months at *The Home News,* I was finally hired as a full-time reporter and was assigned to the police beat. After that it was off to municipal government—you know, zoning-board meetings, school-board meetings, fires, thefts; you name it, you will cover it.

The reporting teaches you the works. From prejudice (which almost made me quit) to the pain and suffering of the people we cover to the joy of doing your job well.

After my newswriting stint began at *The Home News,* I had a yearning to get back to sports. So I asked our sports editor, Gabe Suto, in 1985 if I could cover a college basketball game in New York City. It just happened to pit number-one St. John's against number-two George-town. It was Louie Carnesseca against John Thompson at sold-out Madison Square Garden. It was heaven.

And I filed the longest game story, my first deadline sports reporting, in the history of the paper. They still laugh about it, but it was then that I knew that the sports department was my haven.

I think it's almost a necessity to have a love of sports to be a good sports editor, and I knew from back in my youth in the South Bronx that I had the sports fever. Find out if it is in your blood, because you will need that love to carry you through what I guarantee you will be choppy waters at times.

After *The Home News,* I worked as a sports copy editor at the *Times-Union* in Rochester, New York, and the *St. Petersburg Independent* and the *St. Petersburg Times* in St. Petersburg, Florida, before landing on the copy desk at the famed *Philadelphia Inquirer.*

A sports editor must know how to edit, must know how to leave a good story alone, must know how to fix a story that is obviously broken. That is your top goal. Learn from others, learn from reading other newspapers and magazines, and learn from experience. And there are plenty of great small newspapers that will prepare you for The Office.

At *The Philadelphia Inquirer,* I worked for three years on the copy desk. It proved to be an invaluable lesson for The Office.

David Tucker, our executive sports editor, promoted me to Assistant Sports Editor in 1990 and I was elated. Just as I was taught by veterans early on in my career, you should, must, work as a reporter and then as a copy editor in order to build that solid foundation.

It was time now to do the job.

And I did it by working on special sections, individual stories, and the Sunday section. In a quick four years, I found myself as the bureau chief for *The Philadelphia Inquirer* at the 1994 Winter Games in Lillehammer, Norway.

It was a long journey from the South Bronx, but when I returned from those Games, I was promoted to Deputy Sports Editor at *The Inquirer.* I was just 34 years old. It can happen, I kept telling myself, and you must do the same.

KEEPING THE OFFICE

This last part is the toughest. When Martin Kaiser hired me as the Executive Sports Editor at *The Milwaukee Journal* in May of 1994, I was the only African American sports editor at a major daily newspaper in the United States. Today, there are four who run major sports sections, including my good buddy Leon Carter, the Executive Sports Editor of *The* (New York) *Daily News.*

Once again, I had a tremendous desire to succeed. And I would need that desire, especially after *The Milwaukee Journal* merged with *The Milwaukee Sentinel* in April of 1995 to become the much-improved *Milwaukee Journal Sentinel.*

Mr. Carter would agree that the key part to being a good sports editor is your ability to handle your personnel. Sports reporters, columnists, and copy editors are a tough group to handle, but you do it by being honest. And that is easier said than done.

If a reporter's story is not good enough, tell him or her that. And be as specific as possible. Don't jerk your staff around. They are reporters and they can sense our insincerity and just plain bull.

Promote those who deserve it and create a newsroom environment that is conducive to the individual successes. This is an important part of your job. As an African American beginning my journalism career, there rarely was another Black in the office, and that made me feel awfully lonely. If you want to diversify your sports department, find the best and hire them to do the job. And make sure they are comfortable.

As far as your section, let your assistants and deputies do the job you hired them to do. Don't meddle all of the time. Your opinion obviously matters, but they must feel as if they can stand on their own, and they must be able to stand on their own.

Rely heavily on the Associated Press Sports Editors group; it will guide you through the murky waters. Rely on other sports editors, those with more experience, to help you with your decision making.

Do all of these things and you will survive. And if you do, you can effect a change in your paper's city, bring new life to boring sports pages and be able to enjoy what I feel is the sweetest gig on this earth.

Today, as the Assistant Managing Editor/Sports at the *Journal Sentinel,* I really look forward to going to work on the daily sports section. Bill Windler, the Senior Editor/Sports at the *Journal Sentinel,* is one of the big reasons because of the tremendous job he does at helping me run this department. You will need a right-hand person. Treat your staff well, give them good raises and, above all, show them due respect.

It's time to go now, but if you have any questions, call me at the *Milwaukee Journal Sentinel.* If I can't help you, I'll probably know somebody who can.

Here's to you making it to The Office.

20. Covering Women's Sports: Fair Play?

Michelle Kaufman

Michelle Kaufman is a sportswriter for *The Miami Herald* and previously worked at the *Detroit Free Press* and *St. Petersburg Times.* She has covered seven Olympics, four World Cups, three Pan Am Games, two Super Bowls, five Final Fours, two NBA Finals, two Stanley Cups, three US Open tennis tournaments, one World Series, and numerous college bowl games. When she isn't covering events, she is writing sports feature stories and occasional columns and spending time with her husband, daughter, and stepson.

Four hours before the kickoff of the 1999 Women's World Cup, and Pasadena traffic was at a standstill. The winding, bougainvillea-lined streets leading to the Rose Bowl were packed with sport utility vehicles and minivans. In those vehicles were ponytailed girls in star-spangled face paint, their brothers and dads in Mia Hamm jerseys, and moms carrying hand-painted posters with such slogans as "You Go, Girls!"

President Bill Clinton's motorcade made its way through the crowd. No way was he going to miss the USA-China game, a game he would later call "the most important sporting event of the decade."

Concession booths sold merchandise not usually seen at sporting events—World Cup Barbie dolls, World Cup ponytail scrunchies, and replica soccer jerseys with female-sized neck and arm holes.

By kickoff, 90,185 fans had filled the stadium—the largest crowd ever to attend a women's sporting event. More than 500 journalists were on hand for the occasion. And a television audience of 40 million tuned in, beating the ratings for the 1999 NBA Finals, crushing the ratings for the 1999 Stanley Cup Finals, and doubling the U.S. ratings for the 1998 men's World Cup final between Brazil and France. The "Girls of Summer" had captivated the nation and become such celebrities that they checked into hotels under assumed names to avoid phone calls from the fanatics camped out in the lobbies. What was expected to be a nice little soccer tournament, a tournament buried in newspaper sports sections for the first round (if it was covered at all), was gracing the covers of *Time, Newsweek,* and *People* magazines by July. Late-night talk-show host David Letterman, who dubbed the team "Babe City," was among the team's most ardent supporters.

And yet much of the mainstream sports media took a long time to catch on to the story. Unlike other major sporting events in America, the Women's World Cup did not inspire special preview sections in most U.S. newspapers. If there were preview stories at all, they ran inside. *USA Today* and large metropolitan dailies in New York, Los Angeles, Chicago, and Washington, D.C., covered the tournament from the start. But other newspapers in major markets practically ignored the event, despite its opening-game sellout at Giants Stadium and crowds of tens of thousands at most matches.

Newspapers in Houston, Denver, and Minneapolis did not staff the Cup. When a *Miami Herald* reporter asked her sports editor about traveling to the late-round games, he replied: "Nobody gives a rat's ass about women's soccer." She insisted on covering the final, arguing that the paper would look foolish running wire stories, and wound up paying her own way to Pasadena. *The Herald* ran her stories on page 1-A and the front of the sports section and eventually reimbursed her for half the travel expenses.

Glen Crevier, an assistant managing editor in charge of sports at the Minneapolis *Star Tribune,* admitted that his paper should have covered the tournament. "We blew it on that one," conceded Crevier in the book *The Girls of Summer.* "It's a major blunder at this point. If I had known how big it was going to be, we would have covered it."

If only he had known. Truth is, nobody knew how big this story was until it was unfolding. And even then, skeptics suggested it was a media creation. *Detroit Free Press* columnist Mitch Albom accused American sportswriters of behaving "shamefully" and "irresponsibly" in giving so much ink to a women's soccer tournament. He suggested those 40 million viewers would not have tuned in were it not for the media hype. (One wonders whether the same column could be written about the Super Bowl.)

Women's sports have come a long way since 1972 Title IX legislation, which required schools to offer boys and girls equal sports opportunities. Then, only 1 in every 27 high school girls played varsity sports. Today, the number is 1 in 2.5. Nearly 40 percent of high school and college athletes were female in 2001. The women's Final Four basketball tournament drew 20,000-plus fans in 2000, 2001, and 2002. The WNBA, the women's pro basketball league launched in 1997, averaged 9,075 fans in 2001. The successes of U.S. female athletes at the 1996 Summer Olympics raised the profile of women's soccer, basketball, and softball to unprecedented heights.

There were more than 400 female sportswriters at the nation's 1,600 newspapers in 2002, compared to a few dozen in the 1970s, when *Sports Illustrated* reporter Melissa Ludtke went to the Supreme Court to battle for equal locker-room access. Lesley Visser, then a reporter for *The Boston Globe,* remembers waiting outside the locker room for an interview with Pittsburgh Steelers quarterback Terry Bradshaw. When he emerged and saw a pen and notepad in her hands, he grabbed them from her and—naturally—signed his autograph.

Nowadays, though female sportswriters continue to fight for credibility, the mere sight of them is not so surprising. Ron Rapoport, a *Chicago Sun-Times* columnist who in 1994 compiled an anthology of female sportswriters (*A Kind of Grace: A Treasury of Sportswriting by Women*), wrote: "Today, women cover baseball, football, basketball, hockey and college sports of every description. They write about horse racing, tennis and golf. They do investigative reporting and write columns. A few have even overcome their sports editors' outmoded assignment notions by becoming sports editors themselves."

But media coverage of women's sports has not kept up with the pace. Of *Sports Illustrated*'s 520 covers in the 1990s, only 25 were devoted to female athletes or coaches. (The 10 swimsuit-issue covers don't count.) From 2000 to mid-2002, the magazine had five women on its cover—the Dallas Cowboys cheerleaders, Anna Kournikova in a bedroom pose, and Olympians Marion Jones, Megan Quann, and Sarah Hughes.

Washington Post columnist Sally Jenkins, who in 2002 became the first female to win the Associated Press Sports Editors column-writing contest, spent several years at *Sports Illustrated.* She said the magazine "always viewed women's sports coverage as coming at the expense of male sports coverage."

"An editor once said to me, 'If it's a choice between doing a feature on Jackie Joyner Kersee and Michael Jordan, we're going to do Michael Jordan every time.' I said, 'But that's just it. It's not a choice. Why can't you do both stories?' He looked at me like I'd turned into Patricia Ireland. All I know is, every piece I did on a female athlete wound up in the swimsuit issue."

Newspapers don't have a much better track record when it comes to women's sports. The 2002 University of Connecticut women's basketball team went 39-0 and had four likely first-round WNBA draft picks on its roster; but it wasn't until the final rounds of the NCAA Tournament that most newspapers carried features on the Huskies. And there was no *Sports Illustrated* cover when they completed their perfect season. That week's cover went to the University of Maryland men's team. "If a men's team did what we did, everyone would be drooling all over them," lamented UConn's Sue Bird.

Los Angeles Times columnist Diane Pucin, who covered the 2002 Women's Final Four, said: "I don't think papers do an adequate job of covering women's sports. While I don't think that the LA Sparks should be covered the same as the Lakers, or the UCLA women as extensively as the UCLA men, and while I don't think it is the newspaper's job to abide by Title IX rules, it also doesn't serve the readership to ignore good women's stories. It is not good coverage if the first the LA *Times* readers, for example, hear of Diana Taurasi, a local girl, is how she played in the national championship game. It is not good coverage if no LA *Times* readers know how good a player Sue Bird is."

A study done in 2000 by University of Southern California sociology and gender studies professor Michael Messner found that men's sports received 88.2 percent of the air time on the three Los Angeles network affiliates. Women's sports received 8.7 percent of the time, and gender-neutral topics received 3.1 percent. ESPN's *SportsCenter* devoted just 2.2 percent of its show to women's sports in 1999, according to Messner's study.

A 1997 study done by Vanderbilt University tracked a year's worth of women's sports coverage in *The Tennessean, USA Today,* and *The New York Times.* It found that women received 11 percent of the coverage, compared to 82 percent for men's sports and 6 percent for gender-neutral sports topics.

The Women's Sports Foundation, with the help of DePauw University, compared women's sports coverage in *The New York Times* and *The Indianapolis Star* over 52 Saturdays to see if it had improved from 1989 to 1999. It had. The percentage of space devoted to women's sports increased from 2.7 percent to 8.6 percent in *The Star* and 2.2 percent to 6.7 percent in *The Times*. Still, those numbers lagged far behind men's sports coverage.

"We're second-class citizens," U.S. soccer player Michelle Akers told the *Contra Costa Times* in July 2001. "That's the way it's always been. For some people, it's just ignorance, for some it's sexism, for some it's a power issue. Men have always run the news media and had more input on decision-making, so we don't get the same amount of coverage or the same kind of coverage that male athletes get."

Cynthia Cooper, a guard for the WNBA's Houston Comets, feels the media often "disrespects" female athletes.

"I'm a professional athlete just like they are, so why shouldn't I be covered just like they are," she said, referring to her male counterparts in the NBA. "Why should we have to beg and plead for attention? I am so tired of ignorant journalists interviewing me. I'm so tired of being [mistaken for teammate] Sheryl Swoopes. How many NBA players have to deal with that? We're not getting a fair shake."

USA Today columnist Christine Brennan agreed. She said in a 2000 speech to the American Society of Newspaper Editors: "I think we're doing a poor job of covering women's sports, especially at a time when most of our circulations are dropping and women and girls are potential new readers for our sports sections."

Regarding the Women's World Cup, Brennan said: "The minivan revolution ignored by the mainstream sports media for years was going on whether anyone paid attention or not."

While newspapers have expanded their coverage to include women's sports, their pages oftentimes do not reflect the growing interest in athletes named Brianna, Chamique, and Sarah. Figure skating, which trails only the NFL in sports television ratings and is hugely popular with women, is generally covered only during the Olympics even though there is interest year-round.

"It is not good business [for the LA *Times*] to not cover figure skating world championships, which get excellent TV ratings, when two of the top competitors are LA-area girls," said Pucin. "The same sports editor who will argue that covering the women's Final Four is a waste because, look, the TV ratings are terrible, will then ignore those same TV ratings when it's time to cover world figure skating championships. The point is that there are great women's stories to be told and they aren't getting told often enough or early enough. Want some new readers to the section? Offer the women, who are, after all, 50 percent of the population, something they might enjoy reading."

Women's tennis gets covered, but the most photographed player is Kournikova, a long-legged blonde who has never won a major tournament.

Women's team sports and women's golf—in which women wear shorts rather than skirts and leotards—continue to struggle to get attention. The LPGA, in an effort to get more coverage, came up with "Five Points of Celebrity," a checklist of ways female golfers can get more attention from the media. The five areas players were asked to work on were: performance, approachability, joy and passion, relevance, and—the most controversial of the points—appearance. Critics felt the LPGA was setting women's sports back by bringing up the issue of appearance, saying it shouldn't matter what players look like and that the tour shouldn't stoop to selling sex appeal.

LPGA Commissioner Ty Votaw insists the tour isn't trying to sell sex appeal but a more marketable overall package intended to increase fans' interest. "Sex is just a default position that everyone gravitates to," Votaw said. "This is no different than [baseball stars] Alex Rodriguez and Derek Jeter appearing on the cover of GQ. Those players look good. We want our players to look good. Anybody who says appearance doesn't matter is fooling themselves."

He said he wasn't bothered by a Playboy.com poll asking fans which golfer they'd like to see in a nude pictorial. Carin Koch won but immediately rejected the six-figure offer. Second-place finisher Jill McGill considered it before declining.

"Ultimately, it kept the LPGA's name in the spotlight for a few weeks," Votaw said. The subject of sex appeal in women's sports coverage has been much debated during the past decade as some female athletes have chosen to pose in provocative photos. Figure skater Katarina Witt, volleyball player Gabrielle Reece, and gymnast Svetlana Khorkina posed for *Playboy.* WNBA player Lisa Harrison considered posing for *Playboy,* setting off a firestorm of columns and radio talk-show debates.

Olympic swimmer Jenny Thompson posed topless for *SI* with her fists covering her breasts. The Australian women's soccer team, "The Matildas," sold 60,000 copies of their topless calendar. And U.S. soccer player Brandi Chastain, who became the lasting image of the Women's

World Cup when she ripped off her jersey to reveal a jog bra, posed nude for *Gear* magazine with strategically placed balls covering her private parts.

A June 2000 *Sports Illustrated* cover story on Kournikova featured her in stiletto heels and sexually suggestive poses. The author, veteran sportswriter Frank Deford, wrote: "As Raymond Chandler wrote in Farewell, My Lovely, 'It was a blonde. A blonde to make a bishop kick a hole in a stained glass window.' . . . Anna is that kind of gorgeous, and Anna knows it."

The Women's Sports Foundation issued a formal statement with regard to the subject of female athletes and sex appeal. "*Sports Illustrated* has asked top female athletes to remove their clothes or wear sexy clothes or adopt sexy postures and be photographed in a non-sport setting while it does not ask top male athletes to pose in this way," WSF said. "Male athletes are photographed to display their skill and muscles while in athletic gear and in sport settings. This is a double standard that objectifies women. Because *SI* seldom covers women for their athletic exploits and frequently portrays women as sex objects, such coverage is objectionable and demeaning to female athletes."

The foundation also chastised female athletes who choose to be featured in nude or semi-nude photos: "Because female athletes receive 80 to 90 percent less coverage of their athletic achievements in the print and electronic media than their male counterparts, female athletes who use this opportunity for non-sport exposure allow the media to continue to marginalize the achievements of the female athlete."

The American mainstream media is still trying to figure out how to cover women's sports. Should sports sections—and specifically, female sportswriters—be advocates for women's sports? Should they give the local women's college basketball team the same space as the men's team even though the attendance at the women's games is a fraction of the men's following? Should the WNBA, the women's pro basketball league, and the WUSA, the women's pro soccer league, get the same coverage as their male counterparts even though their television ratings pale in comparison?

Coaches and players in women's team sports say yes. They say if their athletes had better coverage, their attendance and sponsorships would increase. Bonnie DeSimone, a veteran sportswriter for the *Chicago Tribune,* isn't so sure. "I've worked for five different newspapers, and my personal feeling is that in most markets, women's sports are over-covered compared to the actual amount of interest, as measured by attendance, sponsorship etc.," DeSimone said. "Sometimes that is justified in a sort of affirmative action sense, sometimes it's not. One area where I think it is absolutely justified is preps. There has been tremendous growth in girls' sports, and parents are just as interested in reading about their daughters as they are their sons. I'm a lot less sanguine about team sports like the WNBA and WUSA. I don't like being guilt-tripped into thinking we have to cover those because it's politically correct. The women's sports that are truly popular have built their own audiences, and we've followed that (tennis, skating, big events like the Women's World Cup). I don't think it's up to us to try to create a demand by highlighting fledgling sports."

Nearly all sports sections in America are still run by men, so women carry little weight in the daily decision making. Editors tend to come up with story ideas in sports they are familiar with, and most men are not as familiar with women's sports as they are with the NFL, the NBA, the NHL, Major League Baseball, and men's college sports.

Stories about men's sports are far likelier to make the front page of the section. As a result, women's beats are still not as prestigious as men's beats, so ambitious female sportswriters are equally likely to choose to cover men's sports as their male colleagues. If you cover the NBA at a major paper, you travel with the team. If you cover the WNBA, chances are you don't. Which assignment is more glamorous?

If your ambition is to be an NFL writer, chances are you'll get there faster by covering college football than any women's sport, so why hold back your career path by taking on women's beats?

Women's stories are often relegated to inexperienced reporters, or disgruntled reporters, who are forced to do the assignments. This, female athletes say, hurts their coverage.

Pro golfer Meg Mallon said that on more than one occasion a reporter has complained to her about having to cover LPGA events. "I can assure you that no male athlete has had a reporter tell him he had to cover an event because his boss got the good assignment and got to go to the Masters [the men's tournament]," Mallon said. "That happened to me. Another reporter told me, 'You know what? You're lucky I'm here. So dazzle me. Give me a story. Give me something to write about.'"

Cooper, the WNBA player, said she also sees disgruntled reporters at games. "You're a newspaper reporter and you're supposed to be objective when you cover a sport," she said. "Instead of covering it and doing your job, you go in there with preconceived notions, half-heartedly, not really wanting to be there, not really wanting to give your best, which means ultimately, you didn't do a very good job. The article reflects that and then the people in the community who read that article are not motivated and encouraged to come watch us because one gentleman was biased about going to watch a WNBA basketball game."

While the growing number of female sports journalists doesn't guarantee better coverage for women's sports, it certainly has helped. For one thing, many of these reporters are former athletes, so they appreciate women's sports. Brennan played tennis, field hockey, and basketball and was her high school's Senior Athlete of the Year. Visser was captain of her high school field hockey and basketball teams. *Palm Beach Post* columnist Karen Crouse was a collegiate swimmer. Also, female reporters have help create diversified sports sections with stories male reporters might not have thought about. Rapoport's anthology included stories about a breast cancer survivor, female basketball players in Europe, stalkers of female athletes, and the relationship between baseball players who room together a long time. It isn't that male writers couldn't think of those stories, but they're less likely to do so.

The true pioneers of women's sportswriting were women such as Mary Garber (*Winston-Salem Journal-Sentinel*), Billie Cheney Speed (*The Birmingham News, Atlanta Journal*) and Louise Flynn Zerschling (*The Austin Daily Herald, Sioux City Journal*), who began covering sports in the 1940s, when press passes said: "No women or children allowed in the press box."

Zerschling wrote under the pen name "Lou Flynn" so readers would think she was a man. Garber, who was still covering college football and basketball after five decades, remembers being barred from the Duke press box in 1946 even though she had the proper credential because the Football Writers Association (FWA) did not permit women in the press box.

"While I was arguing with the sports information director, a little boy was hopping up and down the press box steps," Garber recalled during a speech to the Association of Women in Sports Media, an organization founded in 1987. "He could sit there, but I could not. I was put in the wives' box, where I tried to cover the game as the coaches' wives gossiped and the kids beat on the table and cheered."

Garber wound up joining the FWA in 1965 and served two terms on its board of directors.

As for the locker-room issue—the issue most people ask about first when they meet a female sportswriter—it is not much of an issue anymore. The National Hockey League opened its locker rooms in 1975, the NBA in 1976, and Major League Baseball in 1978, after being sued by *Sports Illustrated*'s Ludtke, who was denied access to the New York Yankees locker room. A female federal judge ruled that a player's right to privacy could be fixed with a towel or bathrobe and wasn't as important as the constitutional right of female sportswriters to do their jobs.

The NFL was the last league to open locker rooms, leaving it up to individual teams until 1985, when a league-wide "equal access" policy was instituted.

(Sidenote: Critics of women in the locker room often ask why women's locker rooms aren't open to male reporters. Truth is, they often are. The WNBA and Women's Final Four have open-locker-room policies. The difference is that female athletes don't generally disrobe in front of reporters. They stay in their uniforms until interviews are complete, and once the reporters are gone, they shower and change. Male athletes have been unreceptive to that concept, claiming they can't wait to get their uniforms off.)

Female reporters endured verbal—and sometimes worse—abuse in locker rooms through the 1980s, and in 1990 the issue made headlines again when *Boston Herald* reporter Lisa Olson claimed she was sexually harassed by some New England Patriots players who circled her and made lewd gestures. Patriots owner Victor Kiam called her an epithet. She sued and settled out of court, but hate mail, threats, and vandalism to her apartment continued, so Olson moved to Australia for five years, where she covered rugby and cricket. She was hired as a columnist by the New York *Daily News* in 1995.

Locker-room incidents decreased as the 1990s wore on. In 1999, the issue arose again when Green Bay Packer Reggie White and New York Knick Charlie Ward, both devout Christians, said their religious beliefs made them uncomfortable with women in the locker room and lobbied for the policy to be reversed.

"It's insane to think that these men are walking around naked, and the poor boys, they need their privacy," Olson said at a forum on women sportswriters at Fordham University. "The standard players contract says they will be available to the media. It doesn't say they will be available naked. The key weapon has always been a towel, and if that's not good enough, then these guys make enough money to buy a bathrobe."

She is offended by suggestions that women get into sportswriting to see men naked. "Some of us have kids and some of us are married, but most of us have no personal lives at all because we've chosen to work in a profession that consumes our nights and weekends," Olson said. "We do it because we love writing and producing and filming and talking about sports. Not because we might be lucky enough to catch a glimpse of Charlie Ward wrapped in a towel."

Johnette Howard, sports columnist for *Newsday,* says female sports-writers today benefited greatly from the Patriots incident with Olson.

"One of the powerful things that came out of Lisa Olson's case was that teams and leagues have said adamantly that they won't tolerate that kind of behavior," Howard said. "Before that, I think women thought ritual hazing was part of the job they had to get through. The women coming up now have a high degree of self-possession and confidence, and when something like the Reggie White and Charlie Ward thing comes up, they say, of course, 'I don't have to take this.' In the past, women were more conflicted."

The Association of Women in Sports Media was formed in 1987 after *Sacramento Bee* reporter Susan Fornoff received a rat in a gift box from a baseball player she covered. A handful of women sportswriters around the country lamented that there was no group to support Fornoff, and thus the group was formed. It had more than 600 members in 2002 and represents women in sportswriting, broadcasting, public relations, and other sports-media fields.

One has to assume the growing numbers of women and girls who play sports and work in sports fields will change the attitude of the boys and men around them and that someday all of these issues will be moot.

An encouraging sign: Ann Killion, sports columnist for *The* (San Jose) *Mercury News,* was sitting at her desk typing a story one day when her son Connor, then 5, came up and asked: "Mommy, can boys be sportswriters?"

21. Racism and Sports

Abraham Aamidor

Abraham Aamidor is a reporter for *The Indianapolis Star* and the author of *Real Feature Writing* (1999). He has taught journalism at Indiana University, Southern Illinois University-Carbondale, and Georgia Southern University.

There is no issue that has befuddled America—and, before it, the colonies—more than race.

In the eighteenth century, the U.S. Constitution called black slaves three-fifths of a man each, based on a formula for assigning congressional seats to the colonies in order to get the southern colonies to join the new union.

As I write this, a new book, *The Real Lincoln: A New Look at Abraham Lincoln, His Agenda, and the Unnecessary War* by Thomas J. DiLorenzo (2002), notes that the 16th president, also known as the Great Emancipator, once defended a slave owner and made other statements earlier in his career demonstrating his view that slavery was, in effect, a property right.

People live and learn; they change. Most civilized and religious people believe in forgiveness, too. The opposite of forgiveness is vengeance and perpetual war.

I remember my first summer job in college. I was a key clerk at the former Morrison Hotel in downtown Chicago, now the site of one of those ubiquitous corporate bank buildings with a phony street address and a soulless existence. I gave room keys to drunken guests who were coming in after a night on the town—this was in the days when hotels had real brass room keys, not electronic cards—and I'd watch in amusement as the hotel detective (yes, hotels had and have detectives on duty) would shoo away the prostitutes and other lounge lizards who were often hanging around, looking for trouble.

The night auditor (this was the guy who did the accounts, which he or an assistant would slip under guests' doors in the early morning hours) was a basketball fan. This was the 1960s, and black professional basketball players were gaining prominence in the NBA.

"You know what happens when you mix a little white milk with chocolate milk?" he asked me one night. "Nothing. You still got chocolate milk. But when you mix a little chocolate milk with white milk? Then you got chocolate milk, too."

He didn't want to see black players in the NBA. No Bill Russell. No Oscar "Big O" Robertson. No Wilt "the Stilt" Chamberlain.

It's easy enough to decry such attitudes; it takes no real courage anymore to stand and be counted in the fight against racism.

In the popular culture, the struggle today is over group rights versus individual rights, multiculturalism versus a colorblind society, and diversity as a kind of substitute for equality.

These issues all spill over into the sports arena. Here's an excerpt from a column by Jonathan Tilove, carried by the Newhouse News Service on April 15, 2002:

> Robert Obstgarten, a white freshman at the University of Maryland, and Miesha Lowery, a black senior, agree that American life is rife with racial double standards. But they hold precisely opposite views of who is getting away with what.
>
> Obstgarten, 18, wonders why it is OK for Shaquille O'Neal to write in his book, "Shaq Talks Back," about the humiliation of being "dunked on by a white boy." If a white player disparaged O'Neal as a "black boy," Obstgarten suggests, "there would be bloodshed."
>
> Lowery, 22, says she and black friends marveled at the relatively benign reaction to the riots on and around campus when their school won the NCAA basketball championship. Were Maryland a predominantly black school, she said, "I'm sure somebody would have compared it to the Los Angeles riots."

In the early part of the first decade of the twenty-first century, it's big news that the Williams sisters are the first true black superstars of women's professional tennis and that a city like Indianapolis has black coaches running the show for both the Pacers (basketball) and Colts (football). It was big news when Mike Davis, an African American, succeeded the legendary Bob Knight as head basketball coach at Indiana University down the road a bit in Bloomington.

It was news. Think about that for a moment. Is a spate of black coaches news because there are so few, or is it news because we are so obsessed with race in this country still?

The nice thing about sports is that the guys with the most points or the most runs at the end of regulation play, or who ran 100 yards the fastest, or who shot four rounds of golf with the lowest score win. But we still think race matters in sports, 50 years after Jackie Robinson integrated the National League. (Quick: Who integrated the American League? Larry Doby did.)

I played baseball at Theodore Roosevelt High School in Chicago. I was a bench warmer on a losing Blue Division team (the Blue Division was below the Red Division in those days). Baseball is one of those sports that's absolutely better to watch in person at a ballpark rather than on TV. Some people think baseball is boring to watch, but they're always up to something on the field.

I was a rare Northsider who didn't root for the Cubs but rather was a White Sox fan. The White Sox generally struggled for fans, while the Cubs were the toast of the town, even as they had losing season after losing season. The real reason the White Sox didn't draw well in the '50s and '60s and beyond, I knew (I believed, I felt) was that Comiskey Park was on the wrong side of town. A lot of people simply would not ride the "L" train to 35th and Shields and walk a couple of blocks through the "ghetto" to see Nellie Fox or Jungle Jim Rivera or Minnie Minoso play ball.

I always tried to go when the Yankees came to town. This was the late '50s and Mickey Mantle was in his prime, but it was the pitching matchups I cared about more. Yankees manager Casey Stengel and Sox manager Al Lopez had enough respect for each other, and for the game of baseball itself, that they always tried to throw their best pitchers at each other. That meant Whitey Ford for the Yanks and Billy Pierce for the Sox.

My mother, who was a cook at a nursing home in Chicago, sometimes got White Sox tickets from her boss. (She never got Cubs tix.) I and a dishwasher named Wilbur went to a couple of games together. I was still in my teens, he was twentysomething, and this was the late '50s, when the civil rights movement was just arriving in Chicago.

Wilbur was a dishwasher in the nursing home. Get it? He was black. I was white. We both liked Billy Pierce.

Wilbur and I would meet at the park; after all, he could walk to the stadium from where he lived.

Nobody ever called us names or threw bottles at us or told us to get out of there, even though we had pretty good seats; that is, when we had the boss's seats. But they sure stared a lot. Wilbur never said a thing, but I didn't like it. Halfway into a nice 2-1 game when both Pierce and Ford would pitch complete games, though, we'd forget the stares or who we were or even why we would care what other people thought.

Years later, I was to read a story by *New York Times* sportswriter Ira Berkow about the integration of Major League Baseball and the relationship between Robinson (who made a promise to his employers in Brooklyn not to be baited by racial taunts from other players) and Pee Wee Reese, the Dodgers' shortstop and team captain who hailed from Kentucky:

> He [Reese] recalled the first time he learned about Robinson. "I was on a ship coming back to the States from Guam, in the middle of the ocean, and was playing cards. Someone hollered to me: 'Hey, Pee Wee, did you hear? The Dodgers signed a nigger.' It didn't mean that much to me and I kept playing cards. Then the guy said, 'And he plays shortstop!' My God, just my luck, Robinson has to play my position! But I had confidence in my abilities, and I thought, well, if he can beat me out, more power to him. That's exactly how I felt."

Baseball today is the most international and multicultural sport in America. I like it that "multicultural" in this context includes great Hispanic players from Central America and the Caribbean plus an increasing number of stars from the Orient as well as plenty of southern whites, where baseball still matters at the high school and college level. I think that's great.

But issues of race and allegations of racism continue to permeate all levels of sports. Robert Washington of Bryn Mawr University and a colleague reviewed academic treatises on race and sport in the January 2002 issue of *Annual Review of Sociology*: Most focused on disparities in the payment of professional athletes, so-called stacking (discrimination in allocating players' positions in team sports), retention barriers (discrimination in retaining minority athletes who are not stars), and continuing practices of racial exclusion or tokenism.

One study "focusing only on sub-star starters, indicates that whites are paid 18 percent more than blacks, but it goes on to suggest that white sub-star starters are preferred because they increase fan interest."

Sometimes issues of race and ethnicity go beyond the biggest issue of race in this country, which is the relationship between blacks and whites. Stanford University changed the name of its football team to the Cardinal from Indians several years ago; some Native Americans continue to decry the Cleveland Indians baseball team, if not for its name, then for its mawkish, red-skinned, hook-nosed caricature of a Native American. Yet most team names are by their nature positive— nobody names a team the Losers, the Crybabies, or the Turkeys. To be a brave or a chief is a good thing.

I think the issue is not whether naming a team the Braves or the Indians or the Chiefs is racist per se, but it does put real living people and groups on the same level as lost peoples and fabled groups, like the Trojans, or with highly romanticized groups, like pirates.

Salim Muwakkil, senior editor of *In These Times,* wrote about blacks, sports, and lingering racial stereotypes on June 17, 2002, on the pages of the *Chicago Tribune:*

> As Jon Entine notes in his book, "Taboo: Why Black Athletes Dominate Sports and Why We're Afraid To Talk About It," long before [Bob] Cousy made his mark with the Celtics, an all-Jewish team dominated basketball during the 1920s, '30s and part of the '40s.
>
> The South Philadelphia Hebrew Association was the best known and most successful all-Jewish team.
>
> "The Hebrews barnstormed across the East and Midwest, playing in a variety of semipro leagues that were precursors to the NBA," Entine writes. "In an incredible 22-season stretch, they played in 18 championship series, losing only five." Entine reveals that the team was more popular than Philadelphia's two baseball teams.
>
> "The reason, I suspect, that basketball appeals to the Hebrew with his Oriental background," Entine quotes Paul Gallico, former sports editor of the New York Daily News and one of the premier sports writers of the 1930s, "is that the game places a premium on an alert, scheming mind, flashy trickiness, artful dodging and general smart aleckness."

I learned a couple of new old stereotypes in Muwakkil's article. I think it'll be a better day when we can all laugh at all the old stereotypes and when all the winners in the world are the ones who jumped the highest or ran the fastest or scored the most points or skated the most brilliantly or threw the ball the hardest.

22. Ethics

John Cherwa

John Cherwa is the sports coordinator for the Tribune Company, working with the company's 11 newspapers. Previously, Cherwa was the Associate Managing Editor/ Sports for the *Chicago Tribune* and deputy sports editor of *The Los Angeles Times.*

In a time not too long ago, Marje Everett, the former matriarch of Chicago's legendary Arlington Park horse-racing track, was known for her lavish parties and royal treatment of the press. The highlight was always the Christmas party. There were giant ice sculptures carved into likenesses of some of the country's best thoroughbreds, shrimp as big as Rhode Island, and, of course, an endless bar where the words "well drink" were not spoken.

It was the social event of the season, and no member of the press went home empty-handed. One former high-ranking sports executive at the *Chicago Tribune* likes to tell this story.

"I remember eating and drinking until I could do no more of either. It was time to go and there I was walking down the steps with a giant TV in my arms. Do you know why?"

"No, why?" the response would come, always anticipating an unforeseen answer that would justify the indiscretion.

"Because that was all I could carry."

Ah, the days before ethics.

Days of free booze, free meals, free tickets, and free golf. Did I mention free booze? Mostly delivered to your home so the boss wouldn't find out.

Do such practices still go on today? Sure, but not to the same extent as in the past.

At *The Los Angeles Times* and *Chicago Tribune,* two papers I spent 20 wonderful years at collectively, I knew there were such abuses. But who had the time or energy to try to prove something that would be labeled a mere suspicion, especially when it was unlikely you could ever prove a thing?

The Dodgers knew how to handle the press and clearly had a wink-wink arrangement with some of the staffers to offer free tickets. The Angels weren't as smart, but their cheapness could be seen as ethical conduct.

In Chicago, it was much more delicate. The Tribune Company owned both the *Chicago Tribune* and the Chicago Cubs. There was an adversarial relationship between the *Trib* and the Cubs. The team believed it had to bend over backward to prove the newspaper wasn't getting any breaks because of common ownership. You could pretty much guess that if there were any free tickets, they were going across the street to *Chicago Sun-Times* staffers.

However, free golf, always disguised as the innocuously named "press day," was another matter. It was a way to make an out-and-out freebie sound legal.

But if ethics were only a matter of taking freebies then it would be a very simple issue to deal with. In short, don't take things for free. Okay, we've dealt with that.

I stopped worrying about free key chains and T-shirts a long time ago. Where the discussion of ethics goes from black and white to the always-difficult-to-interpret gray is where the fun lies.

Some of my best friends in the business, people whose ethics and sound judgment are unquestioned, disagree with me on some of these topics. What is clear to some is murky to others. But ethical behavior always has the same goal, which is doing nothing to endanger your relationship with your readers. If you lose their trust, you've lost it all. And the chances of getting it back are very slim.

CONFLICT OF INTEREST

The basic concern is not conflict of interest but appearance of conflict of interest. It is this basic tenet that most ethical discussions revolve around. And violating it would most surely cost you your job. Your bosses may rarely look for evidence of a conflict of interest or bias in your reporting, but they don't have to. There is always someone keeping

score, believing that you are either favoring the opposition or not favoring their team. One time in Los Angeles, for example, the sports
information director at UCLA kept a running total of column inches
devoted to his school and to USC. The perception, of course, was that
USC was getting special treatment. The reality is that the count was
pretty even.

Still, you don't want to give the people keeping score any more
ammunition to back their claims of favoritism. Again, the danger often
is in the appearance, not the reality. That's not to say that sportswriters
don't favor certain teams, but the reasons are usually unrelated to free
tickets. Some teams are just better at manipulating sportswriters. Other
times, the people you are covering are just more likeable.

(Advice to sports information officers and team publicists: Sportswriters are very simple creatures. If you want to keep them happy then
don't lie to them, do return their phone calls, and, please, treat them
with respect. This magic formula works almost every time.)

One of the best stories of avoiding conflict of interest happened at
my first big paper job at the *Orlando Sentinel.* One of the sportswriters
was taking money from the local harness track to write stories about
them. But no stories were appearing in the paper. The track, obviously
feeling wronged, called the editor of the paper. The writer was confronted and asked if the charge was true. He said it was, but added this
defense: "The wrong thing to do would have been to take the money
and write about them. This way they don't get any special favors."

It was a novel defense, but the writer was asked to find employment
elsewhere.

TICKETS

If you want to play the ethics card to its utmost, then you need to
reevaluate your policy on buying tickets. Bill Dwyre, the longtime
sports editor of *The Los Angeles Times,* was a pioneer when it came to
cleaning up our business. He started his crusade at the *Milwaukee Journal* by not allowing staffers to buy tickets from the public-relations
departments of local teams. He believed that working in a sports department should not give you any advantage or special status when it
came to dealing with the teams you cover. He wanted nothing the general public couldn't get, such as tickets to ostensibly sold-out games.
It was a wonderful display of principle and was clearly intended to send
a message to the teams that his paper covered.

In part, the ticket decision has been forced upon sports editors by their bosses and colleagues in other departments, the people who un-thinkingly make the majority of requests for tickets. While it's not intended to be disrespectful, it is a complete abridgement of ethical protocol. How would they feel if sportswriters asked for a ticket to an execution or to get into an exclusive political gathering? How about a seat in the Senate gallery?

Dwyre also was uncomfortable about having his writers obtaining free press-box food. Among his adversaries was Bud Selig, then owner of the Brewers, now the commissioner of baseball.

"So, once a year," Dwyre said, "I used to send Selig a check for something like $1,216.17, with a note saying: 'For *Milwaukee Journal* press box food for season.' It drove him nuts, which is why I kept doing it for a couple of years. He'd always call up and scream: 'What in hell am I supposed to do with the 17 cents?'"

I've been fortunate to work at papers where a sports department is valued, but at some papers sports is viewed differently—as entertain-ment, or, heaven forbid, the dreaded "toy department." Every prep night in a sports department is like election night in the newsroom. The only difference is no one orders pizza. The best solution when others ask you for tickets is to get a bunch of business cards from team public-relations people. When a colleague asks to buy tickets, give them the card and let them make the call. It's the cleanest way to handle the situation.

Sometimes sports teams do not have a mechanism to sell you tick-ets. In those cases, simply write a check to the team's charity of choice. Every team has one. And finally, if you are getting tickets for someone else, please remind them that their demeanor and actions at the game reflect on you and, more important, the paper you are working for.

GAMBLING

Sportswriters generally tend to delude themselves into thinking they know more about sports than anyone else. Sometimes it's even true. Wouldn't it be a shame if all that information you know went to waste without the slightest benefit to you? Well, I'm here to tell you, suck it up and live with it.

There is little point in discussing making sports bets with a bookie because that is flat-out against the law in this country. You can get in a lot less trouble betting legally than you can by using a bookie. The reason is simple: A sports book doesn't take credit; a bookie does.

While a sports book will allow you the privilege of betting every penny you have, a bookie will allow you to bet many pennies you don't have. That, and government taxes, is the difference.

But this isn't about the morality or practicality of betting on sports. It usually comes back to the basic tenet of appearance of conflict of interest. It's a sad sight to see some of the best and most noted sports-writers and sports editors in the country enjoying an afternoon in a Las Vegas sports book. It's a common sight. In fact, the western region of the Associated Press Sports Editors holds its annual meeting in Las Vegas.

You should never bet on sports, because if a team does you wrong financially you're going to remember it. Maybe not at the front of the brain but subconsciously you will feel different about this team because of how your bet turned out. Or maybe not. Maybe your slamming down the program in the sports book will be remembered by one of the pa-trons from your city. You rip that team one year later and all that person can remember is how you hated that team for that one instant. Your credibility has been ruined, all for only a $20 (we hope) bet.

If you are an NFL writer, you should never bet on the NFL. Same for baseball if you are a baseball writer. Pete Rose wasn't punished by baseball for betting on football; he bet on his own sport and was placed on baseball's ineligible list in 1989, effectively banishing him from the game and making him ineligible for the Hall of Fame. Some have con-tended that he bet on games he was managing, but that was never proven. If a sportswriter were to bet on a game he or she was covering, I would recommend dismissal.

There was a longtime Los Angeles sports columnist who would call his bookie from press boxes across the city. This lovable caricature of Oscar Madison was known for his indiscretions. He was especially remembered for calling each venue press box before choosing which event to go to. The deciding factor: what food was being served to the reporters that night. Luckily, that isn't a problem anymore as most press boxes now charge for meals, as they should.

This same columnist was also known for bouncing checks in some of the finer horse-racing press boxes across southern California. It's interesting that whenever you talk about ethics, horse racing always seems to come up. Horse-racing public-relations persons are among the most accommodating in the business. You're not sure if it's because they know how to get racing writers to write what they want or they realize how much horse-racing writers contribute to the mutuel handle.

Or maybe both. Some editors, such as Dwyre, insist that their horse-racing writer not gamble or be more than a $2 bettor. Pulitzer Prize–winning columnist Jim Murray loved to go to the track and enjoyed betting $5 or $10 on a horse. No one ever said anything.

Andy Beyer, considered the best horse-racing writer in the country working for *The Washington Post,* bets large amounts of money at the track, and he writes about it. Beyer has had a profound impact on the racing industry, inventing what are now called the "Beyer speed figures" to help handicappers figure out how a horse will likely be rated and perform down the stretch. But Beyer has often said that he if had to choose between betting and writing about horse racing, he would choose the former. *The Post* doesn't seem to mind.

I have only bet on one sporting event I have ever covered. It was Bill Shoemaker's last ride before retiring. I was at the track doing a sports business story on what effect one race could have on the overall mutuel handle. I had not intended to bet the race, thus depriving myself of a keepsake. But Mike Downey, the talented former columnist at *The Los Angeles Times,* talked me into it. Ethics be damned for one race. I had no intention of cashing the ticket. Well, Shoemaker, riding a horse named Patchy Groundfog, came up short and didn't win. My willpower was not really tested.

The most despicable example of ethical malfeasance also came from Los Angeles, where a noted handicapper was known to tout horses other than the one he was going to bet in order to improve the odds. The handicapper, in turn, would bet on the horse he really thought was going to win in hopes that he would win more money. Even in the sometimes shady world of horse racing, this was frowned upon.

POINT SPREADS

One ethical dilemma that sports editors find themselves in without giving it a second thought is the running of point spreads. The way I see it, only the newspapers in Nevada can morally run point spreads as that is the only state that allows sports betting. By running a point spread are you encouraging illegal gambling? Some argue that the point spread helps you weigh the relative strengths of each team. In fact, a point spread is really only designed to equalize betting on both sides of the line. This is why you'll always find New York teams with less favorable point spreads because the bookmakers know that New Yorkers will bet on their team simply out of loyalty.

One common gambling stat for which there is no defense for is the over-under. This is where you bet that the number of points scored in a game is over or under the line set by the bookmaker. When I was sports editor of the *Chicago Tribune,* I often thought about dropping the point spread but didn't have the courage. The opposition paper, the *Sun-Times,* catered to gamblers. I felt that to drop the point spread would put us at a competitive disadvantage. In the end, it proved that my sense of competition was greater than my sense of morality. I'm not proud of that.

There is only one major daily newspaper in the country that doesn't run point spreads; *The New York Times.* Neil Amdur, the former long-time *Times* sports editor, has held firm on this tradition. *The Times* is also the only major paper in the country not to run a horse-racing handicap. Again, the same philosophy. *The Los Angeles Times* also wanted to go in that direction when it came to printing the spread. Dwyre chose to print the NFL line and college football line once a week instead of every day beginning in the early '80s. Still, from an ethical standpoint, some might argue that that's akin to being only slightly pregnant.

WRITING BOOKS

Sportswriters are often sought out to ghostwrite books by athletes and coaches. It makes a lot of sense. The writer more than likely knows the person, is invariably fast, and probably writes in an easy conversational style. Yet what has been the norm for many years is unacceptable in most circles today. In short, you can't enter into a financial arrangement with anyone you cover.

Today, the *Chicago Tribune* has one of the toughest ethics policies among the major papers. Yet in a controversial move, Bob Verdi, the longtime sports columnist at the *Tribune* before leaving to write about golf, wrote a book with Chicago Bears quarterback Jim McMahon in 1986. The *Tribune* benefited from that arrangement, as Verdi was of-tentimes the only writer who could talk to the controversial quarterback. When Phil Hersh, the *Tribune*'s Olympic writer, was offered the chance to ghost the Tara Lipinski book in 1997, he was faced with a decision. If he did the book he would have to stop covering figure skating as long as Lipinski was active. If he didn't do the book, it would be busi-ness as usual. Hersh decided to keep the figure skating beat, where he is acknowledged as one of the most knowledgeable writers in the world.

But one of the best sportswriters in the country, Gene Wojciechowski of *ESPN the Magazine,* has ghosted three books—on Bill Walton, Reggie Miller, and Rick Majerus. While he has since turned his attention to writing hilarious sports fiction, he never saw anything wrong with the conflict.

"Either you have ethics and journalistic integrity, or you don't," Wojciechowski said. "That doesn't change because you co-wrote a book. If I had to write a tough story or column on Walton, I could and would do it. That ability is not compromised."

In the case of Wojciechowski, and just about every other sportswriter I know, I agree. As someone who has worked with Gene twice, I have no question that it would ever influence his judgment. But what concerns me is that there might be one person out there that would bring up the appearance of conflict of interest.

Wojciechowski continues: "Not to put too fine a point on it, but I was able to get a story with Miller during the playoffs a couple of seasons ago because of my prior relationship with him. It was a story no one else had, or could get, because he wasn't doing 1-on-1 interviews. To me, it's simple: if you're a professional, you separate the two relationships. If you're not, it doesn't matter if you wrote a book with someone or not."

The other side of the book-writing dilemma is the unauthorized story, or the story the athlete or team didn't want you to tell. Again, there are ethical issues. Sam Smith, the NBA writer for the *Chicago Tribune,* came under fire after the publication of *Jordan Rules,* the runaway bestseller that got under the skin of Jordan and exposed the underbelly of the Chicago Bulls. Smith gathered all his information for the book during one season he was covering the team. Many said that Smith held back information during the season to use in the book. Smith said there was nothing new in the book but that it just read differently when you took nine months of anecdotes and put them in one place. Smith's point is well taken. It is one of the more infuriating experiences to be covering a big local story day after day only to have *Sports Illustrated* or *The Wall Street Journal* come in and compile all the information in one story. Everyone falls in love with the story, not realizing that all that information had already been in the local paper.

Stories can be holistic in nature, and the final product can be greater than the sum of the parts.

MISREPRESENTING YOURSELF

There are consequences to shoddy ethics that go beyond losing respect and creating appearances of conflict of interest. Sometimes the results can be incredibly costly. You have to understand that the public doesn't particularly trust us. Surveys show that journalists rate somewhere around car salesmen and politicians when it comes to trustworthiness. Never was this more evident then in the 1990s when an ABC-TV documentary crew caught Food Lion stores putting expired meat on the shelves. The story was well researched and well documented, but the producers working on the story went undercover to expose the situation. The problem was that they were not truthful on the job applications that gave them access to the stores.

Food Lion sued, and the jury agreed that the real criminal was not the food store but the deceptive journalists. The jury remanded a huge judgment, which was partially overturned on appeal. Nonetheless, the sentiment was clear and the message was loud. The public will not tolerate journalists lying or deceiving people regardless of the good it might do.

All journalists must wrestle with such questions every day. How clear must you be that you are a reporter and the information may be published? Should we read a journalistic Miranda to our sources?

"You have the right to remain silent, although I really hope you don't. You have a right to consult with someone before saying anything although that will hurt any spontaneous response you may give and lessen my chance of getting a good interview. You have the right to say something stupid but realize that anything you say may appear on the front page of my newspaper and may even be put in a large headline. Do you understand these rules I must live by?"

Yikes. I don't think you have to wear a sign around your neck that says, "I'm a journalist." And I also don't think you should quietly mumble your intentions. Nevertheless, at the start of the interview you should clearly state your name and newspaper—once. If the person has any questions, they can follow it up. If the person is well respected and says something outrageous, I think you owe them a response or question that gives them the chance to understand the implications of what they said.

Never was this point more evident then in Ted Koppel's 1987 *Nightline* interview with Al Campanis, then general manager of the Los Angeles Dodgers. Campanis said that African Americans may lack the "necessities" to be a general manager and even treaded into the area of them not being "buoyant" when it came to water. Koppel and guest Roger Kahn, the noted author of *The Boys of Summer,* among other books, tried to help Campanis by re-asking the question and even went so far as to imply that it wasn't really the answer he meant to give. Campanis wouldn't back down.

Campanis was shown the door by the Dodgers.

You can pretty much figure if you are in a press conference or a locker room with a notepad and pencil that the person knows you are a reporter. No additional identification is necessary. However, if you are at cocktail party, engaged in idle chitchat, I think identification is necessary. In fact, I don't think any interview done late at night in a bar, regardless of how often you identified yourself, is fair to use in print. You have to be mindful of the person's state of mind. A court decision in Chicago backed that up. A simplified version of the story has a *Chicago Tribune* reporter doing an interview with a mother whose son has just died violently. The mother talked about how much better off her son was rather than having to face the life in front of him. The woman knew the person was a reporter; the people around her did, too. Everyone signed off.

Later, the woman sued, saying she wasn't in the right frame of mind to make the decision to be interviewed. She sued. She lost. But an appeals court overturned the ruling.

It's common sense that staying out of court is a good thing. The current practice is to not fight a constitutional issue unless it is absolutely necessary. There is little to gain and a lot to lose. The courts are not going to expand our rights, so there is nothing to gain there. But there is always a chance they will set a precedent that will decrease our rights. Make sure the risk is worth it.

And realize that there will be little sympathy for a reporter who fails to properly inform the person they are talking to that they are a reporter.

SOURCES

I've said that the most important thing a reporter can have is his or her credibility. And what goes hand in hand with that, as it does in life, is their word. Journalism became a glamorous profession after Woodward and Bernstein broke the Watergate story; unfortunately, it also signaled the rise of the off-the-record quote or stories with the phrase "sources said." All our sources saw the movie and read the book, and before you know it, coaches were telling routine stuff, but only "off the record." Like fools, we oftentimes give away the off-the-record card with little resistance. Let me tell you, people like to talk, and most people will tell you stuff even if you deny them the shield of anonymity.

People like the intrigue of talking to a reporter and whispering sweet somethings that, upon reflection, are usually pretty benign comments. There are people who enjoy being part of the process. It's their 15 minutes in the sun.

But what does this have to do with ethics? I believe, and I may be in the minority, that a source has a responsibility to give you accurate information. And if they don't, you have no obligation to them. If you make a deal with a source not to disclose his or her identity and they were less than truthful to you, then I think the deal is off. Those magical movie moments about reporters going to jail to protect their sources are great theater. And if my source is straight up with me, I would go to jail myself. (It's an easy way to get famous and give you job security.)

As a general rule, I always explain that if what they are telling me is blatantly false, then our arrangement is off. About a third of the time, that will freeze the source because they may realize that all they have is rumor and conjecture. Those that stick with you have something to say, and it's probably worth listening to.

A MATTER OF ETHICS

You need an entire book, not just a chapter, to cover how we deal with ethics every day in the sportswriting business. Some of the problems seem to have obvious answers. But rarely is something that's worth discussing easy and obvious. As a general rule, if you have to ask if something is a problem, then it probably is a problem.

Ethics can be very situational. The answer to one situation may change based on the events that led up to it. I've taken meals from public-relations people and sources, but I've had what I believe to be good reasons. You can rest assured that I've reciprocated. I've taken gifts worth more than $5 to avoid an uncomfortable scene. I've also made contributions to charities out of my own pocket because it's just too difficult to explain to the accountants that you're doing a make-up call for something someone has done for you. I've made mistakes. But I tried never to put my newspaper or myself at any risk.

As I've said, it's all about credibility. You do whatever you can to avoid an appearance of conflict of interest. Perhaps the most disappointing part of the job is that our colleagues in other departments think that the ethics in a sports department are different. There was a time that it was true. But not anymore.

The next time you are carrying a television set down a set of steps, make sure you are carrying it to the car for someone else. Please.